# Climate Change, Moral Panics, and Civilization

In recent years, interest in climate change has rapidly increased in the social sciences, and yet there is still relatively little published material in the field that seeks to understand the development of climate change as a perceived social problem. This book contributes to filling this gap by theoretically linking the study of the historical development of social perceptions about 'nature' and climate change with the figurational sociology of Norbert Elias and the study of moral panics.

By focussing sociological theory on climate change, this book situates the issue within the broader context of the development of ecological civilizing processes and comes to conceive of contemporary campaigns surrounding climate change as instances of moral panics/civilizing offensives with both civilizing and decivilizing effects. In the process, the author not only proposes a new approach to moral panics research but makes a fundamental contribution to the development of figuration sociology and the understanding of how climate change has developed as a social problem, with significant implications regarding how to improve the efficacy of climate change campaigns.

This highly innovative study should be of interest to students and researchers working in the fields of sociology, environment and sustainability, media studies, and political science.

**Amanda Rohloff** was a Wellcome Trust Postdoctoral Research Fellow in Sociology at the School of Social Sciences at Brunel University, UK.

**André Saramago** is an Auxiliary Professor of International Relations at Lusíada University-North, Porto, Portugal.

# Routledge Advances in Climate Change Research

**The Anthropology of Climate Change**
An Integrated Critical Perspective
*Hans A. Baer and Merrill Singer*

**EU Climate Diplomacy**
Politics, Law and Negotiations
*Edited by Stephen Minas and Vassilis Ntousas*

**The Global Climate Regime and Transitional Justice**
*Sonja Klinsky and Jasmina Brankovic*

**Climate Justice and the Economy**
Social Mobilization, Knowledge and the Political
*Edited by Stefan Gaarsmand Jacobsen*

**A Critical Approach to Climate Change Adaptation**
Discourses, Policies and Practices
*Edited by Silja Klepp and Libertad Chavez-Rodriguez*

**Contemplating Climate Change**
Mental Models and Human Reasoning
*Stephen M. Dark*

**Climate Change, Moral Panics, and Civilization**
*Amanda Rohloff*
*Edited by André Saramago*

For more information about this series, please visit: https://www.routledge
.com/Routledge-Advances-in-Climate-Change-Research/book-series/
RACCR

# Climate Change, Moral Panics, and Civilization

Amanda Rohloff

EDITED BY ANDRÉ SARAMAGO

Routledge
Taylor & Francis Group
LONDON AND NEW YORK

from Routledge

First published 2019 by Routledge

2 Park Square, Milton Park, Abingdon, Oxfordshire OX14 4RN
52 Vanderbilt Avenue, New York, NY 10017

*Routledge is an imprint of the Taylor & Francis Group, an informa business*

First issued in paperback 2020

*British Library Cataloguing-in-Publication Data*
A catalogue record for this book is available from the British Library

*Library of Congress Cataloging-in-Publication Data*
A catalog record has been requested for this book

ISBN: 978-0-415-62722-1 (hbk)
ISBN: 978-0-367-50770-1 (pbk)

Typeset in Sabon
by codeMantra

Dr Amanda Rohloff (1982–2012).

# Contents

# Preface

*Jason Hughes, André Saramago, and Judy,*
*Maurie, and Jason and Colin Rohloff*

## Jason Hughes, Leicester, 2018

My part in the story behind this book starts in 2008, when I was a Senior Lecturer in Sociology at Brunel University, London. I received an email from Amanda Rohloff in the early part of that year. I had been recommended to Mandy as a potential PhD supervisor by Stephen Mennell of University College Dublin. All three of us – Mandy, Stephen, and I – shared an interest in Norbert Elias: a sociologist whose work figures prominently in this volume. Mandy was at that time looking for somewhere to study for a PhD. She understood the importance of having a supervisor lined up and of having a good institutional and academic 'fit', not least because she was applying for various sources of funding to make possible her dream of studying overseas. In what was to prove to be something of a hallmark of Mandy's nascent academic career, she exceeded all expectations – not least her own – in eventually landing three separate sources of funding from both her home country of New Zealand and her host country and institution.

Like many good research ideas, Mandy's thesis brought together several substantive themes in a way that had not previously been undertaken. These made for somewhat unlikely bedfellows: moral panic, climate change, and figurational sociology. This very combination invited controversy. Surely, I thought, climate change was a topic about which people were not panicking enough. Was she suggesting that the idea of anthropogenic climate change was a kind of overblown reaction engineered by a hysterical popular media? In our first conversations, it was clear that Mandy relished my response. The basis of my reaction, of my immediate questions, was precisely that which she wanted to explore. First, because it revealed much about the notion of 'moral panic', which, as my response serves to illustrate, was a concept that I, like many others, understood to refer exclusively to problems which were not really problems at all: that moral panics were by definition *exaggerated* social reactions perpetuated in the interests of particular groups. Second, because my response highlighted a growing social sensitivity towards the environment that could be understood, she was later to argue, as part of a much more general set of processes involving widening circles of mutual identification, in turn, linked to longer-term civilizing and decivilizing processes. And third, because in presenting this particular combination of topics, Mandy had quite self-consciously violated a whole host of sociological mores: disciplinary norms which, she felt, were ripe for critical interrogation.

Here is how a basic sociological training might lead one to view her proposed thesis topic: exploring climate change as a moral panic – *she must be a climate change denier*; using the concept of moral panic itself – *using this rather unfashionable concept shows that she is not up to speed on developments in sociological theory*; and, perhaps worst of all, use of the term 'civilization' – *she must be either unaware or unashamed of the colonial/ teleological connotations of this term*. I was impressed! Mandy was not frightened of controversy; she was also not, it became quickly apparent, blissfully unaware of the issues attendant upon using these terms and bringing these topics together. As someone who had studied the work of Elias, I understood something of where she was coming from. For instance, Elias's usage of the term 'civilization' (principally a normative term) stands in contrast to the (principally technical) term 'civilizing process' – this is a similar distinction to that maintained by anthropologists in their use of the term 'culture' – as will be discussed at length in this book. Moreover, it soon became clear that Mandy was precisely interested in why it was that the concept of moral panic had somewhat fallen out of vogue; in the problems with the concept and its applications; and in exploring the scope for reworking, perhaps reinvigorating, the concept through a dialogue with developments in social theory. Like Mandy, I was fully signed up to the idea that it is a folly to equate recency or intellectual vogue with conceptual value in relation to developments in social theory; again, it was Elias who taught me that most clearly. In addition, Mandy was interested in exploring the processes by which climate change *came to be* widely understood as an anthropogenic social problem and investigating the shifting behavioural standards that have, to varying degrees, come to accompany this development. For the record, she was anything but a climate change denier. However, importantly, she did not feel compelled to announce that from the outset.

Her combination of topics also tells something of the story of Mandy's thesis and of this book that is based upon it. In the first instance, Mandy was primarily interested in the concept of moral panic. I think it is fair to say that in the early phases of her thesis, the topic of climate change was important only in its role as a kind of empirical testing ground within which to explore that concept. Likewise, figurational sociology, while a pivotal interest that drew us together as supervisor and supervisee, was still a second-order concern that Mandy intended to utilize in order to conceptually rework moral panic. However, as she worked through her thesis, each concern, in turn, began to assume centre stage, with the others becoming secondary. Soon, and no doubt partly influenced by my enthusiasm for the approach, it was figurational sociology that became a prime target, particularly the thorny and by no means fully resolved problem of the relationship between civilizing and decivilizing processes. Then it was climate change itself. From being initially the problem around which she might be able to say interesting things about moral panic, it soon became in itself the central substantive concern. In the Eliasian tradition, Mandy undertook to develop an account of the 'sociogenesis' (the social origins and development) of climate change as an anthropogenic problem. Through her examination of long-term shifts in public and scientific understandings of, and attitudes towards, climate change, Mandy traced the ascendancy of a kind of 'carbon temperance' movement – a 'greening' of demands to restrain and curb our excessive consumption of the planet's finite resources that had parallels with other long-term shifts in behavioural standards involving a *social constraint towards self-restraint*. Today, the movement finds its clearest expression in guides to 'ethical' living; in the rise of corporate 'environmental statements'; and, for instance, in growing demands for 'right-thinking' individuals to account for and 'offset' the carbon emissions that result from the pursuit of interests relating to work, leisure, and spare time activities. Mandy was, of course, ultimately interested in whether these developments might indeed yield the kinds of signal changes in human behaviour required to tackle anthropogenic climate change.

Along with a time-series analysis of various documentary sources, Mandy conducted a number of interviews with environmental activists and non-activists. She piloted her interview questions on me. I remember feeling exhausted at the end of the interview. In the space of about 30 minutes her probing questions and prompts had laid bare my own deeply personal – and, I might add, entirely contradictory and inconsistent – stance on climate change. All of this made for what was to become an exceptional thesis that spoke to literatures on moral panic, on climate change, on figurational sociology, and on the sociology of knowledge more generally. When it was finally submitted, the thesis was already very book-like. I remember discussing with her – and this was some time before her viva – what she would need to do to rework the thesis to form the basis of a book; she had already begun to approach different publishers and draft a proposal plus a plan for its further development. She was awarded her PhD with only very minor corrections, which were quickly completed and approved. Shortly afterwards, in December 2012, Mandy died of an epileptic seizure.

At the point of her untimely and tragic death, Mandy had achieved an incredible amount. Upon her arrival at Brunel, she had rapidly immersed herself in university life, soon becoming centrally engaged with the staff-student liaison committee and subsequently becoming a prominent school representative for postgraduate research students. She later came to take the lead in a series of initiatives, perhaps the most notable of which was her lead role in organizing the 'Moral Panics in the Contemporary World' conference that took place at Brunel in December 2010. The conference was a highly successful international event attended by in excess of 120 delegates, including the most prominent names in the academic field, such as Stanley Cohen and Jock Young. We did not know it at the time, but this was to be the last time Stan and Jock would appear together at a major academic conference. Stan Cohen died aged 70 in January 2013, and Jock Young died in November of that same year aged 71. Other key speakers included high-profile journalists, such as the BBC Panorama documentary maker James Oliver, whose programme on the 'Baby P' affair sparked a major national debate about social care and child protection in the UK. The conference attracted a considerable amount of highly positive media attention, including the likes of the *Times Higher Educational Supplement*, BBC Radio 4's *Thinking Allowed*, and the British Sociological Association (BSA) newsletter *Network*. It is testament to Mandy's superb organizational skills that the conference actually turned a not insubstantial profit. The remaining funds were used, again with Mandy taking the lead in every case, to secure a special reserve collection of books on moral panics in the Brunel University library; for the development of a website with archive footage of all the keynote presentations from the conference; and, most significantly, for the establishment of an international moral panic studies research network, complete with a working paper series and social media feed which attracted a substantial, international membership, including many major figures from the field. Amanda was well known on campus, where she also worked in the library and taught undergraduates to support her PhD research. As a very active member of the postgraduate community, she was greatly admired and came to be known as 'Amanda the Wise'! Exceptionally generous, helpful, and friendly, she had an uncanny ability to tackle bureaucracy to get results – 'ask Mandy' seemed the default answer to many queries on campus from students and, increasingly, from colleagues in the academic faculty. She was successfully nominated for the Jock McKeon prize for inspirational leadership – an award she was due to collect formally together with her PhD at the graduation ceremony in July 2013, and which her parents, Judy and Maurie Rohloff, accepted on her behalf.

In her short but incredibly productive academic career, she had already developed a publications record that rivalled that of some senior members of the academic staff. Alongside articles in prominent sociological journals, including the BSA's flagship journal *Sociology*, numerous book chapters, and a number of international conference presentations, she had already co-edited a special issue of the journal *Crime, Media and Culture*, and had co-edited a book on moral panics entitled *Moral Panics in the Contemporary World*, which was published by Bloomsbury in 2014. The list of her achievements goes on: it includes the establishment of a BSA study group on moral panics, active involvement in another on alcohol research, and her appointment shortly before her death as a Postgraduate Research Fellow in Sociology at Brunel University, funded by the Wellcome Trust.

Among her many achievements was her securing a contract with Taylor & Francis (T&F) to publish a book based on her excellent thesis. I remember discussing this with Mandy shortly after she had landed it. She was absolutely thrilled to be working with such a prestigious publisher. She also wanted to use the book to develop and extend her arguments and ideas. I should imagine that by the time she had completed it to her own exacting standards, there would only be a fraction of the thesis left in it. The book was one project among numerous others that Mandy had planned. I still have a shared Dropbox folder, 'Mandy/Jason Interchange', which contains ideas for numerous conference papers, special issues, journal articles, funding applications, panel sessions, and so forth. These included Mandy's ideas to extend her focus to researching the sociogenesis of alcohol use; a research project that would investigate drugs, sexuality, normality, and the notion of 'problematized consumption'; an article that would explore the development of, and contestation over, the use of 'illegal' drugs in medicine; another on the role of social media in problematized consumption; and a monograph on the methods of moral panic research. These were only (some of) the plans that Mandy had to undertake work with me; she had numerous further plans with other current and prospective collaborators.

Of all the unfinished business, it was the monograph with T&F that was the most frustrating. There was much in the thesis that remained relevant to the fields it covered. As a case in point, at the time of writing this preface, debates about 'fake news' and media portrayals of climate change have never been sharper, particularly following the appointment of Donald Trump as US president. Understandably, Mandy's family were also very keen to see the project reach fruition. However, the contract with T&F was based upon a proposal in which certain themes of the thesis would be retained, but others would be significantly developed and expanded. Without a complete sense of how Mandy planned to write, rework, and extend these sections, it was going to prove very difficult for me or anyone else to deliver on that contract. I had numerous email exchanges and face-to-face discussions with T&F, who, from the outset, were incredibly supportive, understanding, and helpful. In particular, Louisa Earls; Annabel Harris; and, most decisively of all, Margaret Farrelly showed incredible patience and persistent endeavour to help realize this monograph. Part of this undertaking involved looking back at the reviews T&F had commissioned for the manuscript proposal, including any conditions they presented for the book's publication. These exchanges spanned a few years: I moved jobs from Brunel to Leicester, and T&F had changes of the commissioning editors covering different environment and sociology lists. We eventually managed to find a way forward which involved developing a project that was somewhere between the book Mandy promised and an edition of the thesis.

By chance, during this same period, I was approached by André Saramago, again by an out-of-the-blue email. This time the referral was from his former PhD supervisor, Andrew Linklater from Aberystwyth University – a colleague, once more, whom I had met through our common interest in the work of Norbert Elias. André had approached me with a view to my being his supervisor for a postdoctoral fellowship on the relationship between ecology and civilization in a long-term perspective. The similarities to Amanda's project were striking. I did not know it then, but André and I had already met, briefly, at a conference – From the Past to the Present and Towards Possible Futures: The Collected Works of Norbert Elias, Leicester 2014 – where I had not been able to attend André's paper and learn of his interest in this area. For his part, André had heard of Amanda's work and had already read some of her publications. When we eventually turned to the possibility of his having a hand in turning Mandy's thesis into a book, he was, I quote, 'delighted and honoured' by the prospect of fulling the work of an 'impressive scholar who was treading a very promising path'. We shared a Skype together with Mandy's parents Judy and Maurie, and they, like I, immediately warmed to André, all of us getting the instant sense that he was the perfect person to take the project forward. Together, we hatched a plan to dovetail his taking on the role of co-author of this volume with his postdoc project. The original intention was in fact to expand upon Mandy's work and add extra layers to her research. He submitted the application to the Leverhulme Trust. However, unfortunately, the project was not funded.

We were all incredibly disappointed at the knock-back from the Leverhulme, but, ultimately it proved to be the making of this volume. André remained interested in completing the project, now not as co-author but rather in the role of editor responsible for an in-depth editing of her thesis that updated it, highlighted her contribution to her fields of study, and showed her projected future paths of research so that present and future researchers could follow them in her stead. We kept our discussions going, with Mandy's parents, with Margaret Farrelly, and now also with Matthew Shobbrook, with André doggedly pushing ahead with the project in his spare time. What he has helped to produce is an excellent manuscript that does full credit to Mandy's work. I cannot think of a more fitting tribute to Mandy than to see the publication of this book and for a community of scholars to engage with her important, still timely, and path-breaking work. My sincere and wholehearted thanks to André for making this happen.

In the rest of this preface, after André Saramago adds a few words on the project, Mandy's family will add their own reflections on Mandy as a person and on the realization of this monograph. My thanks also to them for their great patience, kindness, and warmth, both in relation to the completion of this project and in all of our exchanges, discussions, and meetings since Mandy's death.

## André Saramago, Setúbal, 2018

The most important aspects of Amanda Rohloff's career path have already been covered by Jason Hughes in the previous paragraphs. As such, I take the opportunity to only add a few words about my relationship with Mandy's research and the pleasure it has been to edit this book.

I first came across Mandy's research at the end of my PhD studies in International Relations. I was supervised by Andrew Linklater at Aberystwyth University, where I developed a deep interest in Norbert Elias's figurational sociology and its application to the study of International Relations. Elias gave me what I still consider to be an original and highly insightful engagement with one of the research questions that occupied me at the time: understanding how to theoretically conceive of the political multiplicity of humanity without losing sight of its embeddedness in non-human nature. This led me to discover Mandy's use of figurational sociology to understand the development of 'ecological civilizing processes' and how these were related to contemporary concerns about climate change. Initially, given the quantity and quality of Mandy's published work, I assumed she was a well-established scholar, clearly years ahead of me. It was with great surprise that I learned that she was just a few years older than me and had just recently finished her PhD!

It was also then that I learned about her untimely death. It struck me as particularly painful that such a young and brilliant academic had departed so suddenly. Even though I never met Mandy personally, her similar age and interests made me relate to her on a personal, emotional level.

That is why when Jason Hughes suggested that I co-author a book with Mandy, based on a substantial expansion of her PhD research as part of a postdoctoral application with the Leverhulme Trust, I naturally accepted and felt honoured to have a role in making Mandy's work more widely known. But the application was not successful, and I ended up assuming other professional obligations that made the envisioned substantial expansion on Mandy's themes impossible. However, neither I nor Mandy's parents, Jason Hughes, Margaret Farrelly, or Matthew Shobbrook wished the project to be dropped as everyone saw it fitting not only to pay this last homage to Amanda Rohloff but also to give others the opportunity to read and develop her work. The solution that was found was for me to become editor of the book, instead of co-author, and to revise Mandy's thesis, updating it and drawing out its core themes and contributions as well as Mandy's envisioned future paths of research.

This book is the outcome of that project. Working on the book has been a true pleasure and quite an experience to reflect upon and draw out the intricacies of Mandy's thinking. Throughout, I was fascinated and humbled by her originality, power of synthesis, and clarity of reasoning. With this book, we hope to pay a fitting tribute to Amanda Rohloff and ensure that her work becomes available to other researchers in the field, who will, hopefully, keep Mandy's memory alive in their own research.

## Judy and Maurie Rohloff, Wellington, 2018

Mandy was more than just our daughter – she was a friend. Mandy's life was full of health challenges which she bore with strength and fortitude, along with a cheerful attitude. She never let anything stand in the way of what she wanted to achieve, whether it be in the field of sport (she was a regional representative in hockey for many years) or academia. Her drive, determination, and passion for life and knowledge saw her awarded three scholarships to Brunel University in London, where she studied her PhD in Climate Change, Moral Panic, and Civilisation from September 2008 until July 2012, when she completed her thesis and was awarded her doctorate with minor revisions. Mandy worked part-time in the Brunel Library and did the occasional bit of teaching while working on her thesis. At the time of her death, on 7 December 2012 at the age of 30 years, Mandy held the position of Wellcome Trust Postdoctoral Research Fellow in Sociology, based at Brunel University. She was working on three research projects – in the areas of epilepsy, alcohol, and end of life care – while teaching a variety of modules in both sociology and media and communications. It is a little ironic that it was epilepsy that ended her life. In addition, she was the Director of the International Moral Panic Research Network and co-convener of separate BSA research groups on Moral Panics and Alcohol.

Mandy's passion for academia, along with her strength and perseverance in the face of adversity, was second to none. She was a gifted academic with a wonderful future ahead of her. She presented at conferences all over the world and had a number of publications in the form of journal articles, chapters in edited books, etc., as well as a signed contract to turn her thesis into a book, which, due to her untimely death, she wasn't able to complete.

Thanks to Mandy's PhD supervisor Jason Hughes and to André Saramago, who was familiar with Mandy's work and has had the role of editor, her book has now become a reality. We have come to know them both on a personal basis, and this has been an added bonus for us.

## Jason and Colin Rohloff

Mandy was our little sister. We first met her when we were four years old, after Dad brought her and Mum home from the hospital. As twins, we had grown up keeping each other company – like living with your best mate... who is exactly like you. So, when Mandy came home it was our first introduction to someone different, someone who we could teach all the things we had learnt in our first four years; we were so full of wisdom and ready to share it!

Mandy looked up to us and was always hanging around, joining us when we had friends over and always willing to step up and play with the 'big boys'. She became very good at backyard cricket and even played a couple of seasons for Wellington Girls; she had a strong arm and terrified the opposition batters with her fast right-arm swing bowling. We only played one or two seasons and were never really that good, but clearly Mandy had learnt what she needed to from us and quickly moved from being the apprentice to the master, a theme that would follow in later years...

In high school we always did very well, getting the sort of grades that made Mum proud. Mandy, on the other hand, less so. She tried hard but somehow just never found her rhythm: B's instead of A's. Mum and Dad were still proud of her achievements, but she could always do better.

Mandy's first year at university was not great as she ended up failing about half her papers. Mum went searching for answers; clearly Mandy just was not trying hard enough, right? Wrong. Mandy had certain expectations set on her that were less about what she wanted to do and more about what we all thought she should be doing. You went to university to get an education, so you could get a job and start earning money, right? That's certainly how we felt about university at the time. So, after a year of trying to keep everyone else happy, Mandy hit reset and a few years later walked out of Victoria University with a degree in Anthropology, Criminology, and Sociology. But that was just a warm up. Next she tackled a BA with honours, delivering one A and the rest A+'s to finish with first-class honours in sociology. First-class!

Mandy then headed to the other side of the world to continue her academic career at Brunel University, funded by not one, not two, but THREE scholarships! Over the next four years she became a part of the Brunel fabric; she had found her calling and was in her element. Her academic studies took her to conferences in exotic parts of the world. She met some exceptionally great people, making friends everywhere she went. This shy, young girl who had stuttered in school had blossomed into a truly gifted academic.

We had always been the big brothers who provided their little sister with guidance and help navigating through life. If anything, she taught us about how to live a full and rich life, about finding something you are passionate about and giving it everything you've got. The apprentice had truly become the master, and she continues to provide a guiding light to this day.

# 1 Introduction

## Introduction

This book explores two main areas of research: (1) the relationship between moral panic and figurational sociology and (2) the development of climate change as a social problem. Its central aims are to question how and to what extent moral panic remains a useful concept in the social sciences, and if so in what formulation, and to understand how climate change has come to be perceived as a social problem. The book does this by combining the concept of moral panic with concepts from figurational sociology and applying these to the empirical analysis of the development of climate change perceptions. These three fields of research have never been combined before (aside from in my own research[1]).

Initially, this research developed out of an interest in using the example of climate change to develop the concepts of moral panic and civilization; I started with concepts, with a theoretical-conceptual framework, and then looked for an empirical example. Climate change was chosen for several reasons: at the time, very little sociological research had been undertaken on it; it was (and still is) a highly topical example; it was a contemporary example in that it was current; it did not seem like a perfect fit to the concepts of moral panic and *decivilization*; and it challenged many of the assumptions associated with the concepts and was therefore a strong 'test' of them.

Gradually, as the research process developed, I came to be increasingly interested in the topic of climate change for its own sake, not just for its role as a research tool to develop concepts. And so, the focus shifted to exploring not just how the perception of climate change as a problem developed (providing new insights to research on climate change) but also how this perception might, and perhaps how it ought to, develop in the future. This then led to a desire to develop research-informed recommendations that could have implications for climate change policy, campaigns, media, and so on.

This brings us to my central research problem and research questions. But before I introduce them, it is necessary to provide a brief overview of the concepts of this book: climate change, moral panic, and civilization.

## Climate change

The prospect of global climate change, as influenced by anthropogenic processes, has come to be viewed by some as an increasingly prominent 'social problem'. Climate change is a 'natural' ongoing process, with or without the involvement of humans, and the greenhouse effect is necessary to sustain present life on the planet. However, research undertaken in the various sciences of climate change has demonstrated how the rapid increase in greenhouse gas emissions (including, but not limited to, $CO_2$) corresponds to increasing overall global temperatures and has projected that these global temperatures will continue to increase, with devastating consequences for various forms of life on earth.[2]

While the *science* of global climate change has been developing since before the twentieth century (Weart, [2003] 2008), it is only comparatively recently that the topic has come to be increasingly commonplace in the 'public sphere'. The last few decades, in particular, have witnessed an increase in attention to the topic, with an acceleration of 'popular' interest. Following a series of extreme weather events in 2005, with associated media coverage (see Lever-Tracy, 2008), 2006 saw the release of the documentary *An Inconvenient Truth* (Guggenheim, 2006), presented by Al Gore, which sought to educate the public about 'global warming' and engender a sense of urgency to address the 'climate crisis'. Numerous popular books, guides, teaching resources, reality TV shows, movies, and other documentaries have since emerged. 'Global warming' clothing, Live Earth concerts, amongst other developments, all suggest that anthropogenic climate change has become at least a popular (though at times contested) social problem.[3] This research seeks to explore how such developments have occurred and what implications they have for dealing with climate change.

This research employs a long-term approach to understanding the development of climate change as a perceived social problem. It explores how different processes – natural processes, intentional campaigns and interventions, and wider social processes – may influence understandings about anthropogenic climate change and, potentially, changes in nature-society relations. Primarily, this research brings together the concept of moral panic with Norbert Elias's theory of civilizing (and decivilizing) processes to explore how and to what extent understandings about and the governance of climate change have developed.

## Moral panic

The development of climate change as a perceived social problem provides an interesting case with which to 'test' and 'develop' the concept of moral panic for it does not fit neatly with the original understanding of the concept. The term 'moral panic' was first taken up by Jock Young (1971) and then more fully developed by Stanley Cohen (1972) in his famous study on the 'Mods' and 'Rockers'.[4] This original, or 'classic', conceptualization of moral panic describes a particular type of *over*reaction to a perceived social problem. As Cohen famously describes it,

> Societies appear to be subject, every now and then, to periods of moral panic. A condition, episode, person or group of persons emerges to become defined as a threat to societal values and interests; its nature is presented in a stylized and stereotypical fashion by the mass media; the moral barricades are manned by editors, bishops, politicians and other right-thinking people; socially accredited experts pronounce their diagnoses and solutions; ways of coping are evolved or (more often) resorted to; the condition then disappears, submerges or deteriorates and becomes more visible. Sometimes the object of the panic is quite novel and at other times it is something which has been in existence long enough, but suddenly appears in the limelight. Sometimes the panic passes over and is forgotten, except in folklore and collective memory; at other times it has more serious and long-lasting repercussions and might produce such changes as those in legal and social policy or even in the way the society conceives itself.
>
> (Cohen, [1972] 2002, p. 1)

Despite Cohen's groundbreaking study (see also Critcher, 2003; Goode & Ben-Yehuda, [1994] 2009; Hall, Critcher, Jefferson, Clarke, & Roberts, 1978; Thompson, 1998), there have been several criticisms of moral panic research, with some authors rejecting the concept altogether (for example, Hunt, 1999; Moore & Ungar, 2001; Valverde, 2000; Watney, [1987] 1997). Criticisms include the normativity of the concept (the reaction to the perceived social problem is presumed to be irrational and innately misguided; see Hunt, 1999; Moore & Valverde, 2000); the short-term focus of much moral panic research (it has tended to focus on the processes involved within the 'panic', without exploring how these relate to wider, long-term social processes; see Rohloff & Wright, 2010; Watney, [1987] 1997); problems of determinism and agency; and the relative lack of theoretical-conceptual development, of continually engaging the concept with developments in social theory[5] (for example, see Hier, 2008; Rohloff & Wright, 2010). In response to some of these criticisms, increasing attention is being given to the theoretical and methodological development of the moral panic concept, with many publications discussing the concept and its adequacy (for example, see Altheide, 2009; Critcher, 2008a, 2009; David, Rohloff, Petley, & Hughes, 2011; Garland, 2008; Hier, 2008, 2011; Jenkins, 2009; Rohloff, 2008, 2011; Rohloff & Wright, 2010; Young, 2009).

One way in which some authors are seeking to develop moral panic is through the utilization of the Foucauldian concept of *governmentality*. Put simply, this involves exploring how governance (i.e. practices of government or regulation) is thought about and how it develops. It incorporates both governance of the self and governance of the other (Dean, [1999] 2010). In this respect, it is similar to Elias's self-constraint and external constraint (except that, for Elias, there is a long-term shift towards increasing self-constraint relative to external constraint). Sean Hier has incorporated governmentality into his reformulation of moral panic; he conceptualizes moralization as a 'dialectic that counterposes individualizing discourses (which call on people to take personal responsibility to manage risk, e.g. drinking responsibly) against collectivizing discourses (which represent more broadly harms to be avoided, e.g. the drunk driver)' (Hier, 2008, p. 174). He argues that during moral panics, this dialectic shifts more towards collectivizing discourses, where the focus is on the governance of the (harmful) other. This concept of governmentality, and how it relates to moral panic and civilizing processes, will be further discussed in Chapter 3.

Drawing from Eliasian and other approaches, an additional aim of this research is to contribute to these debates with a reformulation of the moral panic concept. It is anticipated that, by applying the concept of moral panic to the example of climate change (a social problem that does not fit neatly with many of the assumptions of the original understanding of the moral panic concept), in combination with the original utilization of Norbert Elias's theory of civilizing (and decivilizing) processes, I will develop a reformulation of the moral panic concept, one that begins to address many of the problems and disputes within moral panic research. Some of these disputes include whether moral panics require folk devils, the relationship between panic and denial, the criterion of disproportionality, the extent to which moral panics contribute to deviancy amplification and secondary deviance, and the notion of 'good' (as opposed to 'bad') moral panics. These will all be explored and developed throughout this book, with the aim of developing a new approach to moral panic research, one that is relevant to empirical examples across time and space.

## Civilization

In *On the Process of Civilisation* (formerly titled in English *The Civilizing Process*) ([1939] 2012), Elias explores 'civilization' in two very different ways. First, he explores the development of the *normative* concept of 'civilization': the process whereby one group of people come to see themselves as more 'civilized' than another group of people, thereby legitimizing these self-identified 'civilized' people to establish asymmetrical power relations with those deemed 'uncivilized'. Indeed, the first part of Elias's book is devoted to the 'sociogenesis', or development, of the normative concepts of 'civilization' and 'culture' in everyday language:

> when one examines what the general function of the concept of civilisation really is...one starts with a very simple discovery: this concept expresses the self-consciousness of the West...It sums up everything in

which Western society of the last two or three centuries believes itself superior to earlier societies or 'more primitive' contemporary ones. By this term Western society seeks to describe what constitutes its special character and what it is proud of: the level of *its* technology, the nature of *its* manners, the development of *its* scientific knowledge or view of the world, and much more.

(Elias, [1939] 2012, p. 15)

While Elias did not want to use the term 'civilizing process' to refer to *progress*, he did seek to understand how the concept of 'civilization' in its everyday usage had attained these connotations of 'progress' and 'self-betterment' (as opposed to the 'uncivilized' and the 'barbaric').[6]

In contrast to the former normative, everyday understanding of 'civilization', Elias sought to develop a second, more technical and sociological understanding of 'civilization'. And so after having explored the normative terms of 'culture' and 'civilization', he goes on to provide empirical examples and analyses that feed into his technical concept of civilization. In his examination of the development of Western European societies since the Middle Ages, he develops his 'central theory'[7] of civilizing processes by empirically exploring the interrelationship between long-term changes in standards of behaviour and long-term changes in state formation and other wider processes.

'Elias's intention is to show by the examination of empirical evidence how, factually, standards of behaviour and psychological make-up have changed in European society since the Middle Ages, and then to explain why this has happened' (Mennell, [1989] 1998, p. 30). Psychological make-up is often referred to as 'habitus', and it essentially means 'that level of personality characteristics which individuals share in common with fellow members of their social groups'. So, examining manners and etiquette books (and other texts) provides a window into social habitus and its long-term transformation. From examining these texts, Elias discovers long-term changes in codes of mannerly behaviour, where manners from the medieval period were comparatively 'simple, naïve and undifferentiated' compared with today. Then, during the Renaissance period, 'with the structural transformation of society, with the new pattern of relationships, a change slowly comes about: the compulsion to check one's behaviour increases' (Elias, cited in Mennell, [1989] 1998 p. 42). By the eighteenth century, many 'bad' manners that were discussed in previous centuries were now absent from etiquette books; these proscriptions no longer needed to be mentioned as they were now internalized within people's personality make-up. This 'movement towards many things no longer being spoken about ran in conjunction with a movement towards moving many of the same things *behind the scenes of social life*' (Mennell, [1989] 1998, p. 43). These changes were accompanied by changes in emotions associated with these behaviours, with advancing feelings of shame and repugnance towards bodily functions.

These long-term changes are described by Elias as relating to the balance between external restraint (control by others) and self-restraint (internalized self-control); he argues that there is an overall shift in the balance towards increasing self-restraint. And he adds that the 'super-ego', the inner self that forbids people to do certain things, regulates relations with others via an internalized individual self-control (Mennell, [1989] 1998, p. 105). As Elias puts it,

> the displeasure towards such conduct which is thus aroused by the adult finally arises through habit, without having been induced by [the present action of] another person…Since the pressure of coercion of individual adults is allied to the pressure of example of the whole surrounding world, most children as they grow up, forget or repress relatively early the fact that their feelings of shame and embarrassment, of pleasure and displeasure, are moulded into conformity with a certain standard by external pressure and compulsion. All this appears to them as highly personal, something 'inward', implanted in them by nature… [I]t becomes more and more an inner automatism, the imprint of society on the inner self, the super-ego, that forbids the individual to eat in any other way than with a fork. The social standard to which the individual was first made to conform by *external restraint* is finally reproduced more or less smoothly within him, through a *self-restraint* which may operate even against his conscious wishes.
>
> (Elias, cited in Mennell, [1989] 1998, p. 44)

Elias argues that from the beginning of the Renaissance onwards, 'feelings and affects were first transformed in the upper class, and the structure of society as a whole permitted this changed affect standard to spread slowly throughout society' through a trickle-down process via status aspirations, where people sought to distinguish themselves as members of the 'good society' (Elias, cited in Mennell, [1989] 1998, p. 48).

Elias describes the process of the transformation of these individual personality structures as *psychogenesis* and insists that we can only understand this development by looking at its relationship to *sociogenesis*: the development of long-term, broader transformations in the structure of relations of power and interdependence in human societies (Mennell, [1989] 1998, p. 50). For changes in behaviour and emotion were and are necessary in order to adapt to changes in the structure of relations in societies. Elias describes how, for example, as the function of a knight comes to be needed less and less, for people who are knights to survive or to flourish in such societies they must adapt to another way of life that is more functional and, coincidentally, more restrained (Mennell, [1989] 1998, p. 60).

One important reason why these changes occurred, argues Elias, has to do with processes of state formation. This long-term process of

constitution of an increasingly central single authority (the 'state') involves several mechanisms. There is the *monopoly mechanism*, which
refers to the gradual concentration of the means of violence and taxation (the two principle means of ruling) in the hands of a single ruler
and administration in each territory; and the enlargement of the territory through competition with and elimination of neighbouring rulers.
Second, the *royal mechanism*, which refers to the internal balance of
social forces *within* the developing state. And third, the *transformation
of 'private' into 'public' monopolies.*

(Mennell, [1989] 1998, p. 66)

These three processes intertwine with one another and contribute to and
are affected by changes in personality make-up. Consequently, we can see
an overall shift towards increasingly less and less violence involved in conflicts between people. It is this combination of interconnected processual
transformations – at the micro and the macro levels, in the form of psychogenesis and sociogenesis, in processes of state formation, involving state
regulation and interpersonal self-regulation and socialization – that constitutes Elias's theory of civilizing processes.

While these long-term changes were characterized by trends and
counter-trends, Elias argues that we can still observe an overall long-term
trend that is developing in a particular direction: towards increasing complexity. To simplify this process, temporarily ignoring the counter-trends,
Elias outlines how, as a central state authority grows and gains increasing
monopolization over the control of violence and taxation, and as population grows and the division of labour increases, societies become more
complex, more differentiated, and so people become increasingly reliant
upon one another. This increase in interdependencies exerts pressures
towards changes in behaviour, compelling people towards increased
foresight and increased self-restraint (initially imposed with force by the
state, with a long-term processual shift towards self-imposed constraint).
However, these processes are constantly developing simultaneously with
other counter-trends.

The theory of civilizing processes does not argue that violence has simply
disappeared; rather, it has been transformed. For example, where face-to-face
violence has come to be increasingly viewed as 'uncivilized', through the aid
of technology we witness an increasing shift towards violence at a distance,
where perpetrators increasingly become physically and emotionally distanced
from victims. This is clearly depicted in Elias's own example of the Holocaust
in Nazi Germany (Elias, [1989] 2003). Some of the additional examples of
'killing at a distance' are to be found in the use of long-range weapons in
warfare, 'from machine-guns at a distance through to fighter aircraft and
inter-continental ballistic missiles' (Fletcher, 1997, pp. 50–1), and in transformations in the methods used for the execution of those sentenced to death in
the USA. This relates to the problem of 'civilized barbarism', which is where

'dehumanizing violence [continues] at both an individual and collective level at the very same time that we appear to be becoming increasingly civilized' (van Krieken, 1998, p. 127).

Additionally, while violence within states becomes increasingly monopolized by a central state authority (where intra-state violence changes form), we witness an additional shift from intra- to interstate violence. As (some) state figurations become established, they then seek to monopolize other 'rogue' states or territories. Historically, we can consider the internal violence (including civil wars) that occurred within places like the UK, followed by processes of colonialism, world wars, then other wars with other nations, and 'peacekeeping missions'.

And so it is important to note that Elias did not regard his theory of civilizing processes as being unilinear or inevitable – it was not a theory of 'progress' nor was it a proclamation of the superiority of Western 'civilization' (Kilminster & Mennell, 2008, p. xiii). Elias did not use the word 'civilizing' in any normative sense; 'civilization' is used by him as a more detached, processual term – the dynamic *process* of civilization (Elias, [1939] 2012). Indeed, he observed that the process of civilization is 'in a continuous conflict with countervailing decivilising processes. There is no basis for assuming that it must remain dominant' (Elias, [1986] 2008, p. 4). It is the interplay between these processes – civilizing and decivilizing – that I wish to explore in relation to moral panic and climate change.

Stephen Mennell defines decivilizing processes as 'regressions from earlier standards' ([1989] 1998, p. 20), as reversals of civilizing processes (1990, p. 205). In *Studies on the Germans* ([1989] 2013)[8] Elias explores this notion, referring to the 'regression to barbarism' (for example, p. 231) and the 'decivilizing spurt' (for example, p. 1) that facilitated the rise of the Nazi regime. Mennell (1990, p. 20) suggests that what he calls 'true' decivilizing processes

> would be marked by breaking links and shorter chains of social interdependence, associated with higher levels of danger and incalculability in everyday life, the re-emergence of violence into the public sphere and a decline in mutual identification, reduced pressures on individuals to restrain the expression of impulses (including the freer expression of aggressiveness), changes in socialization and personality formation, and increasing fantasy-content of modes of knowledge [where knowledge becomes farther removed from 'reality'].

In addition to this 'absolute' definition provided by Mennell, Elias refers to the idea that civilizing processes could give rise to decivilizing processes or at least contribute to them – where civilizing and decivilizing processes could occur simultaneously. For example, again in relation to Germany, Elias made the point that the monopolization of physical force by the state, through the military and the police, cuts in two directions and has a Janus-faced character, because such monopolies of force can then be all the more effectively wielded by powerful groups within any given nation-state, as indeed they did under the Nazi regime.

(van Krieken, 1998, pp. 112–3)

Elias also highlights 'that social norms [have] an "inherently double-edged character", since in the very process of binding some people together, they turn those people against others' (van Krieken, 1998, p. 113). In other words, processes of *integration* are accompanied with processes of *disintegration*. This is perhaps most evident in de Swaan's work on compartmentalized genocide, where positive identification with an in-group and disidentification with 'outsiders' occur simultaneously (for example, the cases of Rwanda [de Swaan, 1997; see also de Swaan 2001]). It is this notion of integration and disintegration that I will be exploring in relation to the development of moral panics. The concept of moral panic, and the example of climate change (and other examples examined in Chapter 8), will be used to question and develop the notion of decivilizing processes and their relation to civilizing processes and offensives.

Through exploring the relationship between civilizing/decivilizing processes and moral panics, this research will begin to explore the role of knowledge in decivilizing processes (including the monopolization, democratization, and technization of the dissemination of knowledge). Research on civilizing processes, and decivilizing processes in particular, has tended to focus on the relative state monopolization (or lack thereof) of the means of violence, as is evident in the title of Jonathan Fletcher's (1997) introductory text on Elias: *Violence and Civilization*. In turn, in examining the concept of moral panic in relation to the development of understandings about anthropogenic climate change, this research also aims to contribute to debates about the relation of decivilizing processes to civilizing processes as well as the interplay between *intentional* civilizing offensives and *unintentional* civilizing processes[9] (the latter another area which has received little explicit attention; see Dunning & Sheard, [1979] 2005, p. 280). (These areas of Elias's research, and of figurational sociology more generally, will be discussed in more detail in Chapters 3 and 4.)

*Civilizing offensive* is a term that appears to have first been used by Dutch sociologists in the 1980s and is derived from the work of Elias (for example, see Mitzman, 1987; Verrips, 1987). It refers to intentional campaigns that attempt to change the manners and morals of a group of people. In exploring civilizing processes, Elias largely focusses on long-term unplanned developments – although people act intentionally, he argues that the course of human history was (and is) by and large the unintended outcome of intentional actions. In other words, people's planned actions have many unintended consequences. However, critics of Elias, and those seeking to develop his work, argue that the area of civilizing offensives is relatively neglected (for example, van Krieken, 1990). As such, in this book I will be exploring how long-term changes in relations with and perceptions of 'nature' and 'the environment' relate to more short-term intentional campaigns to change people's behaviour with regard to climate change.

This interplay between offensives and processes, between the planned and the unplanned, is useful to think about when considering the possibility of *ecological civilizing processes*. Aarts et al. refer to the process of 'ecologization' as 'the development of what came to be called "environmental awareness"', encompassing 'attempts to keep the nature of human activity and the numbers of human species within constraints considered "ecologically acceptable"'. It 'strives for optimum welfare within ecological constraints' (Aarts, Schmidt, & Spier, 1995, pp. 1247–8). In their analysis of various campaigning groups' attempts to change people's behaviour towards more 'ecological self-control', Aarts et al. found that '[a]lthough sounding the alarm is a necessary component of efforts to stimulate ecological awareness, positively phrased campaigns to stimulate specific moderation are likely to be more successful than alarmist approaches' (Aarts et al., 1995, pp. 1248). Here, Aarts et al. appear to be exploring the intended and unintended consequences of *ecological civilizing offensives*. In this book, I will be using the concept of moral panic and the related concept of denial to explore the relationship between panic and denial in climate change campaigns (or ecological civilizing offensives). I will also examine how long-term civilizing processes have perhaps unintentionally contributed to ecological civilizing processes.

Aarts et al. additionally explore the role of status aspirations in the relative appeal of ecological self-control, in refraining from consumption. They argue that compared with other forms of consumption, ecological associations have relatively low status appeal but that under certain conditions this status appeal may be strengthened (Aarts et al., 1995). Taking this notion of status aspiration, in this book I will additionally explore how and the extent to which various *current* climate change campaigns attempt to appeal to status aspirations.

This concept of ecological civilizing processes, however, has also faced contestation. For example, as Quilley (2011, p. 85) argues, 'Unfortunately an ecological civilizing process and the inculcation of much more demanding standards of habitual self-restraint, though possible, seems unlikely'. Quilley may or may not be accurate in his prognosis of the future, but for the purposes of this study I will be focussing on a much more limited outlook. Rather than exploring the extent to which ecological civilizing processes may be occurring at a fast-enough rate and be widespread enough to address anthropogenic climate change, I will instead be exploring how and the extent to which ecological civilizing processes have been occurring on the back of a broader civilizing process and how ecological civilizing offensives feed into and are fed by these processes.

Within this notion of ecological civilizing processes, there are different levels that can be explored. First is the personal, individual civilizing process that occurs from birth to death, what is commonly referred to as socialization, enculturation, personality formation, and so forth – 'Whatever it is called, this individual lifetime learning process is closely bound up with processes of biological maturation' (Mennell, [1989] 1998, p. 200). This study will not address this level of civilizing processes in depth, rather focussing on the second level as it is the most relevant to the argument being made.

This second level is explored by Elias through his analysis of table manners, behaviour when at court, and so forth. While these also involve social-psychological transformations, they occur at a slower pace than individual civilizing processes (Mennell, [1989] 1998, p. 200). To examine this level, I will analyze a series of texts from the past 200 years, in a manner similar to Elias, in an attempt to find evidence of the development of ecological civilizing processes in the context of which people's perceptions of, and relations with, external non-human nature have changed. The goal of this analysis is to understand the structure of this change and trace its potential future developments in the context of the conception of climate change as a social problem.

The third level occurs on a much longer timescale, focussing on humanity as a whole. It connects middle-range civilizing processes (such as those explored in *On the Process of Civilization*) with much longer, much more gradual civilizing processes, all of which feed into one another (Mennell, [1989] 1998, p. 201). This level will not be looked at to such an extent in this study, but it is important to keep in mind how such long-term civilizing processes relate to the long-term development of the use of fire (Goudsblom, 1992) and how this, in turn, relates to the emergence of *anthropogenic* climate change.

## Central research problem and research questions

To achieve the aims discussed earlier, and to explore the central research problem of how anthropogenic climate change has developed as a perceived social problem, this research will investigate the following questions:

1 How have ideas about 'nature' and the 'environment' developed over time?
2 How and to what extent has the governance of climate change developed over time?
3 How do these developments relate to wider social processes?
4 How do these developments relate to changes in the production and dissemination of knowledge?

These four research questions will all be explored in relation to two central hypotheses:

1   The development of concern about climate change is part of a broader, long-term *ecological* civilizing process.
2   The development of concern about climate change is part of a broader moral panic about climate change.

Additional questions that I will be exploring in this book relate to moral panic:

1   How and to what extent has the concept of moral panic developed?
2   How and to what extent is it still a useful concept?
3   If it is relatively useful, how and to what extent does it need to be reformulated?

Finally, this exploration of moral panic, and of climate change, will be used to critically interrogate the concepts of civilizing processes, deciviliz-ing processes, and civilizing offensives. The research findings will also be used to develop conclusions that may inform policy, campaigns, and media representations of climate change.

I am aware that there are other approaches beyond Elias and moral panic that could have been of value to this research. However, I did not have time or space to utilize these. Furthermore, an aim of this research is to test Elias, which is why I have predominantly focussed on figurational so-ciology (along with moral panic). Future research could utilize these other approaches. Additionally, there are areas specifically related to climate change, green politics, and the 'environment' which I am aware of but did not have the opportunity to cover. These include such things as corporate politics, government policy, intergovernmental relations, and many more. Again, such topics can be explored in later research.

## Theoretical-conceptual background: moral panic and civilization

Drawing from the work of Norbert Elias and the figurational approach to research, this book builds on the original concept of moral panic and on the moral panic and moral regulation contributions of Alan Hunt (1999, 2003, 2011), Sean Hier (2002a, 2008), and Chas Critcher (2009). My aim is to assess some of the main assumptions of moral panic research and, specifically, to elaborate on the *developmental* research of Hunt, Hier, and Critcher, all of who conceptualize volatile panic episodes *in relation to* long-term, wider social processes. The focus on developmental and re-lational research in this book differs from much moral panic research in that the latter is typically characterized by a short-term focus on the moral panic event while neglecting how the panic develops, where it comes from, and how it is related to more long-term processes.

I will argue that the aim to conceptualize moral panics as short-term episodes that emerge from long-term moralization processes can be enhanced by incorporating the work of Norbert Elias. I am not arguing that we should develop a strictly 'Eliasian' approach to moral panic at the expense of all the other very important work that has been undertaken in this field (for example, focussing on the work of Foucault, governmentality, and moral regulation). Rather, I wish to explore how and to what extent Elias's work is of value to emerging and more traditional moral panic research.

The work of Norbert Elias has been little mentioned in the same context as moral panic, which on one level is surprising (as I will discuss later, the 'figurational approach' of Elias and, in particular, the concepts of civilizing processes, decivilizing processes, and civilizing offensives have much in common with moral panic analyses, albeit there are fundamental differences as well). The first coinciding of Elias and moral panic began in the 1980s with Eric Dunning et al.'s work on football hooliganism (for example, see Dunning, Murphy, & Williams, 1986, 1988, pp. 10, 77–8, 134–5, 141, 145–6, 151–2, 241–2; Dunning & Sheard, [1979] 2005, p. 234; Murphy, Dunning & Williams, 1988; Murphy, Williams, & Dunning, 1990). However, this early work did not attempt to develop a synthesis of Elias and moral panic; rather, these figurational studies on football hooliganism merely mentioned the term 'moral panic' in passing, referring to the media's amplification (or deamplification) of incidences of football hooliganism and the perceived inappropriate reaction by policymakers.

We can find traces of Elias in work on moral panic (for example, see Hier, 2002a, p. 324), which draws upon Alan Hunt's work on moral regulation (Hunt, 1999), along with the works of Mitchell Dean ([1999] 2010) and Philip Corrigan and Derek Sayer ([1985] 1991). This suggests that the field of moral panic studies would be compatible with some of the arguments in this book. While largely rejecting the concept of moral panic, Hunt utilizes both Elias and Foucault to explore historical projects of moral regulation (campaigns that others might classify as moral panics). In his analysis, Hunt explores how moral regulatory projects work to both govern others and govern the self. Sean Hier has since taken up Hunt's analysis and applied it to moral panics, arguing that moral panics are volatile episodes of these everyday regulatory projects, where the focus shifts from ethical self-governance to the governance of 'dangerous' others (Hier, 2002a, 2002b, 2003, 2008). Chas Critcher (2008a, 2009) has now also joined the debate, albeit with some disagreement as to the extent to which we can apply the concept of moral regulation to moral panic.

This book's theoretical framework argues for four main methodological shifts in the focus of moral panic research: (1) exploring panics in relation to wider long-term and short-term processes; (2) exploring the contradictory, countervailing processes that occur before, during, and after panics, thereby exploring the complexity of panics; (3) exploring empirical examples that do not fit the 'classic' model of a moral panic as this forces us to question many of the assumptions about moral panic, including the normative presupposition; and (4) establishing a mode of research that does not entail a normative, debunking *pre*supposition that the reaction, or 'panic', is inappropriate (although research can still be informative in this regard, as will be discussed in Chapters 3 and 4). To achieve these shifts in focus for moral panic research, this book will largely (though not exclusively) be drawing from Norbert Elias's theory of civilizing processes and the figurational approach to research.

In terms of research approach, Elias's work offers several insights to moral panic. His processual/relational approach to research provides the means to avoid the trap of using moral panic as merely a descriptive or taxonomic tool. Asking questions that focus on *how* and to what extent a possible moral panic has come to pass provides greater insight than merely asking *is* a particular example a moral panic. Elias's practice of viewing problems from a long-term perspective has additional value for it allows us to explore how and to what extent various long-term processes are feeding into a moral panic, affecting the panic, and thereby provides us with a greater understanding of the processes involved, leading to a greater chance that researchers will be able to successfully intervene and direct panics. This is further enhanced by Elias's adoption of historical and comparative methods, one of the reasons why there are historical and comparative chapters in this book. These 'values' of a figurational approach to moral panic research will be further explicated in Chapters 3 and 4. For now, let us return to the theoretical-conceptual synthesis of moral panic and civilizing processes.

### Civilizing processes

Following on from the first part of *On the Process of Civilisation*, 'On the Sociogenesis of the Concepts of "Civilisation" and "Culture"', Elias ([1939] 2012) explores how the development of the concept of 'civility' played out in notions of what constituted 'civilized' behaviour. He examines these changes in standards of behaviour by analysing etiquette books and other documents, beginning with Erasmus's 1530 publication 'On Civility in Boys'. Throughout his analysis of these etiquette books, Elias traces an overall pattern of gradual changes in standards of behaviour relating to everyday interactions (e.g. behaviour at the table, blowing one's nose, toileting practices). These books illustrate, for Elias, behaviour that was deemed to be acceptable or 'civilized' as well as behaviour that was seen as unacceptable or 'uncivilized'. Elias observes that, over time, certain behaviours that were seen to be more 'animalistic' (such as bodily functions) came to be associated with shame and disgust, and were increasingly 'shifted behind the scenes'. At the same time, the regulation of these and other behaviours came increasingly to be regulated by self-control rather than external force, what Elias calls 'the social constraint towards self-constraint'.

In relation to state formation and other wider social processes, Elias traces how competition between various groups of people, with associated conflict between these groups, culminated in the establishment of a monopoly of one group and the eventual formation of a state. This process of state formation brought with it changes in the way people were connected with one another, leading eventually to greater integration and greater interdependence between people, which brings with it changes in relations between people. As Elias puts it, as people become more reliant upon one another via increasing differentiation and increasing interdependence,

> more and more people must attune their conduct to that of others, the web of actions must be organised more and more strictly and accurately, if each individual action is to fulfill its social functions. Individuals are compelled to regulate their conduct in an increasingly differentiated, more even and more stable manner.
>
> (Elias, [1939] 2012, p. 406)

This process, Elias argues, is in part dependent upon a gradual stabilization of a central state authority, with an associated state monopolization over the forces of violence and taxation. These processes, Elias argues, contribute towards a notion of stability, where dangers come to be perceived as fewer and, when they do occur, as more predictable (that is, where dangers are known, and so life becomes less uncertain). Elias offers the example of 'When a monopoly of force is formed, pacified social spaces are created which are normally free from acts of violence' (Elias, [1939] 2012, p. 408). When violence does occur, it is often either hidden 'behind the scenes' or legitimated in some way by the state.

To summarize, Elias's theory of civilizing processes holds that, as a central state authority grows and gains increasing monopolization over the control of violence and taxation, people come to be increasingly integrated and interdependent with one another. These changes in wider social processes affect and are affected by changes in behaviour, with an overall direction towards increasing foresight, mutual identification, and increased self-restraint, thus contributing to more even, stable behaviours and relations between people. In later works, Elias further examines how these changes were intertwined with gradual changes in modes of knowledge, from 'magico-mythical' knowledge towards increasingly 'reality-congruent' knowledge[10] (Elias, [1987] 2007).

While this exposition is largely divorced from empirical examples, it is important to acknowledge that Elias developed these theories in relation to empirical observations. And he further built upon these with additional empirical observations, employing historical and comparative methods. And to reiterate a point made earlier in this chapter, it is important to highlight that Elias did not regard these processes as unilinear or inevitable: X does not lead to Y, even though this simplified exposition may provide readers with this misperception. They are not simplified laws, and every empirical example differs and has its own degree of uniqueness. The concept of decivilizing process (along with informalization and other concepts to be explored in Chapter 3) is one of the ways researchers have attempted to explain away simplified misconceptions about Elias's theory of civilizing processes.

### Decivilizing processes

Building on Elias's work, Stephen Mennell has developed some 'possible symptoms of decivilizing'; put simply, 'Decivilizing processes are what happens when civilizing processes go into reverse' (Mennell, 1990, p. 205; see also Fletcher, 1997). One of these potential 'reversals' that Mennell elaborates on is 'a rise in the level of danger and a fall in its calculability' (Mennell, 1990, p. 215). As Elias argues,

> The armour of civilised conduct would crumble very rapidly if, through a change in society, the degree of insecurity that existed earlier were to break in upon us again, and if danger became as incalculable as it once was. Corresponding fears would soon burst the limits set to them today.
>
> (Elias, [1939] 2012, p. 576)

In other words, as danger becomes increasingly incalculable, so too people's behaviour changes accordingly – it is perhaps more conducive for your survival if, where there is a great deal of uncertainty surrounding potential danger, you tend to err on the side of caution in relations with the 'social' and the 'natural' world (for example, the 'fight or flight' response).

Mennell observes that there often exists the perception today that we are living in a more violent world. He refers to Geoffrey Pearson's historical study illustrating the periodic commonality of such 'fears of escalating violence, moral decline, and the destruction of "the British way of life"' (Mennell, 1990, p. 214). Here, Mennell critiques the idea that this qualifies as a decivilizing process, stressing that an *actual* increase in violence may not necessarily be occurring (aside from periodic short-term increases).[11] But perhaps merely the *perception* of an increase in violence may affect the development of other decivilizing trends, as may be the case with some moral panics.

Another possible symptom of decivilizing processes that Mennell suggests relates to 'changes in modes of knowledge':

> During times of social crisis – military defeats, political revolutions, rampant inflation, soaring unemployment, separately or in combination – fears

rise because control of social events has declined. Rising fears make it still more difficult to control events. That makes people still more susceptible to wish fantasies about means of alleviating the situation.

(Mennell, 1990, p. 216)

In other words, there occurs a shift back from 'reality congruent' to increasingly 'magico-mythical' knowledge.

These changes may then potentially coincide with changes in behaviour, where certain acts that were formerly seen as 'uncivilized' or barbaric' become increasingly more acceptable, where there may occur a shift away from violence 'behind the scenes' back to the re-emergence of violence in the public sphere, and where mutual identification between people (or particular groups of people) decreases (Mennell, 1990). A classic example of this is Elias's own study of Nazi Germany in *Studies on the Germans* (Elias, [1989] 2013). Although, as Mennell observes, these decivilizing trends were only partial reversals; the extermination of the Jews still had to be kept 'behind the scenes' to a certain extent, suggesting that there was still a degree of mutual identification with the Jews (Mennell, 1990).

Approaches to decivilizing processes will be more critically explored in Chapters 3, 7, and 8. In this chapter, I have merely introduced decivilizing processes so that we might see how they relate to moral panics.

## Moral panics and decivilizing processes

As already mentioned, decivilizing processes may occur where there is a weakening of the state: for example, in the aftermath of social or natural crises. However, with moral panics, there need not be an *actual* weakening, only a *perceived* weakening. This could include the perception that governmental regulations, and the enforcement of those regulations, are failing to control a particular perceived problem or, conversely, that individuals are failing to regulate their own behaviour and that, therefore, there is a need for a stronger external force (from either within or outside 'the state'[12]) to 'control' these 'uncontrollable' deviants.

Moral panics may further assist with the monopolization of the means of violence by the state. Terming certain behaviours and people as social problems, and mobilizing or sponsoring panics about these social problems, may assist in developing public consent for increasing legislation, thereby spreading the scope of the state's monopolization over violence. For example, this type of development can be seen in the work of Hall et al. (1978), in which they argue that the 'mugging' panic was utilized by the government to legitimate an increasingly more coercive state.

A further indicator of decivilizing processes is the increase in the level of danger posed as well as an increasing incalculability of danger, that is, where danger becomes more prominent and increasingly difficult to predict. In the case of moral panics, it could be argued that the 'exaggeration and distortion' of reporting on phenomena (reporting of both past events and potential future risks) have contributed to a sense that we now live in an increasingly dangerous society, where the occurrence of dangers is perceived to be difficult to predict.

Rather than regarding moral panics as a *complete* decivilizing process, we can see how perceived increase in danger, and/or perceived failure of central state authority to protect its citizens from perceived dangers, may be enough to bring about *partial* decivilizing processes, similar to those outlined earlier. If a particular issue (danger or threat) becomes highlighted and mass communicated (for example, via the media), fears may increase, and danger may come to be perceived as increasingly incalculable with regard to the given issue. In turn, 'folk devils' may develop (though the demonization of them, and the categorization of them as folk devils, may be contested). During this process, folk devils may come to be increasingly dehumanized and come to be seen as the dangerous 'uncivilized' other, thereby enabling the use of more 'cruel' measures that would, under other conditions, be deemed 'uncivilized'. In the haste to address the given issue, solutions may be proposed that are not necessarily well informed and may not function adequately to address the given issue; indeed, they may have the unintended consequence of contributing to the problem. In addition, in attempts to alleviate the perceived problem, the state, or even citizens themselves, may draw upon more violent, 'uncivilized' measures in an attempt to try to contain the problem; for example, the development of new laws that may override certain civil liberties or the development of vigilantism (Rohloff, 2008).

However, while these may apply to *some* cases that have been classified as moral panics, I wish to argue that it is not simply the case that all moral panics are merely decivilizing processes. Indeed, as Elias himself would no doubt have argued, civilizing and decivilizing processes (and thereby, moral panics) are much more complex than this. Potentially, civilizing processes may contribute to the emergence of moral panics, and moral panics may, in turn, feed back into civilizing processes. It is here that we need a shift in the focus of moral panic research in order to attend to the complexity of moral panics.

### Civilizing offensives: towards a dialectical understanding of moral panic and (de)civilization

In his discussion of the complexity of civilizing and decivilizing processes, Robert van Krieken (1998, 1999) draws upon the concept of civilizing offensives. Civilizing offensives have been defined as 'deliberate (but not necessarily successful) attempts by people who consider themselves to be "civilized" to "improve" the manners and morals of people whom they considered to be "less civilized" or "barbaric"' (Dunning & Sheard, [1979] 2005, p. 280). In this way, 'civilizing offensives' bear a strong resemblance to those moral regulation campaigns that are analyzed by Alan Hunt in *Governing Morals* (1999), which, in turn, bear some resemblances to what others have termed 'moral panics' (as well as processes that Howard Becker ([1963] 1991) earlier termed 'moral crusades' by 'moral entrepreneurs').

Robert van Krieken argues 'for a more *dialectical* understanding of social relations and historical development, one which grasps the often contradictory character of social life' (van Krieken, 1998, p. 132). Here, van Krieken is arguing that processes of civilization themselves can give rise to decivilizing trends in the form of 'civilized barbarism', where civilizing and decivilizing are 'opposed sides of the same processes of social development' (van Krieken, 1998, p. 164), and are present at the same time as each other rather than being mutually exclusive processes. To illustrate this point, he draws upon the example of the 'stolen generations' in Australia. In their project to 'civilize' indigenous Australian children, Europeans forcibly removed the aboriginal children from their homes and families in an attempt to make the aboriginal children more like European children (i.e. to 'civilize' them). This project took the form of a 'civilizing offensive' and was carried out in the name of civilization. Civilizing processes were present, with the exception that mutual identification was limited between Europeans and the indigenous population. However, there was still a degree of mutual identification; the 'stolen generations' were integrated amongst the Europeans rather than obliterated (although other aborigines were killed), and it is important to highlight that this civilizing offensive was carried out in philanthropic terms, as an attempt to *improve* (as they saw it) the lives of the aboriginals (van Krieken, 1999).

However, van Krieken's and others' usage of the term decivilizing, while sometimes used alongside civilizing, is still conceptualized as a reversal of civilizing and in that way represents a dichotomy. Throughout this book, I will instead suggest that these concepts need to be conceptualized in terms of degrees: degrees of civilizing and decivilizing – rather than this is a decivilizing process, and that is a civilizing process. This will be further explored in Chapters 3, 7, and 8.

Van Krieken's arguments are still useful for while 'civilizing offensives' can be comparable to projects of moral regulation (and, by extension, episodes of moral panic), they may involve within them a *fusion* of civilizing and decivilizing trends. If we combine this idea of a civilizing offensive involving a fusion of civilizing and decivilizing trends, and then apply it to the concept of moral panic, we can then use this to develop a more encompassing concept of moral panic, one that takes account of the complex (civilizing and decivilizing) processes that intertwine before, during, and after a moral panic, thereby overcoming the dichotomous, normative conceptualization of moral panics as being *either* 'bad' *or* 'good' panics (on the idea of 'good' and 'bad' panics, see Cohen, [1972] 2002, pp. xxxi–xxxv; see also Hunt, 2011, for a critique). One potential way to overcome this normative dichotomy is by integrating some of the aspects of figurational research with moral panic research, which will be further discussed in Chapters 3 and 4. In Chapter 7, I will further develop this by comparing several different empirical examples in order to demonstrate the complex interplay of civilizing and decivilizing processes and civilizing offensives.

As we have already seen, via the concepts of civilizing and decivilizing processes and civilizing offensives, moral panic and figurational research also share an interest in exploring changes in the regulation of behaviour – both regulation of the self and regulation of the other. However, there are also several existing points of departure. Rather than viewing these differences in research approaches as problems, in Chapters 3 and 4 I will discuss how these points of departure can be utilized to further develop moral panic research and to attend to some of the criticisms and debates surrounding moral panic.

### Moral panics as civilizing and decivilizing processes: the example of climate change

A figurational approach to moral panic research might involve exploring the interplay between long-term regulatory processes (moral regulation or civilizing and decivilizing processes) and short-term campaigns (civilizing offensives and moral panics). This could involve the study of how various processes have been gradually developing in the long term, including changes in standards of behaviour, changes in the communication of knowledge, changes in state formation, changes in social and self-regulation, and changes in power relations between people. This could then be combined with an exploration of various short-term campaigns (instances of moral panics) and how these short-term campaigns relate to more gradual and wider social processes. Such a focus on long-term developmental research could then provide us with a greater insight into the complex processes that develop in relation to moral panics.

As an example, let us consider the topic of this book: climate change. There has already been some figurational research that has argued that the development of ecological sensibilities could be seen as a type of civilizing process (Quilley, 2009; Schmidt, 1993). Moral panic research has also been undertaken on the topic of climate change, where it is argued that climate campaigns constitute 'social scares' (a concept derived from moral panics) (Ungar, 1992, 1995). One could also argue, perhaps, that certain outcomes of processes of civilization have given rise to decivilizing consequences, in the form of *excess* capitalism and *over*consumption, to the relative detriment of the environment and social life as a whole (see Ampudia de Haro, 2008). Potentially, campaigns surrounding climate change could be utilized as civilizing offensives, or moral panics, to bring about a civilizing 'spurt'. However, these campaigns could also, potentially, bring with them decivilizing disintegrative processes: for example, via the development of 'good' and 'bad' behaviours into 'good' and 'bad' people (this is already happening, to a certain extent, with some animal rights and environmental activists who prioritize animal/environmental rights over the rights of 'other un-eco-friendly' people, where increasing mutual identification with other animals and the environment goes hand in hand with decreasing mutual identification with other people) (for example, see Quilley, 2009, p. 133). So, potentially, moral panics over climate change, and the civilizing offensives that accompany them in the form of campaigns with a view to promoting eco-friendly patterns of behaviour, could be regarded as both civilizing and decivilizing processes.

Moral panics are highly complex processes. To further tap into the complexity of moral panics, it is necessary to abandon some of the former dichotomous thinking regarding them as this limits our perception of what moral panics might be and what they might entail. Such dichotomies include moral/risk, rational/irrational, 'good'/'bad', intentional/unintentional, and civilizing/decivilizing (these will be further explored in Chapters 3 and 4). Through collapsing these dichotomies, and expanding the scope of moral panic research to other types of examples, as well as longer time frames of analysis, we can gain a greater insight into how moral panics develop and how they relate to more long-term processes.

### Time frames: the relationship between processes, offensives, and panics

To understand how these various developments relate to one another, it is necessary to consider the time frames involved in each concept. As mentioned earlier in this chapter, civilizing processes occur at different levels – at the level of the individual, at the level of mid-range societal transformations, and at the level of humanity as a whole. The latter two developments occur over centuries and millennia. The first – individual civilizing processes – occurs over decades, during one's own lifetime. All three of these processual developments are regarded by Elias as largely unintended developments (unintended consequences of intentional actions). But how do decivilizing processes, civilizing offensives, and moral panics relate to these time frames? If we consider the case of Nazi Germany, Elias ([1989] 2013) shows how long-term developments throughout the history of Germany and its relation to other nation states gave rise to a decivilizing spurt – in short, we can think about a long-term gradual civilizing process giving rise to a short-term accelerated decivilizing process (or spurt). Similarly, civilizing offensives, which consist of intentional attempts to induce change, might also result in a 'spurt' of one sort or another. If some moral panics are akin to some civilizing offensives, it is possible that offensives/panics may bring about a civilizing and/ or decivilizing spurt. The question remains to what extent the personality make-ups associated with these 'spurts' become internalized (and if so how long this takes) or rejected.

The example of *Jamie's School Dinners* is useful to consider for illustrating these time frames. Long-term developments in humanity as a whole (except for a minority of small tribes, amongst others) – in the form of agriculture, technology, global trade, and so forth – have resulted in rapid changes in the types and quantities of food that are available for us to consume. These sociocultural developments have accelerated at a much faster pace than biological developments. Mid-range societal transformations have included the development of increasing moderation in consumption and, with regard to the case of food and eating, in the 'civilizing of appetite' (1987). At the individual level, children are taught table manners, what is considered appropriate to eat, and where and when to eat it in their specific households. Some patterns of eating and types of food, however, are considered by some to be unhealthier and less nutritious than others. And so, there is a constant relationship between those habits learnt within the household and those behavioural standards developing outside of the household (with the two feeding into one another). With the increasing concern about obesity, we have witnessed many campaigns – what might be called civilizing offensives, perhaps moral panics – about food, eating, and obesity. One such campaign was instigated by Jamie Oliver, celebrity chef in the UK, transformed into moral entrepreneur in the 2005 TV series *Jamie's School Dinners*. This show consisted of an attempt by Oliver to improve the nutritional standards of food that was provided to children at school, in their canteens. Following this intervention, Oliver met with the Prime Minister, a petition was submitted to parliament, and various methods of regulation were instilled. However, criticisms of Oliver's campaign soon surfaced, with allegations that students were rejecting the new, healthier school dinners (Clark, 2009), and with revelations that parents were passing 'junk' food through school fences to their children (Weaver, 2006). And so, the extent to which such intentional campaigns to rapidly change people's eating habits are effective is perhaps mixed. From the media reaction it seems that there was at least a certain amount of initial resistance by some – a rejection of the campaign and of the new food standards. However, without a detailed analysis, following up with students who were involved in the intervention, it is unclear whether and to what extent some children's eating habits were modified and how internalized these new habits have become. Such questions will be explored in this book in relation to the example of climate change and ecological civilizing processes.

## Chapter outlines

In the rest of this book, I further develop the themes explored in this Introduction. These can be grouped into three main parts.

In Chapter 2, I provide an overview of the various literature on climate change, drawing upon these different disciplines to contribute to syntheses in later chapters as well as highlighting how my research is unique and fills a large gap within climate change research. The climate change literature then leads into a critical discussion of theories of social change in Chapter 3. Here, I define terms and concepts that are to be used throughout the book and interrogate both moral panic and figurational approaches with other sociological approaches in order to refine and develop my own approach to social problems. My approach to the research is further explicated in Chapter 4, where I discuss my 'methodology' and the methods I employed in various stages of the research process. The aim of this chapter is to clarify my approach to moral panic research, which will be even further developed in the conclusion of this book.

Chapters 5 and 6 primarily utilize historical documentary analysis to explore how and to what extent climate change relates to the development of ecological civilizing processes (Chapter 5) and moral panics (Chapter 6), and how it relates to the interplay of long-term and short-term processes.

Chapter 7 consists of a comparative analysis, with the aim of comparing climate change with several other empirical examples to further flesh out the relationship between civilizing and decivilizing processes, moral panics, and civilizing offensives. I compare several case studies – alcohol, climate change, (illegal) drugs, eating/obesity, terrorism, and tobacco – all of which have been explored separately from a figurational and a moral panic approach. The purpose of the chapter is to critically, comparatively, explore the concepts of moral panic, civilizing processes, decivilizing processes, and civilizing offensives. This feeds into a broader interrogation with the concept of moral panic, the concept of decivilizing processes, and the relationship between civilizing offensives and civilizing processes – these are further developed in the Conclusion (Chapter 8). In the final chapter, I then go on to explicate how the research in this book has informed understandings about the emergence of climate change as a social problem. I outline how, based on this research, I think moral panic should be conceptualized and how moral panic research should be undertaken in the future. This is followed by a similar discussion about the relationship between civilizing offensives and civilizing processes, and the conceptualization of decivilizing processes.

## Notes

1 See Rohloff (2011a).
2 For a comprehensive introduction to climate change, anthropogenic climate change, and the consequences of this, see Houghton ([1994] 2009).
3 This is not to suggest that concern about climate change has only developed since 2005. Rather, 2005 and the events that followed provide an example of a series of incidents that may have spurred acceleration in the development of concern about climate change. This research seeks to explore to what extent this may or may not have been the case at different times.
4 Cohen ([1972] 2002, p. xxxv) acknowledges that both he and Young probably first came across the term 'moral panic' in Marshall McLuhan's Understanding Media.

5  Chas Critcher (2002, 2003, 2008a, 2009, 2011) and Sean Hier (2002a, 2002b, 2003, 2008) have begun an attempt to address this via their differing efforts to connect moral panic with discourse, moral regulation, and risk.
6  For introductions to Elias's work, see Dunning & Hughes (2013), Fletcher (1997), Hughes (2008), Kilminster (2007), Mennell ([1989] 1998), and van Krieken (1998, 2003).
7  Quilley and Loyal (2005) argue that Elias's process sociology can be used as a central theory to integrate sociology and indeed the whole of the human sciences. Conversely, Dunning and Hughes (2013, Ch.3) explore central theory in relation to grand theories and middle-range theories. They argue that while Elias's central theory is similar to Merton's middle-range theory, it goes beyond this via the application to a range of topics and by developing integration and synthesis (which Merton was opposed to).
8  See Elias ([1989] 2013).
9  While civilizing offensives have largely been conceptualized as intentional and civilizing processes as unintentional, this is not necessarily the case. Elias refers to civilizing processes as the largely unintended outcome of intentional action (thereby entailing both the planned and the unplanned), while civilizing offensives are regarded as largely intentional actions with unintended outcomes. In other words, they involve blends of the intended and the unintended. The point of exploring the interplay is to draw attention to the blend of planned and unplanned, and of short-term and long-term changes.
10 It is important to highlight that this shift from 'magico-mythical' to 'reality-congruent' knowledge, like other processual shifts that Elias traces, is never absolute.
11 On the long-term decline of violence, see Johnson and Monkkonen (1996), Pinker (2011), and Spierenburg (2008).
12 This could either come from 'official' authorities, such as those of 'the state', or non-state groups, such as social movement or reform groups, vigilante groups, and 'terrorist' groups.

# References

Aarts, W., Schmidt, C., & Spier, F. (1995). Toward a morality of increasing moderation. In S. Zwerver, R. S. A. R. van Rompaey, M. T. J. Kok, & M. M. Berk (Eds.), *Climate change research: Evaluation and policy implications.* (Vol. 65, part 2, pp. 1247–1250). Amsterdam: Elsevier.

Altheide, D. L. (2009). Moral panic: From sociological concept to public discourse. *Crime Media Culture, 5*(1), 79–99.

Ampudia de Haro, F. (2008). *Discussing decivilisation: Some theoretical remarks.* Paper presented at the First ISA Forum of Sociology: Sociological Research and Public Debate.

Becker, H. S. ([1963] 1991). *Outsiders: Studies in the sociology of deviance.* New York, NY: Free Press.

Clark, L. (2009). 'Jamie Oliver's school meal revolution shunned by 400,000 pupils'. *Daily Mail,* 10th July 2009. Accessed online July 2009 from http://www.dailymil.co.uk/news/article-1198566/Jamies-school-meal-revolution-shunned-400-000-pupils.html.

Cohen, S. (1972). *Folk devils and moral panics.* Herts: Paladin.

Cohen, S. ([1972] 2002). *Folk devils and moral panics: The creation of the mods and rockers* (3rd ed.). London: Routledge.

Corrigan, P., & Sayer, D. ([1985] 1991). *The great arch: English state formation as cultural revolution*. Oxford: Basil Blackwell.

Critcher, C. (2002). Media, government and moral panic: The politics of paedophilia in Britain 2000–1. *Journalism Studies, 3*(4), 521–535.

Critcher, C. (2003). *Moral panics and the media*. Buckingham: Open University Press.

Critcher, C. (2008a). Moral panic analysis: Past, present and future. *Sociology Compass, 2*(4), 1127–1144.

Critcher, C. (2009). Widening the focus: Moral panics as moral regulation. *British Journal of Criminology, 49*(1), 17–34.

Critcher, C. (2011). Double measures: The moral regulation of alcohol consumption, past and present. In P. Bramham & S. Wagg (Eds.), *The new politics of leisure and pleasure* (pp. 32–44). Basingstoke: Palgrave Macmillan.

David, M., Rohloff, A., Petley, J., & Hughes, J. (2011). The idea of moral panic – ten dimensions of dispute. *Crime, Media, Culture, 7*(3), 215–228.

Dean, M. ([1999] 2010). *Governmentality: Power and rule in modern society* (2nd ed.). London: Sage.

de Swaan, A. (1997). Widening circles of desidentification: On the psycho- and sociogenesis of the hatred of distant strangers – reflections on Rwanda. *Theory, Culture & Society, 14*(2), 105–122.

de Swaan, A. (2001). Dyscivilization, mass extermination and the state. *Theory, Culture & Society, 18*(2–3), 265–276.

Dunning, E., & Hughes, J. (2013). *Norbert Elias and modern sociology: Knowledge, interdependence, power, process*. London: Bloomsbury.

Dunning, E., & Sheard, K. ([1979] 2005). *Barbarians, gentlemen and players: A sociological study of the development of rugby football* (2nd ed.). London: Routledge.

Dunning, E., Murphy, P., & Williams, J. (1986). Spectator violence at football matches: Towards a sociological explanation. *British Journal of Sociology, 37*(2), 221–244.

Dunning, E., Murphy, P., & Williams, J. (1988). *The roots of football hooliganism: An historical and sociological study*. London: Routledge.

Elias, N. ([1939] 2012). *On the process of civillisation: Sociogenetic and psychogenetic investigations* (The Collected Works of Norbert Elias, Vol. 3). Dublin: University College Dublin Press [Previous editions published as The civilizing process].

Elias, N. ([1986] 2008). Civilisation. In R. Kilminster & S. Mennell (Eds.), *Essays II: On civilising processes, state formation and national identity (The collected works of Norbert Elias*, Vol. 15, pp. 3–7). Dublin: University College Dublin Press.

Elias, N. ([1987] 2007). *Involvement and detachment (The Collected Works of Norbert Elias*, Vol. 8). Dublin: University College Dublin Press.

Elias, N. ([1989] 2013). *Studies on the Germans (The Collected Works of Norbert Elias*, Vol. 11). Dublin: University College Dublin Press.

Fletcher, J. (1997). *Violence and civilization: An introduction to the work of Norbert Elias*. Cambridge: Polity Press.

Garland, D. (2008). On the concept of moral panic. *Crime Media Culture, 4*(1), 9–30.

Goode, E., & Ben-Yehuda, N. ([1994] 2009). *Moral panics: The social construction of deviance* (2nd ed.). Chichester, West Sussex: Wiley-Blackwell.

Goudsblom, J. (1992). *Fire and civilization.* London: Allen Lane.

Guggenheim, D. (Director). (2006). *An inconvenient truth: A global warning* [Motion Picture]. United States: Paramount Pictures.

Hall, S., Critcher, C., Jefferson, T., Clarke, J., & Roberts, B. (1978). *Policing the crisis: Mugging, the state, and law and order.* London: Macmillan Press.

Hier, S. P. (2002a). Conceptualizing moral panic through a moral economy of harm. *Critical Sociology, 28*(3), 311–334.

Hier, S. P. (2002b). Raves, risks and the ecstasy panic: A case study in the subversive nature of moral regulation. *Canadian Journal of Sociology / Cahiers canadiens de sociologie, 27*(1), 33–57.

Hier, S. P. (2003). Risk and panic in late modernity: Implications of the converging sites of social anxiety. *British Journal of Sociology, 54*(1), 3–20.

Hier, S. P. (2008). Thinking beyond moral panic: Risk, responsibility, and the politics of moralization. *Theoretical Criminology, 12*(2), 173–190.

Hier, S. P. (Ed.). (2011). *Moral panic and the politics of anxiety.* London: Routledge.

Houghton, J. ([1994] 2009). *Global warming: The complete briefing* (4th ed.). Cambridge: Cambridge University Press.

Hughes, J. (2008). Norbert Elias. In R. Stones (Ed.), *Key sociological thinkers* (2nd ed., pp. 168–183). Houndmills, Basingstoke, Hampshire: Palgrave Macmillan.

Hunt, A. (1999). *Governing morals: A social history of moral regulation.* Cambridge: Cambridge University Press.

Hunt, A. (2003). Risk and moralization in everyday life. In R. V. Ericson & A. Doyle (Eds.), *Risk and morality* (pp. 165–192). Toronto, CA: University of Toronto Press.

Hunt, A. (2011). Fractious rivals? Moral panics and moral regulation. In S. P. Hier (Ed.), *Moral panic and the politics of anxiety* (pp. 53–70). London: Routledge.

Jenkins, P. (2009). Failure to launch: Why do some social issues fail to detonate moral panics? *British Journal of Criminology, 49*(1), 35–47.

Johnson, E. A., & Monkkonen, E. H. (1996). *The civilization of crime: Violence in town and country since the Middle Ages.* Urbana, IL: University of Illinois Press.

Kilminster, R. (2007). *Norbert Elias: Post-philosophical sociology.* London: Routledge.

Kilminster, R., & Mennell, S. (2008). Note on the text. In R. Kilminster & S. Mennell (Eds.), *Essays II: On civilising processes, state formation and national identity (The Collected Works of Norbert Elias, Vol. 15, pp. xi–xxii).* Dublin: University College Dublin Press.

Lever-Tracy, C. (2008). Global warming and sociology. *Current Sociology, 56*(3), 445–466.

Mennell, S. ([1989] 1998). *Norbert Elias: An introduction* (rev. ed.). Dublin: University College Dublin Press. [First published as *Norbert Elias: Civilization and the human self-image.* Oxford: Blackwell, 1989].

Mennell, S. (1990). Decivilising processes: Theoretical significance and some lines of research. *International Sociology, 5*(2), 205–223.

Mitzman, A. (1987). The civilizing offensive: Mentalities, high culture and individual psyches. *Journal of Social History, 20*(4), 663–687.

Murphy, P., Dunning, E., & Williams, J. (1988). Soccer crowd disorder and the press: Processes of amplification and de-amplification in historical perspective. *Theory, Culture & Society, 5*(3), 645–673.

Moore, D., & Valverde, M. (2000). Maidens at risk: 'Date rape drugs' and the formation of hybrid risk knowledges. *Economy and Society, 29*(4), 514–531.

Murphy, P., Williams, J., & Dunning, E. (1990). *Football on trial: Spectator violence and development in the football world*. London: Routledge.

Pinker, S. (2011). *The better angels of our nature: The decline of violence in history and its causes*. London: Penguin.

Quilley, S. (2009). The land ethic as an ecological civilizing process: Aldo Leopold, Norbert Elias, and environmental philosophy. *Environmental Ethics, 31*(2), 115–134.

Quilley, S. (2011). Entropy, the anthroposphere and the ecology of civilization: An essay on the problem of 'liberalism in one village' in the long view. *Sociological Review*, 50, 65–90.

Quilley, S., & Loyal, S. (2005). Eliasian sociology as a 'central theory' for the human sciences. *Current Sociology, 53*(5), 807–828.

Rohloff, A. (2008). Moral panics as decivilising processes: Towards an Eliasian approach. *New Zealand Sociology, 23*(1), 66–76.

Rohloff, A. (2011). Extending the concept of moral panic: Elias, climate change and civilization. *Sociology, 45*(4), 634–649.

Rohloff, A., & Wright, S. (2010). Moral panic and social theory: Beyond the heuristic. *Current Sociology, 58*(3), 403–419.

Schmidt, C. (1993). On economization and ecologization as civilizing processes. *Environmental Values, 2*(1), 33–46.

Spierenburg, P. (2008). A history of murder: Personal violence in Europe from the Middle Ages to the present. Cambridge: Polity Press.

Thompson, K. (1998). *Moral panics*. London: Routledge.

Ungar, S. (1992). The rise and (relative) decline of global warming as a social problem. *Sociological Quarterly, 33*(4), 483–501.

Ungar, S. (1995). Social scares and global warming: Beyond the Rio Convention. *Society and Natural Resources, 8*(4), 443–456.

Ungar, S. (2001). Moral panic versus the risk society: The implications of the changing sites of social anxiety. *British Journal of Sociology, 52*(2), 271–291.

van Krieken, R. (1990). The organization of the soul: Elias and Foucault on discipline and the self. *Archives Europeenes de Sociologie / European Journal of Sociology, 31*(2), 353–371.

van Krieken, R. (1998). *Norbert Elias*. London: Routledge.

van Krieken, R. (1999). The barbarism of civilization: Cultural genocide and the 'stolen generations'. *British Journal of Sociology, 50*(2), 297–315.

van Krieken, R. (2003). Norbert Elias and process sociology. In G. Ritzer & B. Smart (Eds.), *Handbook of social theory* (pp. 353–367). London: Sage.

Verrips, K. (1987). Noblemen, farmers and labourers. A civilizing offensive in a Dutch village. *Netherlands Journal of Sociology 23*(1), 3–17.

Watney, S. ([1987] 1997). *Policing desire: Pornography, AIDS and the media* (3rd ed.). London: Cassell.

Weart, S. R. ([2003] 2008). *The discovery of global warming* (Revised and expanded ed.). Cambridge: Harvard University Press.

Weaver, M. (2006, September 18). Parents and head in school dinner talks. The *Guardian*. Retrieved October 15, 2012, from http://www.guardian.co.uk/news/2006/sep/18/food.foodanddrink.Young, J. (1971). *The drugtakers: The social meaning of drug use*. London: Paladin.

Young, J. (2009). Moral panic: Its origins in resistance, ressentiment and the translation of fantasy into reality. *British Journal of Criminology, 49*(1), 4–16.

## 2 On climate change, 'nature', and the 'environment'

### Introduction

While there has been much written about climate change in the sub-discipline of environmental sociology, as well as in literature on the public understanding of the science of climate change, there has not been a lot of mainstream sociological literature on the topic (see also Lever-Tracy, 2008a). It is only very recently that climate change has emerged as a 'problem' in mainstream sociology. Articles were published in the *British Journal of Sociology* in 2008 (Urry, 2008a), in *Current Sociology* in 2008 and 2009 (Brechin, 2008; Leahy, 2008; Lever-Tracy, 2008a, 2008b; Redclift, 2009; Yearley, 2009), and in a special issue of *Theory, Culture and Society* in 2010 (Szerszynski & Urry, 2010). Books were published in 2009 (Beck, 2009; Giddens, 2009), 2010 (Lever-Tracy, 2010), and 2011 (Lever-Tracy, 2011; Urry, 2011). In 2010, the American Sociological Association (ASA) published conference proceedings from a workshop on sociological perspectives on global climate change (Nagel, Dietz, & Broadbent, 2010), and the British Sociological Association (BSA) held a Presidential Event on 'How to Put "Society" into Climate Change' (BSA Postgraduate Forum, 2010)[1] – this was closely followed by the formation of the BSA Climate Change Study Group and their launch event in January 2011. Indeed, this emerging sociological interest in climate change is perhaps a reflection of the more general interest on the topic, the development of climate change as an increasingly popular social problem.

In accordance with some of these publications, anthropogenic climate change can be approached from disciplines other than environmental sociology[2] and other than the public understanding of science. While both these disciplines have provided useful insights, they have their limitations in that they have theoretical, methodological, or empirical focusses that concentrate on certain things while neglecting others (as with any approach to research). And so, the overall purpose of this chapter is to demonstrate gaps within the research and how those gaps will be addressed by this book (which will employ some of the literature discussed here).

For the purpose of this chapter, what has already been written on climate change, along with other literature that relates, will be artificially broken up into several groups. The first section focusses on exploring the sudden changes that may be necessary to address human impact on climate change, drawing from eco-Marxist and complexity theory approaches. The next few sections explore the gradual changes that are occurring and/or that may occur, including ecological modernization work on the greening of production, consumption, and lifestyles as well as literature on ecological civilizing processes. The public understanding of the science of climate change, encompassing media representations of climate change, is discussed in the following sections. The final section of the chapter explores 'climate change denial', focussing primarily on the role of emotions and psychoanalysis in understanding how some people increasingly avoid the topic of climate change and the unpleasant emotions associated with it. The areas of literature explored here are not restricted to sociological analyses; some of the same concepts employed by social scientists are to be found in popular works and in the media. Indeed, in some cases perhaps, some of these sociological analyses may have been informed by popular ideas about anthropogenic climate change.

In the next chapter (Chapter 3), I will critically examine different theories and concepts that have been used in relation to climate change, moral panics, or civilizing processes. This critical review of the literature on social processes and social change in Chapter 3 will be used to refine my own theoretical-conceptual-methodological approach to this research, which will be explicated in Chapter 4. For now, let us return to the literature on climate change, 'nature', and the 'environment', with an examination of eco-Marxist approaches.

## Eco-Marxism and a relatively static capitalism

Perhaps one of the more critical (environmental) sociological positions is that of eco-Marxism, or the neo-Marxist treadmill of production perspective, which takes its lead from Allan Schnaiberg's analysis of the 'treadmill' of production. In *The Environment: From Surplus to Scarcity*, Schnaiberg (1980) explores the cooperative and competitive relationships between capital, labour, and states. For the cooperative relationships, both capital and labour contribute to production and consumption – capital aims to maximize consumption for profit; labour seeks to maximize consumption, for example, for well-being and perceived increased happiness (Schnaiberg, 1980, p. 210).

Schnaiberg and his colleagues later argue that 'economic criteria remain at the *foundation* of decision making about the design, performance and evaluation of production and consumption' (Schnaiberg, Pellow, & Weinberg, 2002, p. 16, original emphasis). This primacy of economic influences over all others leads Schnaiberg and other eco-Marxists to the conclusion that the 'treadmill of production' must be reversed, which can only be done via the education of labour: making members of the working class realize that they do not need or want a 'comfortable life'. This must then be combined with a 'sufficient political support for production apart from the treadmill' (Schnaiberg, 1980, p. 249), for a different form of capitalism, or for something else altogether.

Combined with James O'Connor's 'second contradiction of capitalism' (O'Connor, 1996, 1998) – expanding forces of production with finite conditions of production – this leads some eco-Marxists to argue that capitalism is not sustainable. The search for 'absolute' sustainability leads them to the conclusion that, to address climate change, *radical* reorganization of social life, including capitalism, is required (Lever-Tracy, 2008a; Mol & Spaargaren, 2005).[3]

While this approach draws attention to the structural changes that might be necessary to address climate change (and other ecological issues associated with capitalism), thereby diverting attention away from neo-liberal approaches to climate change (such as those that focus on individualistic changes made by individual consumers), it does have its limitations. One problem with this approach is that it characterizes capitalism as being relatively static and unchanging (excluding, of course, its ever-expanding forces of production). As we will see in the section on ecological modernization (and other more optimistic approaches), this is perhaps not an accurate conceptualization; capitalism, like everything else, adapts and changes as relations between social processes, and between social and natural processes, change. It assumes that concern about climate change, and other changes, will not affect significant changes in capitalism.

Additionally, the focus on the economic causes of climate change reduces the problem to a single cause while neglecting to explore the various other (non-economic) processes that contribute to climate change. While it is important to highlight and address these economic factors, they are only part of the puzzle – all cannot be reduced to economic causes.

## Complexity theory and tipping points: 'switching' to a post-carbon future

In his work on climate change (utilizing complexity theory), John Urry (2008a, 2008b, 2008c, 2009b, 2010, 2011) has incorporated some aspects of eco-Marxism – notably, the argument that capitalism is inherently unsustainable. He uses the example of the car 'system' to illustrate his arguments. This 'system' consists of 'networks' and 'flows' between the 'components' of cars, technology, people (drivers, passengers, pedestrians), signs, symbols, cultures, objects, and so on, which together form a 'locked-in' system.

He describes these locked-in systems, such as the use of cars or the QWERTY keyboard, as difficult to change or reverse (akin to eco-Marxist arguments about capitalism). Only with a particular combination of many small changes and interactions between components in the system can the system reach a 'tipping point', at which time the system may suddenly 'switch' (and then become 'locked in' to a different trajectory) rather than change in a gradual, linear way (he gives the examples of a liquid suddenly 'switching' to a gas and of small temperature increases suddenly producing global heating). This seems to suggest rapid change, followed by stasis.

Such a conceptualization focusses on the sudden (or apparently sudden) changes that occur, to the relative neglect of gradual change. In this way, Urry appears to contradict himself: he talks about systems being 'locked in' to a particular trajectory, yet at the same time he argues that all systems are dynamic and processual, and generate emergent contradictions, especially through feedback loop mechanisms. Interestingly, his focus seems to be only on the negative side of these contradictions and feedback loops – how they *gradually* contribute to climate change, etc. Yet he argues that, to address climate change, we need 'a massive reorganisation of social life, nothing more and nothing less' (Urry, 2008b, Climate Change and Peak Oil section, para. 13). But even then, he argues that the 'fateful' twentieth century, with its development of 'high carbon forms of life', has 'massively constrained the future possibilities of life on Earth' (Urry, 2009a, p. 9).

These arguments about 'tipping points', in particular, describe a specific type of social change – that of continuity followed by discontinuity, of 'ruptures' similar to those described by Thomas Kuhn ([1962] 1970) in *The Structure of Scientific Revolutions*. This relates to debates about gradual versus sudden change and intentional versus unintentional developments. I will return to these debates, and to Urry's complexity theory approach, in Chapter 3.

One possible criticism of Urry's arguments relates to his utilization of disciplines outside of the social sciences, of direct applications of theory from the physical sciences to the social sciences, such as the idea of a chaos point, without perhaps a critical assessment as to whether or not such concepts can be applied in this exact way to social sciences (for example, see Newton, 2003). It does not follow that those natural processes *are the same* as social processes, as much as Urry may want to transcend the divide between the physical and the social sciences, between nature and society (see Urry, 2003, p. 18, in Mol & Spaargaren, 2005, p. 100).

There appears to be an underlying moralistic element to Urry's latest work on climate change. He argues that the late twentieth century has been characterized by a *capitalism of excess*, where 'there is only pleasure no guilt' – the only 'guilt is not to consume to the "limit"' (Urry, 2008b, Excess Capitalism section, paras. 5 & 7). Drawing from a newspaper article by Giddens (2007), Urry conceptualizes the past as characterized by 'disciplined excess', where such institutions as the family, school, and so on confined and disciplined to regulate consumption. These 'societies of discipline', he argues, have shifted towards 'societies of control', where increased freedom (from 'sites of confinement') has gone hand in hand with 'freedom to become "addicted", to be emotionally and/or physically dependent upon certain products of global capitalism' (Urry, 2008b, Excess Capitalism section, para. 6). Dubai is Urry's example of a capitalism of excess in societies of control. In Dubai, he argues, the focus is on 'overconsumption, prostitution, drink and gambling where guilt is not to consume to the "limit"' (Urry, 2008b, Excess Capitalism section, para. 7). However, this focus on 'overconsumption' ignores other trends that may be occurring in opposite directions: towards decreasing consumption, towards self-control of consumption levels. (This will be looked at in the next section in relation to ecological modernization and ecological civilizing processes.) It also appears to be a departure from previous research by Urry, which suggested that consumers *do* feel guilt about their consumption and its impact on the environment (see Macnaghten & Urry, 1998).

This usage of complexity and 'tipping points' has not been restricted to social (and natural) sciences; it is also used by the media and by climate change campaigners, including in popular books on the topic. References to 'tipping points' include the 'point of no return', that is, once a 'tipping point' is reached, it will be too late to act on climate change, with different predictions as to whether or not we have reached, or are approaching, a tipping point. Tipping points are also used as the point at which people act on climate change – a tipping point of knowledge (for example, see Walsh, 2007, October 12th). This popular usage of the terms is similar in some ways to that of Urry's and demonstrates the transference of ideas between academia and popular culture (not necessarily that one is influencing the other but rather that academics are part of the same world as those who write in popular media and have some of the same influences).

Both academic and popular usages of 'tipping points' have some similarities to moral panic (though I do not wish to suggest that these publications are representative of a moral panic in the popular or even the original understanding of the term). Certainly, with some of Urry's work, we get the sense that the past, low-carbon 'societies of discipline' are better than the present, high-carbon 'societies of control' (and also the possible futures, see Urry, 2010, 2011). In the apparent shift from external control to self-control, Urry appears to see the latter as failing to regulate consumption. Thus, as with moral panics, campaigners and academics are arguing that something drastic must be done now before it is too late (before the tipping point is reached). Indeed, the dramatic nature of such films and documentaries as *The Day After Tomorrow* and *An Inconvenient Truth* (both of which Urry refers to) perhaps exaggerates the sudden change in climate that may result (or they at least focus on worst-case scenarios). This application of complexity theory to climate change, like the eco-Marxist perspective, argues that current developments in the governance of climate change are not sufficient to address the problem.

In this way, the eco-Marxist and complexity approaches, along with those of climate change campaigners, suggest that individuals, corporations, governments, and so on have not put in place changes to adjust adequately nature-society relations to decrease the human impact on climate change. And so, perhaps like those campaigners during moral panics, they believe that drastic, sudden change is required to avert the climate crisis.

## Ecological modernization and an intentional restructuring of capitalism

In counter to these positions, which argue that sudden substantial change is necessary to address climate change, several approaches have begun to explore how the regulation of consumption may already be occurring. In an attempt to move beyond the central focus on the state for the formal regulation of consumption, the concept of *citizen-consumers* has been used by ecological modernization scholars to explore the role of individuals in relation to states, markets, and lifestyles in the greening of consumption (Spaargaren & Mol, 2008).

Citizen-consumers, as *ecological citizens*, demand environmental security and, at the same time, have a responsibility to contribute towards greater security (Spaargaren & Mol, 2008). However, the global nature of *some* environmental problems creates the requirement for international ecological citizenship. Spaargaren and Mol (2008) note that the increasing development of international political (e.g. Greenpeace) and governmental (e.g. the Intergovernmental Panel on Climate Change (IPCC)) organizations increases public environmental awareness and pressure for environmental governance. In their capacity as 'ecological citizens', there has been some focus on the need to consciously instil some form of 'global citizenship' where people come to have 'some concept of duty towards and sense of belonging to, not just their locality, but humanity or nature and the planet as a whole' (Macnaghten & Urry, 1998, p. 152). However, this greening of consumption focusses on deliberate, conscious attempts to affect changes in people's understandings of nature-society relations, with a concomitant change in their behaviour. As I will suggest later (in the section on ecological civilizing processes and in Chapter 5), unplanned processes, which are not primarily the outcome of intentional campaigns, may also affect changes in nature-society relations and in consumption.

At another level, environmental labelling (or 'eco-labelling') provides 'responsible' citizen-consumers (and -producers) with the identifiers for *political consumerism* (Spaargaren & Mol, 2008), and globally organized boycotts of products and corporations can, in some situations, create the financial need for corporations to (at least appear to) become more 'socially responsible' (for example, Friends of the Earth campaigns against CFC products and the Greenpeace organized consumer boycott of Shell over the intended sinking of Brent Spar (see Macnaghten & Urry, 1998, pp. 56, 68–69)). Indeed, this pressure, from both boycotts and market pressures as other competing companies 'go green', may affect the increasing visibility of 'the environment' in corporations' branding and advertising, and in their policies and strategies. For example, BP's rebranding from 'British Petroleum' to 'Beyond Petroleum', their logo change from the shield to a green and yellow flower, and their vocal investment in alternative energy and stance on climate change (although this was all 'lost' following the BP oil spill in the Gulf of Mexico). Prior to the BP oil spill in the Gulf of Mexico, this contrasted with the much-criticized Exxon-Mobil, but interestingly even they now have an 'environment' section on their website and (at least appear to) have begun to adopt a precautionary stance regarding climate change.[4]

These developments – eco-labelling, rebranding, and so on – exemplify more wider changes in production-consumption; developments that, contra the eco-Marxist and complexity approaches discussed earlier, appear to suggest that capitalism does develop, react, and adapt over time, as the development of 'neat capitalism' (Rojek, 2007) illustrates. Using the terminology of eco-Marxists, 'neat capitalism' occurs where labour (individuals) works with capital (corporations; the market), rather than the state, to try and improve the environment.

However, such neat capitalist companies, with their appeals to ecological citizenship and political consumerism, are to a certain extent only appearing to be green. There exists an inherent conflict within these companies and not just in terms of profit versus the environment. Some of those mentioned earlier, such as BP and ExxonMobil, deliver a product that further contributes to climate change and other ecological issues.[5] Subsidizing research into alternative energies, for example, does not change the fact that the burning of fossil fuels creates greenhouse gasses that contribute to climate change. And so 'green' is used as a branding device to make companies appear to be less 'bad' than others, and to make consumers feel better by buying those products (or using those services) that seem on the surface to be greener alternatives. Paradoxically, the emotional reassurance associated with 'buying green' may lessen the likelihood that someone will engage in other means to try to change broader social, structural factors that might be necessary to alleviate climate change and other ecological issues.

Philip Sutton argues that green consumerism is reliant upon an 'environmentally enlightened' population to be able to identify mere 'greenwash' (Sutton, 2004, pp. 138–139). Perhaps this is why there has been such a development of websites and books that allegedly demonstrate the 'real' versus the 'false' 'green' credentials of corporations.

The socially responsible notion to 'care for the self' and to 'care for the other' in neat capitalism (Rojek, 2007) may not be the only motivating factor for green consumerism. Indeed, McCormick (in Macnaghten & Urry, 1998, p. 60) notes how, throughout the late 1980s (at a time when the first guides to living green emerged), green consumerism 'became one of the most fashionable concepts in public life, shared by media, supermarkets, political parties, and industry'. With the 2006 release of *An Inconvenient Truth* (Guggenheim, 2006), with its calls for self-governance of consumption, and Al Gore's continuing campaign to educate the public about climate change (for example, see Haag, 2007), we can once again witness the rise of green consumerism as a popular status. In 2006, *Vanity Fair* published the first of their annual 'Green Issues'; guides on how to live green have had a upsurge, some of them directly linked to climate change; phrases such as 'green is the new black' and guides with titles like 'how to live green in style' further suggest that green consumerism is about more than being 'socially responsible'.

In 2008, the Oprah Winfrey Show held an Oprah's Earth Day Event[6] on 'going green', with 'eco-celebrities' and campaigners Julia Roberts, Sandra Bullock, Al Gore, and *Gorgeously Green* author Sophie Uliano (Oprah also has a 'going green' section on her website[7]). Following Schmidt (1993), the focus on eco-celebrities could possibly be seen to fulfil the function of lifestyles to aspire to. For example, Boykoff and Goodman (2009) note how, since 2005, there has been a rapid increase in newspaper coverage of celebrities *and* climate change, which has included a focus on celebrities as 'heroic individuals' seeking 'conspicuous redemption' through 'eco-friendly' actions such as the purchasing of 'green goods' (Boykoff & Goodman, 2009). Yet, at the same time, 'eco-celebrities' are criticized when their lifestyles 'deviate' from their 'eco-friendly' messages. And so, celebrities' actions may be played out in the media as 'good' and 'bad' behaviour, that is, behaviour to emulate or not to emulate ('dos' and 'don'ts'). This may aid in the development of ecological sensibilities, but again the focus on individual behaviour to the relative neglect of structural processes may serve as a distraction away from more significant and necessary changes to alleviate climate change.

## Ecological civilizing processes

At another level, the 'popular' status that green and other 'socially responsible' products have attained may mean that status aspirations also play a part in the greening of consumption. For example, Schmidt (1993) notes that, despite trends such as those introduced earlier regarding 'excess-capitalism' (Urry, 2008b), or the 'attraction of potency' with 'new capitalism' (Sennett, 2006), there have also been other counter-trends in consumption in general, towards increasing self-restraint, contributing towards trends of consuming less. Importantly, Schmidt adds, these trends begin with the more 'civilized' groups and then 'trickle down' to other groups via status aspirations (see also Aarts, Schmidt, & Spier, 1995; Vlek, 1995). Such developments (along with the development of environmentalism in general) – the overall process of 'ecologization' – could be conceived of as a civilizing process, as an *ecological* civilizing process

(Quilley, 2004, 2009a, 2009b). Stephen Quilley (2004) notes that such processes are unlikely to occur at a rapid rate, given the gradual changes in sociogenesis and psychogenesis an ecological civilizing process would entail. Therefore, to 'test' the idea of 'ecological civilizing processes', it is important to carry out an analysis that covers a long period of time (over several generations). Therefore, in this book I will be exploring primarily developments over the past 200 years.

Civilizing processes have already begun to be explored in relation to climate change. In their report, *Toward a Morality of Moderation*, Aarts et al. hypothesized that long-term trends in changes of behaviour towards increasing moderation – including body size, number of offspring, tobacco consumption, driving, flying – are occurring as part of unplanned civilizing processes and are not the intentional outcome of environmentalist movements (in the case of climate change) or moralistic rhetoric (Aarts, Goudsblom, Schmidt, & Spier, 1995). While the results of their study were largely negative in relation to climate change – suggesting that these developments towards increasing moderation are not yet widespread in relation to climate change – their hypothesis that such developments may occur is worth investigation, although it may be that intentional interventions do play a role in these developments. Their research was also carried out between 1990 and 1995; many developments have occurred since then, including the apparent increasing popularity of climate change as a social problem.

In *On the Process of Civilisation*, Elias briefly refers to changes in understandings about 'nature' and the 'environment'. He argues that as 'nature' – forests, meadows, mountains – gradually came to be less dangerous (as populations grew and came to be increasingly pacified, and as non-human-threatening species were eliminated or came under greater human control), so too people's perceptions of nature gradually changed towards one of beauty and pleasure (instead of danger): the aestheticization of nature (see Elias, [1939] 2012, pp. 461–2). Sutton (2004) further develops this notion by arguing that there have occurred long-term changes in what constitutes a 'civilized' relationship between 'nature' and 'society', and how these developments, along with the development of environmentalism, might be comparable with civilizing processes. For example, 'ecological identifications' may be indicative of expanding mutual identification (Sutton, 2007, p. 45).

We can explore how these suggested long-term developments may relate to campaigns to change behaviour in response to climate change, that is, where ecological civilizing processes might be occurring but are either not perceived to be occurring or not rapidly enough to counter the perceived problem. For example, Al Gore's campaign, widely disseminated in the documentary *An Inconvenient Truth* (Guggenheim, 2006), calls for changes that could already be occurring as part of civilizing processes, such as increasing self-restraint regarding consumption, increasing foresight and recognition of interdependencies between humans and 'the environment', and increasing mutual identification with 'the environment' (see Rohloff, 2011a). It is a bit presumptuous to dismiss these intentional 'civilizing campaigns' as irrelevant. Rather, it is worth exploring the interplay between these intentional campaigns and more long-term, unplanned developments (such as civilizing processes).

Stephen Quilley (2009b) has begun to explore such an interplay, by examining Aldo Leopold's writings on 'The Land Ethic' in relation to the development of ecological civilizing processes. Quilley argues that Leopold's essay, which was first published in 1949, bears some similarities to etiquette manuals – as a treatise to try and bring about changes in attitudes, including the development of an environmental ethic. Sharing similarities with the etiquette books Elias examined, Leopold's work included writings on 'processes of *distinction* and *social pressure* as conduits for the diffusion of the land ethic', and 'the prospect of conservation and ecology transforming the "foundations of conduct"' (Quilley, 2009b, p. 127). In this way, Quilley begins to explore how environmentalist writings – intentional attempts to change attitudes – may relate to ecological civilizing processes: 'Ethical reform and political activism are revealed as moments in an ongoing process of *psychogenesis*—the moulding of the personality structure in tandem with a wider transformation of society' (Quilley, 2009b, p. 132). While only examining the writings of Leopold, Quilley's argument does suggest that one should not ignore the writings of reformers in the development of ecological civilizing processes and, by extension, the development of climate change as a perceived social problem.

Quilley's analysis of Leopold's writing points towards an informalization of manners regarding the environment – 'The Land Ethic' is a more reflexive essay about how nature-society relations ought to be, without explicit prescriptions on how one should behave. However, an important question remains unanswered: as these texts, directed at imparting ideals, are being written, what is being written in (the more general) etiquette/manners books? What references, if any, are there to nature-society relations in etiquette/manners books, and in other documents, and how and to what extent have the content of these changed over time? Such questions will be explored in this book, in Chapters 5 and 6, where I examine the changing discourses in a wide variety of texts.

## Climate change and the public understanding of science

Another area of research has focussed on climate change and the media, including many publications in the journals *Public Understanding of Science* and *Science Communication*. This area of research has included several focusses, such as how climate change has been mediated and how it ought to be effectively communicated, how climate change is represented in the media and what factors influence this representation, what the function is or should be of the media in communicating climate change and bringing about changes, how the media is perceived by viewers (in relation to climate change), what other factors (other than the media) may influence people's perceptions about the science of climate change, and to what extent it is a social problem that they will be both concerned about and act on.

Several studies have analyzed the media coverage of climate change in different countries, highlighting variations both between and within different countries. Olausson's (2009) study on the Swedish press explored 'framing contests' between three Swedish newspapers. Overall, Olausson found general frames rather than contesting frames. 'The collective action frame of mitigation as a transnational responsibility' occurred where media reporting of international summits and other events framed climate change as a transnational concern, and where industrialized countries were deemed to be responsible for mitigation. Interestingly, this frame contained a 'us' and 'them' divide between Europe and the USA – those who were perceived to be taking the issue seriously and acting responsibly, and those who were not (respectively). Conversely, 'the collective action frame of adaptation as a national and local responsibility' places responsibility at the local and national level rather than at an international or global level. While all of this is interesting, it is limited in that it only looks at newspaper articles. However, there now exists such a variety of media on climate change, from reality TV shows, films, and documentaries to podcasts, iPhone applications, and websites. Discourses and frames within these different media may vary considerably to those within newspapers. Therefore, I will be examining a wide variety of media (this will be further explicated in Chapter 4).

An additional frame in Olausson's (2009) research, 'the frame of certainty', stands in contrast to studies on media coverage in other countries. In Sweden, so it seems from this study, the newspaper media frame climate change science as a certain social problem that is anthropogenic, and that is already having direct, immediate consequences.

In contrast with the Swedish press's 'frame of certainty', several studies from other countries suggest that media coverage of climate change is framed in quite a contrasting way. Max Boykoff has carried out several analyses of newspaper and television news coverage of climate change in the USA and other countries (Boykoff, 2007a, 2007b, 2008a, 2008b, 2008c; Boykoff & Boykoff, 2004; Boykoff & Boykoff, 2007; Boykoff & Mansfield, 2008; Boykoff & Roberts, 2007). He identifies a trend for the media to report 'both sides of the story', which can give credence to minority, or fringe, claims (Boykoff & Boykoff, 2004). Thus, we may witness a disparity between what experts claim amongst themselves and how their claims are then represented to the public. For example, although Oreskes's (2004) analysis of peer-reviewed journal articles on 'global climate change' found no study that disagreed with the apparent scientific consensus, Boykoff and Boykoff's (2004) analysis of USA newspaper articles on global warming found the journalists employing a 'balancing' style that, they argue, misrepresented the science and contributed to misunderstandings about global warming. For example, the 'balanced', 'equal-time' style of reporting in USA newspapers has contributed to biases in reporting (Boykoff & Boykoff, 2004), suggesting there is more of a debate within the scientific community than what the apparent scientific consensus in peer-reviewed science journals indicates (Oreskes, 2004).

This suggests several possible implications for considering moral panic in relation to climate change. First, the notion that the discourse about climate change is contested within the media suggests a need to try to establish a dominant discourse through various campaigns, campaigns that might be called moral panics (Rohloff, 2011a). Second, it provides an insight into the power relations that are at play in the context of (potential) moral panics, thereby assisting with a rethinking about how we conceptualize moral panic and how we practice moral panic research. Third, the variation within the media suggests that dominant discourses are not always present, and that there is the possibility to contest some moral panics, as per McRobbie and Thornton (1995).

Interestingly, in a later study, comparing several USA and UK newspapers, Boykoff found a shift in this style of reporting, with less of an emphasis on 'balancing' (and thereby more representative of the climate change science) (Boykoff, 2007a). This suggests the need to explore long-term developments in the discourses surrounding climate change and moral panics more broadly. It also suggests a shift in the way climate change is conceived beyond the news media. Perhaps, it is a sign that climate change is becoming a more established phenomenon, as the creation of the term 'climate change denier', with its allusions to holocaust denial, suggests.

During such media contestations over the 'reality' of climate change, 'moral panics' (or something similar) may develop as an attempt to establish a dominant discourse over the extent of climate change and what should be done about it. Thus far, only one other researcher, Sheldon Ungar (1992, 1995, 2001, 2011), has utilized moral panic to explore global warming. However, excluding his chapter in *Moral Panic and the Politics of Anxiety* (Hier, 2011), these studies were carried out in the late twentieth century and are thus not up to date with recent developments. His research also does not consist of long-term, developmental research of the sort that I wish to pursue. Ungar did, however, develop a reformulation of the moral panic concept: he removed the *necessity* (but not the possibility) of two moral panic criteria – disproportionality and folk devils – and then re-termed these 'moral panics' over 'real-world events' (such as hurricanes, heat waves, nuclear disasters) as 'social scares'. In part, Ungar develops this reformulation via the inclusion of Beck's work on the 'risk society'; Beck has some points of overlap but also points of departure with Elias's writings on knowledge and civilization – this comparison between Beck and Elias will be explored in Chapter 3, where I will also critically discuss moral panic in more detail.

Concern about the accurate communication of climate change science could be predicated upon an assumption of a knowledge deficit model. Early approaches to the communication of science took a 'knowledge deficit' approach, where it was assumed that the communication about science to a relatively ignorant public would translate directly into concern and action. However, there have been several alternative models that have emerged in critique of the knowledge deficit model: the contextual model, the lay-expertise model, and the public engagement model (Kahlor & Rosenthal, 2009). There have been several pieces of research that have also criticized the model, such as Whitmarsh's.

In criticism of the knowledge deficit model, Whitmarsh utilized a UK survey study that investigated the public understanding of climate change. She concludes that, paradoxically, scepticism or uncertainty about climate change appears to be influenced by greater rather than less scientific knowledge (Whitmarsh, 2009), thereby negating the knowledge deficit model approach. Whitmarsh also concludes that there should be a distinction drawn between 'public understanding' and 'engagement', where the former refers to communicating the science and the latter to engaging concern and action. Whitmarsh's research found that respondents tended to devolve responsibility for causes of climate change, and for mitigation and adaptation, towards international organizations (dissociating themselves).

Other UK survey research suggests that there exists a gap between awareness about climate change and engagement with activities that may mitigate climate change. Ockwell, Whitmarsh, and O'Neill, (2009) found that, while survey findings suggested that people had high levels of awareness about what lifestyle changes would contribute to a smaller carbon footprint, results demonstrated low levels of actual behaviour change accompanying the awareness. This confirms the critique of the knowledge deficit model – where it is not sufficient to just provide people with information to effect behavioural changes. To combat this gap, Ockwell et al. discuss various grass-roots initiatives that appear to have had some success in engaging some people; they argue that these initiatives could facilitate civic engagement with climate change and, thereby, public acceptance of a more flexible regulation. Their research, however, does not provide much in the way of guidelines as to how to achieve such ambitious aims.

An additional model, the reinforcing spirals model (see Slater, 2007), combines both the media effects approach with an active, selective, audience to produce a model of a dynamic, interactive process. Zhao (2009) has applied the reinforcing spirals model to climate change, 'to investigate the mutual influence between individuals' media use and their global warming perceptions' (p. 715), and to explore how this might relate to future searching out of information about climate change. Using survey data, Zhao concludes from the results that types of media use varied amongst different groups: for example, with people of different age groups utilizing different formats of media (the implication being that communication must cover a variety of formats). Zhao also confirms the hypothesis that perceived knowledge and concern about climate change would contribute to future information seeking about climate change, where actors are conceptualized as *active* information seekers. However, this research does not tell us about the interaction amongst the audience, or between the audience and other people. The interaction is focussed on the individual viewer and the media. And while it begins to explore changes in behaviour over time – future information seeking behaviour – it tells us little about the biographical journey whereby people, over time, come to have particular opinions about climate change, etc.

Some research has explored the role of emotions, in particular fear, in media coverage of climate change. In a study undertaken in the UK, O'Neill, and Nicholson-Cole (2009) explored the effect of fear in engagement about climate change. As they outline, many climate change campaigns, imagery, and media coverage have utilized fear and a 'language of alarmism' (p. 358). O'Neill and Nicholson-Cole utilize Witte's (1992) typology of a 'fear appeal', which consists of three parts: (1) the existence of the threat (that is, how risky it is perceived to be and whether it is a personal risk), (2) the emotion of fear, and (3) the perceived efficacy of the proposed response (including aspects of self-efficacy: to what extent the individual feels like they can make a difference). They used semi-structured interviews, Q-sorting[8] images, and focus groups to explore perceptions about climate change. Their results found that most participants had rather negative outlooks about the future of climate change. 'Many [participants] specifically talked about feeling fearful, depressed, scared, or distressed at the thought of climate change' (O'Neill & Nicholson-Cole, 2009, p. 369). They found that fear contributed to a feeling that climate change is a faraway issue (either far in the future or happening elsewhere), concluding that the global fearful imagery, in order to be engaging, needed to be connected to everyday spatial and temporal issues. In addition, the role of fear also served to contribute to a feeling of 'fatalism', thereby contributing to a sense that there was nothing that could be done, leading to disengagement with climate change. So, while participants were largely concerned about climate change, the role of fear appeared to contribute to a lack of engagement.

Conversely, the study found that those images that were found to be empowering – the local personal images – did not get participants attention in the same way; so, while those images were empowering, they were regarded as being less important. They conclude with the suggestion that perhaps fear appeals may be utilized to hook an audience, but they must be combined with other messages that provide a sense of self-efficacy. Otherwise, the authors warn, fear may lead to denial, apathy, and avoidance.

## 'Climate change denial' and 'climate sceptics'

Particularly in the USA, there has been a concern with 'environmental scepticism' and, in particular, with the linkage between scepticism about climate change and conservative think tanks (CTTs). Jacques, Dunlap, and Freeman (2008) carried out an analysis of 141 environmentally scep- tical books that were published between 1972 and 2005. They found that over 92% of the books published since 1992 can be linked to CTTs (mostly in the USA). They conclude that 'environmental sceptics are not, as they portray themselves, independent and objective analysts. Rather they are predominantly agents of CTTs, and their success in promot- ing scepticism about environmental problems stems from their affiliation with these politically powerful institutions' (p. 351). However, some of these links are merely that the CTT published the book. This does not necessarily mean that the author has been corrupted by the CTT. Given the growing disgust that is directed at so-called sceptics or deniers, it may merely be the case that other publishers would refuse to publish such books for fear of being associated with 'climate change denial'.

Moving beyond CTTs and the debunking of 'climate change denial', Mike Hulme ([2009] 2011) looks instead at individual and societal reac- tions to climate change in order to understand the 'reasons why we disagree about climate change'. Highlighting the increasing variability of what dif- ferent people believe, and what matters most to different people, suggests the need to explore different approaches to climate change engagement, utilizing different media and other sources of engagement in different ways. Before we can make suggestions about how these things should be devel- oped, however, it is necessary to first explore how they have already been developing. This will be done in Chapters 5 and 6.

Adding to this line of research, Norgaard (2006, 2011) explores how the desire to avoid unpleasant or clashing emotions contributes to emotion management and the avoidance of climate change: in other words, the de- nial of climate change in the form of 'not seeing' and 'not knowing' – a form of implicatory denial (also see Cohen, 2001). From ethnographic research undertaken in Norway, Norgaard demonstrates how the emotion norms within the community clashed with those induced by climate change (fear, helplessness, guilt). To manage those clashes, then, required residents to avoid thinking about climate change, which contributed to a lack of climate change activism. She found that people would deflect responsibil- ity for climate change onto others, or they would turn their attention to something else.

A related publication is Michael Rustin's chapter on climate change and psychoanalysis (Rustin, 2013). He explores not only the development of de- nial, and how it relates to unconscious desires, but also the relationship be- tween denial and morally outraged responses to denial. Such contributions from psychoanalysis can be incredibly insightful to moral panic studies and to exploring the relationship between various players involved in moral panics. After all, moral panic has within its core an inherent contribution from Freudian psychoanalysis (Garland, 2008).

# Conclusion

Throughout this review of some of the literature on climate change and environmental sociology, I have identified several gaps in the research that I will explore in the following chapters. I have demonstrated how some of the existing research in environmental sociology and on climate change relates to moral panic and to Elias's theory of civilizing processes. These theories and concepts, along with some of the debates I have introduced here, will be taken up in Chapter 3.

## Notes

1 Held at the British Library on Monday 8 February 2010, speakers included John Urry, Elizabeth Shove, Tim Jackson, Alan Warde, and Brian Wynne.
2 Environmental sociology can be defined as a sub-discipline of sociology that attempts to integrate biological and ecological sciences into sociological theory, thereby attending to the interdependence between humans and ecosystems (see Sutton, 2004).
3 See also the 'Ecosocialist Manifesto' on the Capitalism Nature Socialism website: cnsjournal.org/manifesto.html
4 exxonmobil.com/Corporate/safety_climate.aspx
5 One could argue that this is not just the case for energy companies but for all companies because production and consumption in general produce carbon (and other) emissions.
6 oprah.com/showinfo/Oprahs-Earth-Day-Event_3
7 oprah.com/packages/going-green
8 Q-sorting is a method used in psychology to assess participants' viewpoint – in this case, their viewpoint of climate change media images.

## References

Aarts, W., Goudsblom, J., Schmidt, K., & Spier, F. (1995). *Toward a morality of moderation: Report for the Dutch National Research Programme on Global Air Pollution and Climate Change.* Amsterdam: Amsterdam School for Social Science Research.
Aarts, W., Schmidt, C., & Spier, F. (1995). Toward a morality of increasing moderation. In S. Zwerver, R. S. A. R. van Rompaey, M. T. J. Kok, & M. M. Berk (Eds.), *Climate change research: Evaluation and policy implications* (Vol. 65, part 2, pp. 1247–1250). Amsterdam: Elsevier.
Beck, U. (2009). *World at risk.* Cambridge: Polity Press.
Boykoff, M. T. (2007a). Flogging a dead norm? Newspaper coverage of anthropogenic climate change in the United States and United Kingdom from 2003 to 2006. *Area, 39*(4), 470–481.
Boykoff, M. T. (2007b). From convergence to contention: United States mass media representations of anthropogenic climate change science. *Transactions of the Institute of British Geographers, 32*(4), 477–489.
Boykoff, M. T. (2008a). The cultural politics of climate change discourse in UK tabloids. *Political Geography, 27,* 549–569.

Boykoff, M. T. (2008b). Lost in translation? United States television news coverage of anthropogenic climate change, 1995–2004. *Climatic Change, 86*(1), 1–11.

Boykoff, M. T. (2008c). Media and scientific communication: a case of climate change. In D. G. E. Liverman, C. P. G. Pereira, & B. Marker (Eds.), *Communicating environmental geoscience* (Vol. 305, pp. 11–18). London: Special Publications.

Boykoff, M. T., & Boykoff, J. M. (2004). Balance as bias: Global warming and the US prestige press. *Global Environmental Change, 14*(2), 125–136.

Boykoff, M. T., & Boykoff, J. M. (2007). Climate change and journalistic norms: A case-study of US mass-media coverage. *Geoforum, 38*, 1190–1204.

Boykoff, M. T., & Goodman, M. K. (2009). Conspicuous redemption? Reflections on the promises and perils of the 'Celebritization' of climate change. *Geoforum, 40*, 395–406.

Boykoff, M. T., & Mansfield, M. (2008). 'Ye Olde Hot Aire': Reporting on human contributions to climate change in the UK tabloid press. *Environmental Research Letters, 3*, 1–8.

Boykoff, M. T., & Roberts, J. T. (2007). Media coverage of climate change: Current trends, strengths, weaknesses. *Human Development Report 2007/2008: Fighting climate change: Human solidarity in a divided world*: Occassional Paper 2007/3, Human Development Report Office.

Brechin, S. R. (2008). Ostriches and change: A response to 'Global warming and sociology'. *Current Sociology, 56*(3), 467–474.

BSA Postgraduate Forum (Producer). (2010) BSA Presidential Event 2010: How to put 'society' into climate change. Retrieved May 24, 2010, from http://pgforum.libsyn.com/index.php?post_category=BSA%20Presidential%20Event%202010.

Cohen, S. (2011). Whose side were we on? The undeclared politics of moral panic theory. *Crime, Media, Culture, 7*(3), 237–243.

Elias, N. ([1939] 2012). *On the process of civillisation: Sociogenetic and psychogenetic investigations (The Collected Works of Norbert Elias, Vol. 3)*. Dublin: University College Dublin Press [Previous editions published as *The civilizing process*].

Garland, D. (2008). On the concept of moral panic. *Crime Media Culture, 4*(1), 9–30.

Giddens, A. (2007, October 16th). All addictions turn from pleasure to dependency. *Guardian*. Retrieved April 11, 2009, from http://www.guardian.co.uk/commentisfree/2007/oct/16/comment.health.

Giddens, A. (2009). *The politics of climate change*. Cambridge: Polity Press.

Guggenheim, D. (Director). (2006). *An inconvenient truth: A global warning* [Motion Picture]. United States: Paramount Pictures.

Haag, A. (2007). Al's army. *Nature, 446*(7137), 723–724.

Hier, S. P. (Ed.). (2011c). *Moral panic and the politics of anxiety*. London: Routledge.

Hulme, M. ([2009] 2011). *Why we disagree about climate change: Understanding controversy, inaction and opportunity*. Cambridge: Cambridge University Press.

Jacques, P. J., Dunlap, R. E., & Freeman, M. (2008). The organisation of denial: Conservative think tanks and environmental scepticism. *Environmental Politics, 17*(3), 349–385.

Kahlor, L., & Rosenthal, S. (2009). If we seek, do we learn?: Predicting knowledge of global warming. *Science Communication, 30*(3), 380–414.

Kuhn, T. S. ([1962] 1970). *The structure of scientific revolutions* (2nd ed.). Chicago, IL: University of Chicago Press.

Leahy, T. (2008). Discussion of 'Global warming and sociology'. *Current Sociology, 56*(3), 475–484.

Lever-Tracy, C. (2008a). Global warming and sociology. *Current Sociology, 56*(3), 445–466.

Lever-Tracy, C. (2008b). Reply. *Current Sociology, 56*(3), 485–491.

Lever-Tracy, C. (Ed.). (2010). *Routledge handbook of climate change and society.* London: Routledge.

Lever-Tracy, C. (2011). *Confronting climate change.* London: Routledge.

Macnaghten, P., & Urry, J. (1998). *Contested natures.* London: Sage.

McRobbie, A., & Thornton, S. L. (1995). Rethinking 'moral panic' for multi-mediated social worlds. *British Journal of Sociology, 46*(4), 559–574.

Mol, A. P. J., & Spaargaren, G. (2005). From additions and withdrawls to environmental flows: Reframing debates in the environmental social sciences. *Organization & Environment, 18*(1), 91–107.

Nagel, J., Dietz, T., & Broadbent, J. (2010). *Proceedings of the workshop "Sociological Perspectives on Global Climate Change"*, Arlington, VA, May 30–31, 2008: National Science Foundation; American Sociological Association.

Newton, T. (2003). Crossing the great divide: Time, nature and the social. *Sociology, 37*(3), 433–457.

Norgaard, K. M. (2006). "People want to protect themselves a little bit": Emotions, denial, and social movement nonparticipation. *Sociological Inquiry, 76*(3), 372–396.

Norgaard, K. M. (2011). *Living in denial: Climate change, emotions, and everyday life.* Cambridge, MA: MIT Press.

O'Connor, J. (1996). The second contradiction of capitalism. In T. Benton (Ed.), *The greening of Marxism* (pp. 197–221). New York, NY: Guilford Press.

O'Connor, J. (1998). *Natural causes: Essays in ecological Marxism.* New York, NY: The Guilford Press.

O'Neill, S., & Nicholson-Cole, S. (2009). "Fear won't do it": Promoting positive engagement with climate change through visual and iconic representations. *Science Communication, 30*(3), 355–379.

Ockwell, D., Whitmarsh, L., & O'Neill, S. (2009). Reorienting climate change communication for effective mitigation: Forcing people to be green or fostering grass-roots engagement? *Science Communication, 30*(3), 305–327.

Olausson, U. (2009). Global warming—global responsibility? Media frames of collective action and scientific certainty. *Public Understanding of Science, 18*(4), 421–436.

Oreskes, N. (2004). Beyond the ivory tower: The scientific consensus on climate change. *Science, 306*(5702), 1686.

Quilley, S. (2004). Social development as trophic expansion: Food systems, prosthetic ecology and the arrow of history. *Amsterdams Sociologisch Tijdschrift, 31*(3), 321–347.

Quilley, S. (2009a). 'Biophilia' as an 'Ecological Civilising Process': The Sociogenesis and Psychogenesis of Litterlouts and Recycling Eco-Citizens (Working Paper).

Quilley, S. (2009b). The Land Ethic as an Ecological Civilizing Process: Aldo Leopold, Norbert Elias, and Environmental Philosophy. *Environmental Ethics, 31*(2), 115–134.

Redclift, M. (2009). The environment and carbon dependence: Landscapes of sustainability and materiality. *Current Sociology, 57*(3), 369–387.

Rohloff, A. (2011a). Extending the Concept of Moral Panic: Elias, Climate Change and Civilization. *Sociology, 45*(4), 634–649.

Rojek, C. (2007). *Cultural studies.* Cambridge: Polity Press.

Rustin, M. (2013). How is climate change an issue for psychoanalysis? In S. Weintrobe (Ed.), *Engaging with climate change: Psychoanalytic and interdisciplinary perspectives* (pp. 170–185). London: Routledge.

Schmidt, C. (1993). On economization and ecologization as civilizing processes. *Environmental Values, 2*(1), 33–46.

Schnaiberg, A. (1980). *The environment: From surplus to scarcity.* New York, NY: Oxford University Press.

Schnaiberg, A., Pellow, D. N., & Weinberg, A. S. (2002). The treadmill of production and the environmental state. In A. P. J. Mol & F. Buttel, H. (Eds.), *The environmental state under pressure* (Vol. 10, pp. 15–32). Amsterdam: Elsevier Science.

Sennett, R. (2006). *The culture of the new capitalism.* New Haven, CT: Yale University Press.

Slater, M. (2007). Reinforcing spirals: The mutual influence of media selectivity and media effects and their impact on individual behaviour and social identity. *Communication Theory, 17*(3), 281–303.

Spaargaren, G., & Mol, A. P. J. (2008). Greening global consumption: Redefining politics and authority. *Global environmental change, 18,* 350–359.

Sutton, P. W. (2004). *Nature, environment and society.* Houndmills, Basingstoke, Hampshire: Palgrave Macmillan.

Sutton, P. W. (2007). *The environment: A sociological introduction.* Cambridge: Polity Press.

Szerszynski, B., & Urry, J. (Eds.). (2010). *Special Issue on Changing Climates: Theory, Culture & Society, 27*(2–3).

Ungar, S. (1992). The rise and (relative) decline of global warming as a social problem. *Sociological Quarterly, 33*(4), 483–501.

Ungar, S. (1995). Social scares and global warming: Beyond the Rio Convention. *Society and Natural Resources, 8*(4), 443–456.

Ungar, S. (2001). Moral panic versus the risk society: The implications of the changing sites of social anxiety. *British Journal of Sociology, 52*(2), 271–291.

Ungar, S. (2011). The artful creation of global moral panic: Climatic folk devils, environmental evangelicals, and the coming catastrophe. In S. P. Hier (Ed.), *Moral panic and the politics of anxiety* (pp. 190–207). London: Routledge.

Urry, J. (2003) *Global complexity.* Cambridge: Polity Press.

Urry, J. (2008a). Climate change, travel and complex futures. *British Journal of Sociology, 59*(2), 261–279.

Urry, J. (2008b). *Complexity and climate change.* Paper presented at the BSA Annual Conference 2008: Social Worlds, Natural Worlds, University of Warwick.

Urry, J. (2008c). Governance, flows, and the end of the car system? *Global Environmental Change, 18,* 343–349.

Urry, J. (2009a). Complexity and climate change: An interview by David Morgan. *Network, 101*(Spring), 8–9.

Urry, J. (2009b). Sociology and climate change. *Sociological Review, 57*(s2), 84–100.

Urry, J. (2010). Consuming the planet to excess. *Theory, Culture & Society, 27*(2–3), 191–212.

Urry, J. (2011). *Climate change and society.* Cambridge: Polity Press.

Vlek, C. A. J. (1995). Assessment report on subtheme "Culture, consumption and lifestyles in relation to sustainable development". In S. Zwerver, R. S. A. R. van Rompaey, M. T. J. Kok & M. M. Berk (Eds.), *Climate change research: Evaluation and policy implications* (Vol. 65, part 2, pp. 1201–1225). Amsterdam: Elsevier.

Walsh, B. (2007, October 12th). A green tipping point. *Time.* Retrieved October 11, 2008, from http://www.time.com/time/world/article/0,8599,1670871,00. html.

Whitmarsh, L. (2009). What's in a name? Commonalities and differences in public understanding of "climate change" and "global warming". *Public Understanding of Science, 18*(4), 401–420.

Witte, K. (1992). Putting the fear back into fear appeals: The extended parallel process model. *Communication Monographs, 59*(4), 329–349.

Yearley, S. (2009). Sociology and climate change after Kyoto: What roles for social science in understanding climate change? *Current Sociology, 57*(3), 389–405.

Zhao, X. (2009). Media use and global warming perceptions: A snapshot of the reinforcing spirals. *Communication Research, 36*(5), 698–723.

# 3 Theories of social processes and social change

## Introduction

This chapter reviews literature on social processes and social change in order to explore the theories and concepts that can be used in relation to climate change, moral panics, and/or civilizing processes. This review has several purposes: (1) to provide definitions of the theories and concepts that will be used throughout this book for readers who are unfamiliar with any of them; (2) to discuss critically different approaches to social processes and social change in order to draw out core debates within the literature, debates which will be explored throughout this book; (3) to highlight some of the limitations with existing concepts and theories since one of the aims of this book is to critically assess and reformulate the concept of moral panic and the relationship between civilizing and decivilizing processes and civilizing offensives; (4) to demonstrate how different theories and approaches compare and contrast, to facilitate dialogue between them, and to allow them to inform one another; and (5) to utilize this literature to further refine my own theoretical-conceptual-methodological approach to this research.

I have broken up this chapter into thematic sections based on the theories or concepts I will be discussing rather than the purposes outlined earlier. In the first part of this chapter, I will provide a detailed, critical overview of the theories and concepts of Norbert Elias that I will be using throughout this book. I will then go on to do the same with moral panic, looking critically at different approaches to panic. I will then go on to examine denial and the role of emotions in moral panic. Following on from this, I will compare Elias (and moral panic) with several other theorists and approaches, including Foucault, Beck, complexity theory, and practice theory. To enable these comparisons between Elias and others, it is first necessary to provide a more detailed exposition of some of his work.

## Norbert Elias: the civilizing process

Elias's ([1939] 2012) most famous publication, *On the Process of Civilisation*, relied significantly on observations from various texts. These included manners and etiquette books, paintings, and poetry, amongst others. He explored the relationship between these texts, looking for differences between them – what was present in some texts and then left out in subsequent ones, what was not present in texts and was then added to subsequent ones. In this way, he traced the emergence and disappearance of concern with certain behaviours, inferring how people's standards of behaviour were changing over time. He therefore presented his analysis in time series, clearly demonstrating these appearances and disappearances, along with changes in the way things were presented – how things were said. Through tracing these changes in behaviour, Elias illustrated the development of particular emotional or psychic structures: what he termed *psychogenesis*.

Several other processes occurring simultaneously influenced psychogenesis (or psychic development), and these processes, in turn, were influenced by psychogenesis. Various figurations at different times influenced the spread of new behavioural standards. This included royal and aristocratic courts (Elias, [1939] 2012, [1969] 2006) and still includes any other social figuration that is regarded as 'good society'. These model-setting centres effectively disperse ideals for how one should behave for those who are not part of this figuration but want to ascend and become one of the 'good society'.

Elias uses the term *figuration* as a means of overcoming the problem of the structure-agency dichotomy that arises when talking about individuals and society. Figuration describes a network of interdependent people in any form of grouping (e.g. a university figuration, a family figuration, a state figuration, and so on) (Elias, [1970] 2012). He utilizes the example of a dance to illustrate how the term figuration overcomes some of the problems with sociological terms, such as society or structure:

> One can certainly speak of 'dance' in general, but no one will imagine a dance as a structure outside the individual or as a mere abstraction. The same dance figurations can certainly be danced by different people; but without a plurality of reciprocally oriented and dependent individuals, there is no dance. Like every other social figuration, a dance figuration is relatively independent of the specific individuals forming it here and now, but not of individuals as such.
>
> (Elias, [1939] 2012, p. 526)

Individual developments associated with psychogenesis went hand in hand with broader, structural, societal developments; the latter, Elias termed *sociogenesis*. In *On the Process of Civilisation* in particular, he explored how sociogenetic developments, such as the formation of states through elimination contests between smaller groupings and subsequent state monopolization over violence and taxation, affected, and was affected by, psychogenetic developments. As states became larger, with individuals becoming increasingly interdependent and therefore increasingly reliant upon one another, given advances in the division of social functions, so too they were pressured by social interdependence to take greater account of one another, to increase their mutual identification, and to develop more stable and all-round emotional controls that were more predictable. This process was also a shift from external constraint to self-restraint, from external social controls to internalized self-controls.

Initially, this involved a *formalization* of standards of behaviour associated with a phase of social development characterized by greater power asymmetries between interdependent social groups, with increasing and stricter rules on how one should behave and the development of manners and etiquette books. From the beginning of the twentieth century, however, this process of formalization came to be increasingly overshadowed by processes of *informalization*, associated with decreasing power asymmetries between interdependent social groups, where modes of conduct that were formerly forbidden have increasingly become tolerated and approved (Wouters, 1977, p. 439). Such things that would formerly have been frowned upon but in the twentieth century were becoming increasingly accepted include using less formal greetings (e.g. calling people by their first names); wearing clothing that exposes more of the body; and talking with other people more openly about sexual experiences, menstruation, and other bodily functions. Rather than merely representing a relaxation in social and self-controls, informalization instead brings with it a greater demand on individuals to exercise self-restraint. For example, relaxation on what constitutes appropriate sexual behaviour, while constituting a lessening of external controls and of more repressive and automatic self-controls, goes hand in hand with an increase in more conscious and reflexive self-control to ensure that individuals

> do not overstep the more lenient and differentiated standard of today. Thus, the self-control of these young people, at least as far as sexuality is concerned, has so much increased that they today *are able* to a greater extent to think about expressing or repressing sexual urges and emotions. They have become more conscious of social and individual possibilities and restrictions...and this heightened consciousness enables them more than their parents and grandparents to restrain *and* express their impulses and emotions. This might indicate a higher level of consciousness and possibly also a higher level of self-controls.
>
> (Wouters, 1977, p. 447)

And so informalization is about a balance between restraining and expressing, with this balancing act requiring *increasing* self-control (to get the balance right) and increasing reflexivity.

The various developments discussed thus far encompass what Elias means by the term *civilizing process*: the long-term development of sociogenetic and psychogenetic processes, where changes at the individual level and changes at the social or societal level are inextricably intertwined. Elias contrasts this technical definition of civilizing *process* with the normative, everyday usage of the term *civilization*. Normatively, 'civilization' is used to denote superiority to those who are deemed to be less civilized, 'uncivilized', 'primitive', or 'barbaric'. It has also been used as a static thing to refer to 'civilizations' or to those 'material and technical aspects of society' (Goudsblom, 2006, p. 292).

It is important to reiterate that Elias did not regard developments in civilizing processes as being unilinear. This point will be returned to in a later section of this chapter, when I discuss the notion of *decivilizing* processes.

Elias is most known for his book *On the Process of Civilisation*, but his writings extend far beyond this, covering such topics as sport and leisure, dying, time, knowledge, technology, and much more. Before we go on to explore the application of Elias's research to natural processes and ecological issues, let us first examine what he had to say about what might be called 'epistemological' issues.

## Sociology of knowledge versus philosophy of knowledge

In contrast to the dominant modes of sociological research that follow a philosophical approach that defines how research should be carried out, Elias argued that sociology must develop its own sociology of knowledge, its own approach to research design that is, itself, informed by empirical research (Elias, [1987] 2007, [1971] 2009). Throughout various publications, he defines and elaborates upon a host of concepts that he developed in his approach to research.

His concept of *involvement–detachment balance* was key to overcoming several static dichotomies in the social sciences; chief among these were subjective or objective, involved or detached, irrational or rational. With this concept Elias refers to how people can be more or less emotionally involved in their perceptions of, and relations with, phenomena in the three dimensions of human existence: i.e. people's individual internal psyches, external non-human nature, and the social processes that people collectively constitute. Elias argues that one could never be completely involved or completely detached; instead, we can only speak of *degrees* of detachment and involvement.

> As far as one can see, the very existence of ordered group life depends on the interplay in [people's] thoughts and actions of impulses in both directions, those that involve and those that detach keeping each other in check. They may clash and struggle for dominance or compromise and form alloys of many different shades and kinds.
>
> (Elias, 1956, p. 226)

These alloys and blends of involvement–detachment are constantly in flux, and a greater degree of one does not always correspond to a lesser degree of the other.

In trying to contribute to the development of sociology as a discipline, Elias argues that it needs to become more detached in the valuations that orientate its research. He differentiates between *autonomous valuations* and *heteronomous valuations*. The former refers to those values that are developed within and for the discipline, whereas the latter refers to values that intrude from 'outside' the discipline (Elias, [1987] 2007, pp. 72–73). Dunning and Hughes (2013, p. 131) elaborate on this distinction by characterizing autonomous valuations as 'a commitment to understanding the world *as it is* and *as it has developed*', whereas heteronomous valuations 'instead privilege the world *as we want it to be*, or, indeed, *don't want it to be*'. By attempting to avoid the intrusion of heteronomous valuations into research, Elias argued that one was more likely to contribute to research that has a greater degree of reality congruence (that is, where it is increasingly more likely to approximate reality[1]).

And so, we can begin to see how *reality congruence* – the degree to which our concepts and theoretical orientating models corresponds with (though never equates to) reality – relates to the concept of *value congruence*[2] (and value bias). As Elias argues, the kinds of values that are employed or that influence research affect the quality of the research – the degree of potential reality congruence (for a discussion of the relationship between reality congruence and value congruence, see Dunning & Hughes, 2013).

While Elias encouraged his students to research areas they felt passionate about, that they were relatively involved in (Dunning & Hughes, 2013), he also urged them to exercise an increase in detachment – a *detour via detachment* – in order to produce knowledge with a greater degree of reality congruence. Kilminster argues that during the process of research, involvement should instead be devoted to a form of *involved detachment*, where the researcher channels the 'kind of passion normally associated with political and religious beliefs...into the pursuit of a kind of detached sociological knowledge that transcends the one-sidedness of involved viewpoints of society' (Kilminster, 2007, p. 123). Kilminster goes on to state that this form of involved detachment amounts to a *secondary involvement*:

> Sociologists embracing such greater detachment in their enquiries themselves become secondarily involved in that activity and take pleasure from the comprehensive understanding made possible by the standpoint and to relish its potentialities. But for others in society to become secondarily involved in the comprehensive understanding of a certain kind of detached sociology is dependent upon the state of social tension that generates fears and hence the further involvements that hinder it.
>
> (Kilminster, 2007, p. 123)

This is characterized by Kilminster as being chiefly about secondary *sociological* involvement to facilitate the development of the discipline rather than secondary *political* involvement to inform social issues of the day.

However, as will be discussed in Chapter 4, this complete abandoning of political interests and concerns is not conducive with Elias's arguments, nor is it desirable for the development of sociology and the human sciences more generally. Many discoveries would or may not have been made were it not for secondary political involvement. And, indeed, if we avoid the 'impact' sociological research can have by engaging with policy, user groups, practitioners, the media, and so on, we are endangering the future of sociology as a discipline – policymakers, journalists, and other practitioners must have something to work with; why do we not provide them with our own knowledge, which potentially has a greater degree of reality congruence?

## Eliasian approaches to natural processes and ecological issues

An additional concept Elias discusses is the *triad of controls*. In *What Is Sociology?*, he refers to the relationship between control over natural processes, social processes, and psychic processes:

> Among the universal features of society is the *triad of basic controls*. The stage of development attained by a society can be ascertained:
>
> 1   by the extent of its control-chances over non-human complexes of events – that is, control over what are normally called 'natural events'
> 2   by the extent of its control-chances over interpersonal relationships – that is, over what are usually called 'social relationships'
> 3   by the extent to which each of its members has control over himself as an individual – for, however dependent he may always be on others, he has learned from infancy to control himself to a greater or lesser degree.
>
> (Elias, [1970] 2012, p. 151)

He argues that each component of this 'triad' is interdependent with the other. And while he suggests that an overall trend towards greater control can be discerned, not all of these levels of control develop at the same rate; for example, he argues that increasing control over natural processes has occurred at a much faster rate than control over social processes (as reflected in the stage of development of the various sciences associated with these processes – the 'natural' sciences versus the 'social' sciences).

For the purposes of this book, one of the most interesting points Elias makes about the triad of controls is that

> the less amenable a particular sphere of events is to human control, the more emotional will be people's thinking about it; and the more

emotional and fantasy-laden their ideas, the less capable will they be of constructing more accurate models of these nexuses, and thus of gaining greater control over them.

(Elias, [1970] 2012, p. 152)

Applying this to moral panic, and to climate change, we can suggest that the greater the perception that things are 'out of control' or 'beyond control', the more likely it is that there will be increasing emotional involvement, with proposed solutions that may have more unintended than intended consequences. Potentially, this may further contribute to the problem rather than alleviating it. It is therefore important to consider the relationship between these three levels of control.

Furthermore, Sutton (2004, pp. 176–182) argues that the notion of the triad of controls, and Elias's sociological approach more generally, can be usefully applied to develop a sociology of the environment, thus overcoming divides between realist and social constructionist approaches. Importantly, as Sutton demonstrates, Elias's conceptualisation of power relations necessitates an understanding of society–nature relations as being one of degrees, where one never completely subjugates or dominates the other. As Sutton argues, this allows us to move beyond environmentalist claims about 'saving the planet' from an 'ecological crisis'. However, humans do exert influence over the direction of natural processes, and so one must look at the development of climate change in terms of the interplay between natural, social, and psychic processes. Furthermore, discourses of 'crisis' and 'saving the planet' might still be functional, in an intended way, but they must be analyzed critically to assess the extent to which they will have more intended than unintended consequences.

One application of the triad of controls to research is Goudsblom's research on *Fire and Civilization* (1992), where he traces the development of the control and use of fire. Goudsblom clearly illustrates how the triad of controls also corresponds to what he terms a 'triad of dependencies', where, for example, 'as the human capacity to *control* fire has increased, so has people's inclination to *depend* upon social arrangements guaranteeing its regular availability and minimizing the hazards it involves' (Goudsblom, 1992, p. 10, original emphasis). He goes on to discuss some of the unintended consequences of the development of fire use, such as increasing population, increasing use of natural resources, and increasing pollution (Goudsblom, 1992, pp. 209–215). Such unintended developments are important to consider when exploring how ecological civilizing processes relate to counter-trends or unintended developments that have contributed to increasing anthropogenic climate change. These will be explored in Chapter 5.

Following Aarts et al. (1995; see also Schmidt, 1993), Stephen Quilley (2004, 2009a, 2009b) introduces the concept of an *ecological civilizing process*. Here, he is referring to the sociogenetic and psychogenetic transformations associated with the development of an increasingly more ecological relationship with and awareness of the biosphere. Looking at the examples of littering and recycling (Quilley, 2009a), and such seminal texts as Aldo Leopold's 'The Land Ethic' (Quilley, 2009b), Quilley demonstrates how calls for changes in conduct and the actual development of changing standards of behaviour regarding the environment correspond with developments associated with civilizing processes; for example, how identification with other humans has increased and expanded to include non-human nature (Quilley, 2009b). In this book, I will expand upon Quilley's research in this area by exploring how and to what extent ecological civilizing processes in the long term relate to the emergence of concern about anthropogenic climate change.

## Decivilizing processes

As mentioned earlier, civilizing processes – whether they be ecological or not – entail the potential, according to some, of *decivilizing processes.* Several authors have developed Elias's initial ideas about decivilizing. For example, Jonathan Fletcher has further elaborated on the concept by providing 'three main criteria of decivilization': (1) 'a shift in the balance between constraints by others and self-restraint in favour of constraints by others'; (2) 'the development of a social standard of behaviour and feeling which generates the emergence of a less even, all-round, stable and differentiated pattern of self-restraint'; and (3) 'a contraction in the scope of mutual identification between constituent groups and individuals' (Fletcher, 1997, p. 83). He adds that such developments of decivilization are more likely to occur where there is

> a decrease in the (state) control of the monopoly of violence, a fragmentation of social ties and a shortening of chains of commercial, emotional and cognitive interdependence. It is also likely that such societies would be characterized by: a rise in the levels of fear, insecurity, danger and incalculability; the re-emergence of violence into the public sphere; growing inequality or heightening of tensions in the balance of power between constituent groups; a decrease in the distance between the standards of adults and children; a freer expression of aggressiveness and an increase in cruelty; an increase in impulsiveness; an increase in involved forms of thinking with their concomitantly high fantasy content and a decrease in detached forms of thought with an accompanying decrease in the 'reality-congruence' of concepts.
>
> (Fletcher, 1997, pp. 83–84)

Despite the fact that this implies a reversal of civilizing processes, Fletcher is quick to clarify this by arguing that, due to the learned aspects involved in civilizing processes – the changes in behaviour and social relations that people learn throughout their lifetime – these processes cannot be completely reversed, as such, for people do not simply forget what they have learnt. So, like Mennell, Fletcher conceptualizes decivilizing processes as reversals but only as *partial* reversals.

In his research on punishment, John Pratt has added to this in exploring possible decivilizing processes as they relate to recent developments in punitiveness in some Western countries. Rather than involving simply reversals, Pratt (2005, p. 260) suggests that instead 'we are likely to see the emergence of new practices, behaviours, and cultural values that represent a *fusion* of these influences rather than the exclusive ascendancy of one or the other': in other words, a fusion of civilizing and decivilizing trends rather than the dominance of civilizing processes or decivilizing processes. Using the example of Nazi Germany, he demonstrates how civilizing and decivilizing processes occurred in tandem. He combines the arguments of Elias and Fletcher on the decivilizing processes that culminated in the holocaust, with Fletcher's argument that these decivilizing trends were put into effect through civilizing trends such as a systematic, state control over the means of violence, with long chains of interdependence, and where many people were only a *part* of the process that culminated in the systematic extermination of individuals. He then goes on to relate how different civilizing trends combine with different decivilizing trends in the development of the new punitiveness. In relation to the 'war on terror' in Britain, these themes of partial decivilizing, and of a fusion of civilizing and decivilizing, are taken up by Vertigans (2010). He argues also that counterterror strategies, and current public reactions to terrorism, are indicative of an interweaving of civilizing and decivilizing trends.

In a different way, de Swaan (2001) seeks to overcome the problem of the relationship between civilizing and decivilizing processes by introducing the concept of *dyscivilization*. This refers to compartmentalized decivilizing processes, where decivilizing occurs in a sequestered area that is hidden from the rest of the population; where disidentification and cruelty is directed only at a designated group; where the rest of society maintains conditions of civilizing processes. In other words, decivilizing is spatially compartmentalized within a broader civilizing process. Such a concept is useful to consider when thinking about how and why some folk devils during some moral panics are treated in such a radically different way to others.

This is similar in some ways to how Robert van Krieken relates civilizing processes to decivilizing processes. He argues that these two processes 'interpenetrate each other so that, under certain circumstances, societies are "barbaric" precisely in their movement towards increasing civilization' (van Krieken, 1999, p. 297). Using the example of the 'stolen generations' in Australia to illustrate this – where, in the pursuit of 'civilization', and as civilizing processes themselves were developing, some aboriginal children were forcibly removed from their families in order to 'civilize' them to become more like the European colonists – he demonstrates how civilizing processes were occurring but that a part of this involved decivilizing trends directed towards aboriginal people. Van Krieken terms this campaign to 'civilize' the indigenous aboriginals as a *civilizing offensive*, a concept that is particularly useful to consider when thinking about the relationship between civilizing and decivilizing processes, and also how moral panics relate to these processes.

Moral panics can be regarded as a type of civilizing offensive. While moral panics may not always invoke discourses of civilization and civilizing, there is the underlying theme within them to influence the behaviour and the morals of particular groups of people, or to at least protect from those who are deemed to be 'immoral' and 'dangerous' (similar to how civilizing offensives might aim to protect the 'civilized' from the 'uncivilized'). And while, as van Krieken demonstrates, civilizing offensives involve civilized barbarism – a fusion of civilizing and decivilizing – so too moral panics may involve a fusion of these trends. This will be most explicitly demonstrated in Chapter 7, where I comparatively explore how civilizing and decivilizing processes and civilizing offensives relate to a selection of moral panic case studies.

## Moral panic

As outlined in Chapter 1, moral panics have typically been defined as over-reactions to perceived social problems. As Cohen describes it in *Folk Devils and Moral Panics*:

> Societies appear to be subject, every now and then, to periods of moral panic. A condition, episode, person or group of persons emerges to become defined as a threat to societal values and interests; its nature is presented in a stylized and stereotypical fashion by the mass media; the moral barricades are manned by editors, bishops, politicians and other right-thinking people; socially accredited experts pronounce their diagnoses and solutions; ways of coping are evolved or (more often) resorted to; the condition then disappears, submerges or deteriorates and becomes more visible....Sometimes the panic passes over and is forgotten...at other times it has more serious and long-lasting repercussions and might produce such changes as those in legal and social policy or even in the way the society conceives itself.
>
> (Cohen, [1972] 2002, p. 1)

As Nachman Ben-Yehuda (2009, p. 1) observes, the concept of moral panic 'has benefited from several theoretical innovations', including initially, in the work of Cohen and others, symbolic interactionism (SI) and labelling theory. This early influence of SI is important for, as Goudsblom illustrates in *Sociology in the Balance* (1977), SI approaches share many similarities with figurational approaches to theory, concepts, and empirical research.

This suggests that moral panic research, or at least the research from the likes of Cohen, would be compatible with a synthesis with Eliasian theories and concepts.

SI greatly influenced a substantial proportion of moral panic research that has utilized a constructionist approach to the study of social problems (Best, 2011). That line of research focusses on exploring how and why particular claims get made and who is involved in the claims-making process (Best, [1995] 2009). It explores the relations between the people involved in the claims and the claims-making rather than focussing on assessing/alleviating the social problem about which the claims are being made. In this respect, it is only a partial approach for it does not explore the interplay between how the 'reality' of problems is developing and how the 'construction' of them is developing, that is, how they effect and are affected by one another. Through synthesising moral panic with Elias, we can begin to overcome this problem of the objective/subjective divide, as I will suggest in the following chapter.

A more recent development has employed the arguments of Ulrich Beck's 'risk society' thesis to moral panic. Shelly Ungar argues that moral panic is no longer sufficient to consider exploring the development of social problems associated with the risk society, specifically, those surrounding 'real-world events' that are unintended outcomes of the risk society. He attempts to integrate natural processes into his approach to research: for example, by exploring how 'real' weather events influence the reception of climate change as a social problem (Ungar, 1992).

In contrast with earlier models of moral panic, Ungar argues that a 'risk society' (Beck, 1992) perspective brings a new dynamic to the creation of folk devils and the issue of disproportionality (Ungar, 2001). Potential risk society 'accidents' (that may lead to moral panics or social scares) do not necessarily involve clearly identifiable targets for blame – the fault may be more institutional rather than with an identified deviant group. Thus, instead of 'classic' moral panics (where the public are drawn together in their mutual hatred towards evil folk devils), risk society accidents and scares 'tend to create "corrosive communities" as the different actors try to deny their culpability' (Ungar, 2001, p. 284). Instead of creating certain 'us' and 'them' cohesive groups – bringing people together in uncertain times – they give rise to uncertainty, doubt, and a decrease in trust. That is, they expose the fallibility of these longer chains of interdependence but do not provide any object with which to direct the accompanying anxieties. As a result, there may be no violence (state or public) directed at a folk devil (as may have been the case with 'classic' moral panics).

Through looking at failed panics/scares, such as the greenhouse scare of the summer of 1988, Ungar (2001) examines how their success or failure is dependent upon external factors that are beyond claims-makers' control, such as dramatic real-world events, the timing of the claims-making, the receptivity of the audience, and the diffusion of claims. This relates back to how we conceive of the relationship between intended and unintended consequences in the development (or non-development) of moral panics.

One of the most important contributions to the development of the concept of moral panic comes from the synthesis of Foucault, governmentality, moral regulation, discourse, and risk. This began primarily in the work of Sean Hier and, Chas Critcher. Hier (2002, 2008) draws upon the sociologies of governance and risk to situate panics as short-term volatile regulatory episodes occurring within more routine practices of moral regulation. These episodes of 'volatile moralization' occur where grievance over a past event (such as the death of a child) becomes associated with future risk from dangerous, risky others. During such episodes, the responsibility for individual management/avoidance of risk is temporarily displaced to responsibility of the 'other'. Here, the other is seen to be as responsible for both past grievance and future risk as they are considered to be inadequately regulating their behaviour. This allows for exploring the interplay between developments that occur *before* moral panics as well as those that occur *during* panics. An important point of departure in Hier's work is his emphasis on moral panics (volatile episodes of moral regulation) as being *rational*. However, like the notion of a 'good' moral panic, conceptualizing moral panics as rational is useful to aid us in thinking beyond limited understandings, but it is still merely the other side of a normative dichotomy (irrational versus rational, bad versus good). In this way Elias's work is useful in helping us to think beyond these dichotomies and instead explore the *degrees* and *blends* of various different *relations* and *processes* involved in moral panics.

Moral panic may be linked with current campaigns about climate change in the following way. Some campaigners have implicitly or explicitly attributed recent natural disasters to climate change. Grievances over these past events are then used as indicative of future disasters, future risks that will occur in greater frequency and severity if something is not done to regulate everyone's behaviour. In contrast with Hier's conceptualization, and much moral panic research, it is not as if there is a dangerous, risky other that can be avoided, controlled, or regulated; we are all seen to be failing at the project of regulating our consumption. And so, we witness the development of various calls for intentional interventions aimed at regulating consumption, both formally, at the level of the state, and informally, at the level of the individual (the latter, encouraged by the proliferation of guides – books and television programmes – on how to live green and stop climate change) (see Rohloff, 2011a).

## Informalization, reformalization, and moral panic

While not exploring moral panics or nature-society relations, Cas Wouters (2004) has compared changes in manners and emotions from the fifteenth to the twenty-first century. He describes how the regulating of behaviours has changed over time, where, up until the end of the nineteenth century, there occurred a long-term process of formalization, where 'more and more aspects of behaviour were subjected to increasingly strict and detailed regulations that were partly formalized as laws and partly as manners' (Wouters, 2004, p. 204). This went hand in hand with the development 'of a type of personality with a rather stringent mode of self-regulation and a rather rigid conscience, functioning more or less as a "second nature"' (Wouters, 2004, pp. 193–194). In contrast with this, during the twentieth century there occurred a process of informalization, characterized by a re-laxation of some of these rules, while others came to be less formal and less specific. This informalization could thus be described as the development of a 'third nature':

> a balance between ... 'second-nature' self-regulation and a more reflex-ive and flexible one .... The term refers to a level of consciousness and calculation in which all types of constraints and possibilities are taken into account. It is a rise to a new level of reflexive civilization.
>
> (Wouters, 1998, p. 139)

More recently, the emergence of books and guides in response to the 'climate crisis' perhaps points towards a partial phase of *reformalization* (Wouters, 2007), where the ideals (of the likes of Leopold) are still present, but there is a shift towards increasing prescriptions – what behaviour to do, and what not to do, to 'save the planet' and 'stop global warming'. It is almost as if the potential future crises from climate change have engendered a sense that changes in behaviour regarding the environment have not been occurring at a fast-enough rate (or they have gone into 'reverse'). And so, this perceived social crisis has brought about a phase of reformalization, where (some) nature-society relations are written down in the form of guides containing prescriptions and prohibitions. But at the same time, the way these green guides are written is as if they are appealing to a 'third-nature personality', reflexive and self-regulating. Therefore, it is not as if the process of infor-malization has gone into reverse, as such.

We can now begin to see how moral panic may be used to understand how climate change has developed as a perceived social problem. There are many potential examples of reformalizing phases in response to infor-malizing that have been explored through a moral panic framework: for example, reactions to new media and to sex and violence in the media, and reactions to marijuana smokers (and 'youth' in general) in the 1960s. It is worth noting that some episodes of 'moral panic' involve looking back to a 'golden age' in the past, where 'social stability and strong moral discipline acted as a deterrent to delinquency and disorder' (McRobbie & Thornton, 1995, p. 561; see also Thompson, 1998, p. 4). In contrast, the 'present' is viewed as one of continual moral decline, where right and wrong are no longer certain and so a return to rules and regulations is deemed necessary.

And so, the ideas mentioned earlier, where an idealized past is compared with today's 'societies of excess', of 'overconsumption', are perceived as being indicative of a failure in more informal self-controls, and so implying the need for more specific guidelines on how to live.

As with manners books, as examined by Elias ([1939] 2012) in relation to civilizing processes, and self-help books, as examined by Rimke (2000) and others in relation to Foucault's concept of governmentality, guides to living green may be viewed as both reflecting and contributing to changes in standards of behaviour regarding nature-society relations. This shift towards *self*-governance of climate change may also reflect a wider *informalizing* of governance and can then be explored in relation to calls to return to more formal means of governance, such as those measures of social control enacted by state authorities. So, in addition to exploring the relationship between green guides and civilizing processes, we could (in future research) contrast this with other 'crises' and the differing degree of measures that have been enacted as a result, be they formal or informal. This could then be looked at in relation to the relative closeness or distance between campaigners and those who are the target of such campaigns. This returns us to the concept of moral panic and its relationship to long-term changes in regulation, in particular, to Hier's conceptualization of moral panic as volatile moral regulation and the question of the degree of 'volatility' of such episodes.

The conceptual incorporation of moral panic into long-term projects of behavioural regulation creates additional space for the incorporation of Elias's civilizing and decivilizing processes. Hier's notion of moral panics occurring during crises of the governing of morals can be comparable, in some ways, to *short*-term decivilizing processes. However, in the context of anthropogenic climate change, moral panics could, potentially, contribute to ecological civilizing processes. Thus, the interplay between civilizing and decivilizing trends during such processes that could be termed moral panics, and how these relate to broader social processes, could inform understandings about civilizing and decivilizing processes.

## Decivilizing processes, civilizing offensives, and moral panics

As mentioned in Chapter 1, I have already begun to synthesize parts of Elias's work (and of those who use Elias) with the concept of moral panic. I initially argued that moral panics are a type of partial decivilizing process (Rohloff, 2008). However, that argument was based upon considering a limited number of case studies (of other people's empirical research). As I began to consider a wider variety of empirical examples including climate change, it became apparent that moral panics were much more complex than this and, indeed, the relationship between civilizing and decivilizing processes is more complex than this. I therefore went on to suggest that moral panics are a type of civilizing offensive that may involve a blend of civilizing and decivilizing processes (Rohloff, 2011a, 2011b). And so, in this book I will explore, test, and develop this theoretical conceptual synthesis in relation to the example of climate change and to additional examples in the comparative analysis in Chapter 7.

## Panic and denial

A few authors have hinted at a relationship between moral panic and denial. Michael Welch (2004) has written on both in relation to terrorism (moral panics about terrorism, and denial about the human rights violations directed against those who are suspected of being involved in terrorism). He sees panic and denial as being conceptual opposites, the former in the direction of overreaction, the latter underreaction (Welch, 2007). Similarly, Garland sees moral panic and denial as two opposing poles within the study of social reaction (Garland, 2008). Cohen himself suggests that 'good' moral panics might be deliberately engineered to overcome the denial of atrocities (Cohen, 2001, [1972] 2002, 2011). In contrast, I wish to also explore the possibility of how moral panics themselves can contribute to denial. With the example of climate change, we have allegations (beyond academia) of 'climate change denial', yet we also have allegations of moral panic. And, as introduced in the previous chapter, the work of Norgaard (2006, 2011) and O'Neill and Nicholson-Cole (2009) on emotions and climate change suggests that fear and other undesirable emotions that may be present in claims and campaigns associated with moral panic can lead to denial. And so, it is important to consider these potential unintended consequences of moral panics. This brings us to the role of emotions in moral panic research.

## Emotions and panic

Other than conceptualizing panics as irrational, there has been little in the way of research to explore the emotions involved in panics. Both Cohen and Young have alluded to this, however, in looking at how various actors involved in panics enjoy the spectacle and/or experience feelings of resentment towards those who are seen to be rule breakers (Young, 2009). But not much has been done beyond this. This is perhaps not surprising, given that the sociology of emotions is a relatively young area of research. Kevin Walby and Dale Spencer (2011) have begun to contribute to this area. They argue that moral panic research should explore emotions in the following ways:

> by empirically investigating what emotions do,[3] how emotions align certain communities against others, and how emotions move people towards certain (sometimes violent) actions against others whose actions pose alleged harms.
>
> (Walby & Spencer, 2011, p. 104)

They add that one criticism of moral panic research is its over-reliance on the analysis of media (Walby & Spencer, 2011, p. 105).

## Elias and Foucault

As demonstrated in the work of Critcher, Hier, and others, much of the Foucauldian literature on moral panics shares many commonalities with the small amount of figurational research on moral panics (the latter, mostly consisting solely of my own research). This sparked an initial interest for me to compare Elias and Foucault throughout this research. In addition, several researchers have written on the relationship between Elias and Foucault already (for example, see Dunning & Hughes, 2013; Hughes, 2010; Smith, 1999, 2001; van Krieken, 1990) but not in relation to either moral panics or the 'environment' (least of all climate change). In comparing Elias and Foucault, I highlight commonalities and points of departure, and contribute to dialogue between these two areas of research.

Rather than devoting space here to providing an exposition of these existing comparisons, I wish to instead introduce several areas to which I will return in Chapter 7. I am primarily interested in utilizing Foucault in the form of his apparent or alleged focus on epistemic ruptures, of sudden changes, of continuity followed by discontinuity. As mentioned in the previous chapter, this focus on rapid change, akin to punctuated equilibrium, stands in contrast to Elias's predominant focus on more gradual change. It therefore provides a useful interrogation of Elias's work, to consider these different approaches when exploring empirical examples. Another useful comparison is between Elias and Beck. In contrast to Foucault, from what I am aware, no comparison with Beck has been done before.

## Elias and Beck: knowledge, science, risk, and civilization

In *World at Risk* (2009), Ulrich Beck brings together his earlier ideas about risk, reflexive modernization, and cosmopolitanism to explore the current different examples of financial crises, terrorism, and climate change. While acknowledging that the past was characterized by greater uncertainties and dangers associated with illness, violence, and other threats, Beck argues that these need to be discerned from the more recent developments associated with the anticipation of future threats that, he claims, are 'often a product of the success of civilization' (Beck, 2009, p. 4). The attempt to anticipate future threats, the forecasting of risks, corresponds with an increasing foresight – increasingly looking further into the future at the possibility of potential catastrophes and adjusting behaviour in accordance with these risks – and is in this way conducive with Elias's writings on knowledge and civilization. However, there are several points of departure. Beck argues that catastrophes, and risk (the anticipation of catastrophes), are often an outcome of civilization: for example, climate change as an unanticipated outcome of the success of industrialization. Whereas Elias argues that the dangers that seem to be produced by science – such as the possibilities of nuclear and chemical warfare – are not a product of science, as such, but are instead related to how the development of science occurs in interdependence with shifting power relations between different rival groups (Elias, [1987] 2007).

In relation to the potential dangers of technology, Elias refers to the tandem processes of technization and civilization; the development of different tools requires increasing levels of foresight and detachment, yet at the same time the utilization of those tools requires increasing self-regulation – the exercising of self-restraint – in an attempt to gain increasing control over the possible outcomes of the usage of technology. Elias provides the example of a civilizing process that interacted with the technological development of the motorcar. While not a unilinear process, the interplay of technization and civilization involved decivilizing spurts: '[the development of the motor car] revealed previously undreamt-of possibilities and, at the same time, unforeseen dangers…Viewed in terms of the theoretical concept of civilisation, the motor vehicle had two faces' (Elias, [1995] 2008, p. 66). So, Elias *does* allow for the possible outcome of unintended, unforeseen dangers (a view echoed by Goudsblom (1992) when he discusses the unforeseen outcomes of the control of fire). Indeed, Beck also notes that technology is a 'double-edged sword', which can lead to both 'chance and danger'.

Yet while Elias draws attention to the unintended outcomes of civilization, Beck seems to argue that these unforeseen outcomes are increasing, with the realization that, as the sciences have developed, we have come to increasingly realize that the more we know, the more we do not know. This brings into question Elias's argument of developing more 'reality-congruent' knowledge but perhaps not. The awareness of this not-knowing is perhaps more conducive to decreasing the 'fantasy content' of knowledge, as, if we follow Beck's argument, it brings us closer to the 'reality' of how little we know. However, at times Beck verges more towards the idea that knowledge leads to increasing dangers:

> World risk society is a *non*-knowledge society in a very precise sense. In contrast to the premodern era, it cannot be overcome by more and better knowledge, more and better science; rather precisely the opposite holds: it is the *product* of more and better science.
>
> (Beck, 2009, p. 115)

In contrast, Elias does not argue that knowledge alone can contribute to levels of danger; it is a combination of many part-processes. While Beck does examine this, in part, via his discussion of how crises may or may not lead to enforced cosmopolitanism, one gets the sense that he sees knowledge and technology as inherently dangerous and in need of control. But perhaps this is not too dissimilar to Goudsblom's (1992) discussion of fire and civilization and Elias's of technization and civilization (1995), where increasing technology requires increasing self-control.

Beck argues that risks – potential future catastrophes – are uncertain and, therefore, it is difficult to make a judgement about perceptions of risk; it is difficult to discern between 'hysteria and fear mongering' and 'appropriate fear and precaution' (Beck, 2009, p. 12). This argument problematizes judgements about dis/proportionality of the reactions to social problems in moral panic research.

In addition, Beck points towards how the increasing democratization of knowledge has enabled the continual questioning of science and technology; indeed, the democratization of claims to knowledge has assisted the development of the side effects of industrialization. Not only does this contribute to declining 'ontological security' (according to Beck and Giddens, at least) – where states, sciences, and economies are perceived to be failing to provide security – but it also creates space for increasingly competing and countering claims, thereby further contributing to uncertainty about potential catastrophes.

Beck's argument for opening up scientific debates to the public raises some questions over the relative autonomy of science that may be compromised as a result. To what extent are the public equipped to make such judgements? Reactions to numerous developments in science, including vaccines, the Large Hadron Collider, Evolution, to name but a few, suggest that if the public were to play a role, there needs to be more development in the area of science communication and consultation with the public. Furthermore, this 'reflexivity' that Beck speaks of does not appear to be applied equally to all spheres. It seems that there is more distrust of some areas – such as sciences, big corporations – with the opposite occurring with other areas: for example, 'natural' and 'alternative' therapies. Indeed, Beck notes how 'no new medicine can be hailed without listing the associated known and unknown risks' (2009, p. 60), but this level of scrutiny does not apply to 'alternative' medicines to the same degree.

Beck argues that these global risks, as they affect everyone, are in contrast to violent conflicts of the past – between 'us' and 'them'. However, these risks could also, potentially, produce outsiders, such as the person/organization that does not regulate their behaviour in accordance with the potential risk. And so, the 'irresponsible' may come to be regarded as 'dangerous'. Beck argues that, as new incalculable risks occur with growing interdependence and increasing complexity, it becomes increasingly more difficult to determine a single cause of a catastrophe or to predict them. But he does also acknowledge that some people still try to assign blame, particularly when this risk becomes individualized. This is partly addressed by Beck, when he discusses the risks of terrorism and smoking and how they may contribute to further divisions. We can perhaps see the potential for this with campaigns about other behaviours that are viewed as being not only dangerous to the self but also to the rest of us. Perhaps some behaviours associated with 'non-eco-friendly' lifestyles may come to be viewed as such, and thus, via status aspirations and other pressures, contribute to changes in behaviours.

Beck argues that this decrease in trust in institutions, along with the perceived inability of institutions to 'define or control risks in a rational way', has contributed to the emergence of the individual management of risk via 'responsible' consumerism. This relates to developments discussed earlier, such as the development of 'green' consumerism as well as the more recent emergence of guides on how to 'live green'. This is exemplified in the creation of the individual carbon calculator, where one can measure one's carbon footprint and get advice on how to decrease their individual footprint. Beck argues that with this reductionism of ecological crisis to forms of 'green' consumerism, there is a danger of coming up with only a technocratic answer to how we can mobilize and redefine modernity (Beck, 2008). He adds, against this 'don't to this' (limiting) discourse, that this individualized approach to climate change is not enough – the problem is too big and requires not just the involvement of states but of 'global alliances between states and businesses' (2009, p. 62). He adds that events such as Hurricane Katrina highlight the limitations of individual responsibility as not everyone has the means to 'care for the self'.

Beck appears to focus on the integrative possibilities for world risks. He argues that when risks are perceived as being 'omnipresent, three reactions are possible: *denial, apathy,* or *transformation*' (Beck, 2009, p. 48). For the latter, the transformation he refers to is the 'cosmopolitan moment' of 'world risk society'. Interestingly, despite a brief mention of it when discussing terrorism, for the most part Beck ignores the disintegrative possibilities accompanying world risks. Thus, while Elias tends to focus on 'double-binds' and 'decivilizing processes' in times of crisis, Beck is perhaps more optimistic and sees catastrophes as moments where new beginnings can occur (though this perhaps has something to do with the different examples each of them have explored, thereby highlighting the need for a *comparative* analysis). Taken together, Beck and Elias can perhaps be used to highlight a 'dialectical understanding' (van Krieken, 1998) of the ambivalent (Burkitt, 1996) processes of civilization (see also van Krieken, 1999).

For Beck, the 'cosmopolitan moment' refers to an unintended enforced development, where people increasingly come to be living and cooperating together, and sharing the world with others who, in the past, they might have excluded. It is a process whereby the formerly excluded come to be increasingly included in a continual process in which the increasing interdependence of nations means that helping the other helps the self (Beck, 2009, Ch. 3). Thus, it shares many similarities with Elias's idea of civilization, including increased interdependence contributing to increased mutual identification. However, this process may create further tensions, where groups come to be increasingly excluded if the risk or catastrophe that could bring about this 'cosmopolitan moment' can be blamed on a particular group of people. Indeed, Beck hints towards this possibility in his discussion of the reactions to terrorism.

This comparison between Beck and Elias, with references to climate change and moral panics, further assists with a critical assessment of Elias's theories and concepts, and in conceiving of the relationship between knowledge, moral panic, and decivilizing processes.

## Knowledge, panic, and decivilization

As mentioned earlier, the role of knowledge in decivilizing processes has also been underdeveloped, yet it is especially relevant to moral panic, given the focus on the role of the media in moral panics, where the exaggeration and distortion of events in the media (Cohen, [1972] 2002), or, conversely, the deamplification of events (Murphy et al., 1988), may affect understandings about social problems and the development of moral panics. This is particularly pertinent to anthropogenic climate change, where the public understanding of the science, and the media representation of the science, has been widely discussed. Developments in disparities between representations of climate change in academic literature and popular media could perhaps be related to wider social processes, namely, to changes in the production and the dissemination of knowledge.

The increasing specialization of the production of knowledge, particularly with regard to scientific knowledge, has, according to Ungar (2000), coincided with a relative 'knowledge-ignorance paradox', where the expansion of specialized knowledge has coincided with an increase in ignorance (as specialized knowledge increases, the proportion of information one can be knowledgeable about decreases). While scientific establishments may monopolize the production of scientific knowledge, the knowledge products themselves are, in theory, not so easily monopolized (Elias, [1982] 2009, 1984); scientific establishments cannot monopolize the distribution of knowledge either. The proliferation of multiple media, allowing space for counterclaims (McRobbie & Thornton, 1995) and the fabrication of claims (Ungar, 2000), as well as the relative scientific illiteracy of non-specialists necessitating alterations to knowledge, may affect understanding about topics such as anthropogenic climate change.

And so, the specialization of knowledge, along with the democratization of the distribution of knowledge, while potentially allowing the 'increasing power potential' of the governed via increasing education (Elias, 1984, pp. 277–278), may also, potentially, contribute to the democratization of multiple claims to knowledge and, thereby, increasing uncertainty about dangers. This is perhaps evident with differing understandings about the science of anthropogenic climate change. During such instances of multiple knowledge claims, moral panics may perhaps be an attempt to re-monopolize knowledge (as well as an attempt to perhaps re-formalize governance). This raises questions as to how lengthening chains of interdependence can contribute to decivilization.

## Elias and complexity

As mentioned in the previous chapter, John Urry's application of complexity to sociological understandings of climate change appears to have some dissimilarities with some of Elias's arguments about social change. However, it also has some similarities. Although Urry does not refer to Elias in these works, he does draw from Marx, particularly Marx's idea of the contradictions (including unintended consequences) in capitalism; indeed, Urry goes so far as to refer to Marx as the first 'complexity' theorist (see Urry, 2009). This usage of Marx shares similarities with the way Elias (and others) conceives of the relationship between intentional action and unintended developments, Elias's use of game models, and the relationship between civilizing and decivilizing processes.

And in his book on *Climate Change and Society*, Urry alludes to Elias though never actually refers to him. He introduces four possible future scenarios, possible outcomes from climate change: 'Orwellian scenario', 'perpetual consumerism', 'local sustainability', and 'regional warlordism'. The latter is characterized by a complete breakdown of civilization, what Norbert Elias would call a process of decivilization. Urry (2011, p. 149) writes, 'In this de-civilizing energy-starved future...' and outlines many 'reversals' that could be seen as examples of Elias's symptoms of decivilizing.

However, where the two differ is on the rate of change, and how change occurs. While Elias refers at times to 'spurts' of civilizing or decivilizing – that is, accelerations in the development of civilizing and decivilizing processes (see Elias, [1989] 2013) – he largely conceptualizes social change as occurring at a very gradual rate and largely as the unintended outcome of planned actions. In contrast, and as mentioned in the previous chapter, Urry argues that we become locked into different systems, and only a radical reorientation of social life can bring about a sudden 'switch' from the current system to a different system. This notion of system switching is in keeping with Thomas Kuhn (normal science, followed by revolution, leading to the establishment of a 'new' normal science, and so on) and Michel Foucault's idea of 'epistemic ruptures', of continuity followed by discontinuity. This question of the rate of change, of gradual versus sudden change, will be explored later in this book. Indeed, this is why in Chapter 5 I explore climate change in the long term, looking at in relation to ecological civilizing processes, and in Chapter 6 I look at it in the short term, in relation to moral panics.

## Elias, practice theory, and climate change

One sociological approach to climate change that I have thus far failed to mention utilizes social theories of practice. In the work of Shove, Hand, Southerton, and others, social practices are in some instances seen as separate from the people and the objects involved in the social practice. They focus on understanding how social practices develop, emerge, and dissipate in a relational and processual way (Shove, 2010). In looking at the examples of using a freezer (Hand & Shove, 2007) and showering (Hand, Shove, & Southerton, 2005), making many arguments that are similar to those made by Elias. They explore the long-term development of changes in showering practices. Looking at the development in the nineteenth century of the increasing medicalization and the high status associated with cleanliness, washing, and water, they make observations that are in keeping with Elias's and others' regarding civilizing processes and offensives (for example, see Goudsblom, 2003).

However, like Urry on complexity theory and climate change, these authors utilize practice theory to seek to understand how disjunction between dimensions of practices emerges so that they can then take advantage of these opportunities to 'establish...a less resource intensive form of "normal practice"' (Hand et al., 2005, para. 6.9). Indeed, the use of the phrase *normal* practice indicates a nod towards Kuhn's ([1962] 1970) 'normal science' mentioned earlier. Yet their exploration of gradual developments similar to civilizing processes suggests that they are instead conceptualizing social processes in both ways – as gradual developments and as sudden changes. This potential combination is worth considering as it relates to climate change and to synthesizing various approaches to social processes.

## Conclusion

In this chapter, I have provided an overview of the theories and concepts developed by Elias and others that I will be referring to throughout this research. I have also given an introduction to some of the approaches to moral panic research that I have considered when developing my own theoretical-conceptual-methodological approach to moral panic research. Finally, I have compared Elias, and moral panic, with several other approaches to sociology, namely Foucault, Beck, Urry and complexity theory, and practice theory. In the next chapter, I will develop my approach to this research – my 'methodology' and my 'methods' – with a further critical discussion of the relationship between figurational and moral panic research.

## Notes

1 Reality, as with every process that Elias explores, is dynamic, not static – it is always changing as relations between and within things change. Therefore, one can never 'know' reality for it is always changing; one can only ever

aim to develop knowledge that is more (rather than less) reality-congruent. Additionally, one can never 'stand outside' to view reality, to know whether one has achieved 'absolute reality' for reality is not separate from the self, just as 'society' is not separate from 'individuals'.

2  The term 'value congruence' is developed by Dunning & Hughes (2013).

3  One criticism of Walby and Spencer is that the way they write about emotions devolves them from people, conceptualizing emotions as separate things that act on their own.

## References

Aarts, W., Goudsblom, J., Schmidt, K., & Spier, F. (1995). *Toward a morality of moderation: Report for the Dutch National Research Programme on Global Air Pollution and Climate Change.* Amsterdam: Amsterdam School for Social Science Research.

Beck, U. (1992). *Risk society: Towards a new modernity* (M. Ritter, Trans.). London: Sage Publications.

Beck, U. (2008). Climate for change: Global warming as political opportunity, LSE Public Lecture.

Beck, U. (2009). *World at risk.* Cambridge: Polity Press.

Ben-Yehuda, N. (2009). Foreword: Moral panics—36 years on. *British Journal of Criminology, 49*(1), 1–3.

Best, J. ([1995] 2009). Typification and social problems construction. In J. Best (Ed.), *Images of issues: Typifying contemporary social problems* (2nd ed., pp. 3–10). New Brunswick, CA: Transaction Publishers.

Best, J. (2011). Locating moral panics within the sociology of social problems. In S. P. Hier (Ed.), *Moral panic and the politics of anxiety* (pp. 37–52). London: Routledge.

Burkitt, I. (1996). Civilization and ambivalence. *British Journal of Sociology, 47*(1), 135–150.

Cohen, S. ([1972] 2002). *Folk devils and moral panics: The creation of the mods and rockers* (3rd ed.). London: Routledge.

Cohen, S. (2001). *States of denial: Knowing about atrocities and suffering.* Cambridge: Polity Press.

Cohen, S. (2011). Whose side were we on? The undeclared politics of moral panic theory. *Crime, Media, Culture, 7*(3), 237–243.

de Swaan, A. (2001). Dyscivilization, mass extermination and the state. *Theory, Culture & Society, 18*(2–3), 265–276.

Dunning, E., & Hughes, J. (2013). *Norbert Elias and modern sociology: Knowledge, interdependence, power, process.* London: Bloomsbury.

Elias, N. ([1939] 2012). *On the process of civillisation: Sociogenetic and psychogenetic investigations (The collected works of Norbert Elias*, Vol. 3). Dublin: University College Dublin Press [Previous editions published as The civilizing process].

Elias, N. (1956). Problems of involvement and detachment. *British Journal of Sociology, 7*(3), 226–252.

Elias, N. ([1969] 2006). *The court society (The collected works of Norbert Elias*, Vol. 2). Dublin: University College Dublin Press.

Elias, N. ([1970] 2012). *What is sociology? (The collected works of Norbert Elias,* Vol. 5). Dublin: University College Dublin Press.

Elias, N. ([1971], 2009). Sociology of knowledge: new perspectives. In R. Kilminster & S. Mennell (Eds.), *Essays I: On the sociology of knowledge and the sciences (The collected works of Norbert Elias,* Vol. 14, pp. 1–41). Dublin: University College Dublin Press.

Elias, N. ([1982] 2009). Scientific establishments. In R. Kilminster & S. Mennell (Eds.), *Essays I: On the sociology of knowledge and the sciences (The collected works of Norbert Elias,* Vol. 14, pp. 107–160). Dublin: University College Dublin Press.

Elias, N. (1984). Knowledge and power: An interview by Peter Ludes. In N. Stehr & V. Meja (Eds.), *Society and knowledge: Contemporary perspectives in the sociology of knowledge* (pp. 251–291). New Brunswick, CA: Transaction Books.

Elias, N. ([1987] 2007). *Involvement and detachment (The collected works of Norbert Elias,* Vol. 8). Dublin: University College Dublin Press.

Elias, N. ([1989] 2013). *Studies on the Germans (The collected works of Norbert Elias,* Vol. 11). Dublin: University College Dublin Press.

Elias, N. ([1995] 2008). Technisation and civilisation. In R. Kilminster & S. Mennell (Eds.), *Essays II: On civilising processes, state formation and national identity (The collected works of Norbert Elias,* Vol. 15, pp. 57–92). Dublin: University College Dublin Press.

Fletcher, J. (1997). *Violence and civilization: An introduction to the work of Norbert Elias.* Cambridge: Polity Press.

Garland, D. (2008). On the concept of moral panic. *Crime Media Culture, 4*(1), 9–30.

Goudsblom, J. (1977). *Sociology in the balance: A critical essay.* Oxford: Basil Blackwell.

Goudsblom, J. (1992). *Fire and civilization.* London: Allen Lane.

Goudsblom, J. (2003). Public health and the civilizing process. In Dunning & S. Mennell (Eds.), *Norbert Elias* (Vol. 4, pp. 141–161). London: Sage.

Goudsblom, J. (2006). Civilization: The career of a controversial concept [Review of the book Civilization and its contents]. *History and Theory, 45*(2), 288–297.

Hand, M., & Shove, E. (2007). Condensing practices: Ways of living with a freezer. *Journal of Consumer Culture, 7*(1), 79–104.

Hand, M., Shove, E., & Southerton, D. (2005). Explaining showering: A discussion of the material, conventional, and temporal dimensions of practice. *Sociological Research Online, 10*(2), 1–13.

Hier, S. P. (2002). Conceptualizing moral panic through a moral economy of harm. *Critical Sociology, 28*(3), 311–334.

Hier, S. P. (2008). Thinking beyond moral panic: Risk, responsibility, and the politics of moralization. *Theoretical Criminology, 12*(2), 173–190.

Hughes, J. (2010). Emotional intelligence: Elias, Foucault, and the reflexive emotional self. *Foucault Studies, 8,* 28–52.

Kilminster, R. (2007). *Norbert Elias: Post-philosophical sociology.* London: Routledge.

Kuhn, T. S. ([1962] 1970). *The structure of scientific revolutions* (2nd ed.). Chicago, IL: University of Chicago Press.

McRobbie, A., & Thornton, S. L. (1995). Rethinking 'moral panic' for multi-mediated social worlds. *British Journal of Sociology, 46*(4), 559–574.

Murphy, P., Dunning, E., & Williams, J. (1988). Soccer crowd disorder and the press: Processes of amplification and de-amplification in historical perspective. *Theory, Culture & Society, 5*(3), 645–673.

Norgaard, K. M. (2006). "People want to protect themselves a little bit": Emotions, denial, and social movement nonparticipation. *Sociological Inquiry, 76*(3), 372–396.

Norgaard, K. M. (2011). Living in denial: Climate change, emotions, and everyday life. Cambridge, MA: MIT Press.

O'Neill, S., & Nicholson-Cole, S. (2009). "Fear won't do it": Promoting positive engagement with climate change through visual and iconic representations. *Science Communication, 30*(3), 355–379.

Pratt, J. (2005). Elias, punishment, and decivilization. In J. Pratt, D. Brown, M. Brown, S. Hallsworth, & W. Morrison (Eds.), *The new punitiveness: Trends, theories, perspectives* (pp. 256–271). Cullompton, Devon: Willan Publishing.

Quilley, S. (2004). Social development as trophic expansion: Food systems, prosthetic ecology and the arrow of history. *Amsterdams Sociologisch Tijdschrift, 31*(3), 321–347.

Quilley, S. (2009a). 'Biophilia' as an 'ecological civilising process': The sociogenesis and psychogenesis of litterlouts and recycling eco-citizens (working paper).

Quilley, S. (2009b). The land ethic as an ecological civilizing process: Aldo Leopold, Norbert Elias, and environmental philosophy. *Environmental Ethics, 31*(2), 115–134.

Rimke, H. M. (2000). Governing citizens through self-help literature. *Cultural Studies, 14*(1), 61–78.

Rohloff, A. (2008). Moral panics as decivilising processes: Towards an Eliasian approach. *New Zealand Sociology, 23*(1), 66–76.

Rohloff, A. (2011a). Extending the concept of moral panic: Elias, climate change and civilization. *Sociology, 45*(4), 634–649.

Rohloff, A. (2011b). Shifting the focus? Moral panics as civilizing and decivilizing processes. In S. P. Hier (Ed.), *Moral panic and the politics of anxiety* (pp. 71–85). London: Routledge.

Schmidt, C. (1993). On economization and ecologization as civilizing processes. *Environmental Values, 2*(1), 33–46.

Shove, E. (2010). Beyond the ABC: Climate change policy and theories of social change. *Environment and Planning, 42,* 1273–1285.

Smith, D. (1999). "The civilizing process" and "The history of sexuality": Comparing Norbert Elias and Michel Foucault. *Theory and Society, 28*(1), 79–100.

Smith, D. (2001). *Norbert Elias and modern social theory.* London: Sage.

Sutton, P. W. (2004). *Nature, environment and society.* Houndmills, Basingstoke, Hampshire: Palgrave Macmillan.

Thompson, K. (1998). *Moral panics.* London: Routledge.

Ungar, S. (1992). The rise and (relative) decline of global warming as a social problem. *Sociological Quarterly, 33*(4), 483–501.

Ungar, S. (2000). Knowledge, ignorance and the popular culture: Climate change versus the ozone hole. *Public Understanding of Science, 9*(3), 297–312.

Ungar, S. (2001). Moral panic versus the risk society: The implications of the changing sites of social anxiety. *British Journal of Sociology, 52*(2), 271–291.

Urry, J. (2009). Complexity and climate change: An interview by David Morgan. *Network, 101*(Spring), 8–9.

Urry, J. (2011). *Climate change and society*. Cambridge: Polity Press.

van Krieken, R. (1990). The organization of the soul: Elias and Foucault on discipline and the self. *Archives Europeenes de Sociologie / European Journal of Sociology, 31*(2), 353–371.

van Krieken, R. (1998). *Norbert Elias*. London: Routledge.

van Krieken, R. (1999). The barbarism of civilization: Cultural genocide and the 'stolen generations'. *British Journal of Sociology, 50*(2), 297–315.

Vertigans, S. (2010). British Muslims and the UK government's 'war on terror' within: Evidence of a clash of civilizations or emergent de-civilizing processes? *British Journal of Sociology, 61*(1), 26–44.

Walby, K., & Spencer, D. (2011). How emotions matter to moral panics. In S. P. Hier (Ed.), *Moral panic and the politics of anxiety* (pp. 104–117). London: Routledge.

Welch, M. (2004). Trampling human rights in the war on terror: Implications to the sociology of denial. *Critical Criminology, 12*(1), 1–20.

Welch, M. (2007). Moral panic, denial, and human rights: Scanning the spectrun from overreaction to underreaction. In D. Downes, P. Rock, C. Chinkin, & C. Gearty (Eds.), *Crime, social control and human rights: From moral panics to states of denial* (pp. 92–104). Devon: Willan Publishing.

Wouters, C. (1977). Informalisation and the civilising process. In P. R. Gleichmann, J. Goudsblom, & H. Korte (Eds.), *Human figurations: Essays for Norbert Elias* (pp. 437–453). Amsterdam: Amsterdams Sociologisch Tijdschrift.

Wouters, C. (1998). How strange to ourselves are our feelings of superiority and inferiority? *Theory, Culture & Society, 15*(1), 131–150.

Wouters, C. (2004). Changing regimes of manners and emotions: From disciplining to informalizing. In S. Loyal & S. Quilley (Eds.), *The sociology of Norbert Elias* (pp. 193–211). Cambridge: Cambridge University Press.

Wouters, C. (2007). *Informalization: Manners and emotions since 1890*. London: Sage.

Young, J. (2009). Moral panic: Its origins in resistance, ressentiment and the translation of fantasy into reality. *British Journal of Criminology, 49*(1), 4–16.

# 4   On Methodology[1]

## Introduction

On first impression, combining the concept of moral panic with Norbert Elias's theory of civilizing processes in order to explore how climate change has developed as a social problem may raise many objections and apparent contradictions. For example, the concept of moral panic is commonly associated with a perceived irrational overreaction to an exaggerated social problem. Such assumptions may lead one to judge this book as just an exercise in 'climate change scepticism' or as an example of 'climate change denial'. Furthermore, the concept of moral panic entails within it many assumptions that, at first glance, appear incompatible with Elias's approach. For example, the concept of moral panic entails normative assumptions, where the reaction to a perceived social problem is *pre*supposed to be misguided and misdirected. Such a political, ideological presupposition seems at odds with Elias's conception of attempts to reduce the intrusion of heteronomous evaluations into sociological research by way of a 'detour via detachment'.

I therefore want to begin this chapter by addressing some of these apparent contradictions through a discussion of my particular theoretical-methodological approach to 'moral panic' research, which will be largely informed (but not dictated) by Elias's figurational approach. I will contrast this approach to other approaches in order to highlight some of the commonalities between different approaches to research. I will also critically reflect and question aspects of Elias's theories and concepts by 'testing' them against other approaches and theories, and, eventually, empirical data. Additionally, this chapter will begin to question the relevance and adequacy of the concept of moral panic; this critical assessment of 'moral panic' will be further developed in Chapters 7 and 8.

## Involvement and detachment in moral panic research: normativity and the 'Political Project'

The history of the moral panic concept – how it developed and in what particular context – has left a legacy of several associated assumptions about what moral panic research is, what the concept signifies, and the purpose of the concept. As Garland observes, the sociology of moral panic originated in the 1960s, at a time when the concept's originators (Stan Cohen and Jock Young) were 'often culturally closer to deviants than to their controllers'; moral panic thus emerged as a critique of what Cohen, Young, and others 'regarded as uninformed, intolerant, and unnecessarily repressive reactions to deviance by conservative authorities' (Garland, 2008, p. 19). We can see this 'critical', 'political' characteristic of moral panic research in Cohen's own observations (in his introduction to the third edition of *Folk Devils and Moral Panics*):

> It is obviously true that the uses of the concept to expose disproportionality and exaggeration have come from within a left liberal consensus. The empirical project is concentrated on (if not reserved for) cases where the moral outrage appears driven by conservative or reactionary forces...the point [of moral panic research] was to expose social reaction not just as over-reaction in some quantitative sense, but first, as *tendentious* (that is, slanted in a particular ideological direction) and second, as *misplaced* or *displaced* (that is, aimed – whether deliberately or thoughtlessly – at a target which was not the 'real' problem).
>
> (Cohen, [1972] 2002, p. xxxi)

It is evident, from this extract, that there exists an assumption (or presupposition) that, with moral panic research, the particular reaction to a perceived social problem under investigation is somehow inappropriate and, therefore, wrong. To be sure, some moral panic studies have consisted of analyses of reactions to *imagined* social problems (as was undoubtedly the case with panics over 'satanic ritual abuse'; see de Young, (2004)). However, a concept and a mode of research that carries with it a debunking presupposition is limited in what it may achieve. It limits moral panic research to only those examples that are deemed to consist of inappropriate reactions, thereby limiting the development of the concept (Rohloff, 2011a). It extends an additional bias by assuming, prior to the research, that the reaction is inappropriate – indeed, a central aim of the research is to uncover this. Such a bias might mean that researchers neglect the various different functions that some moral panics may have. (Although this is partly beginning to be questioned through such notions as 'good' moral panics, which may function to overcome the denial of social problems (see Cohen, [1972] 2002, pp. xxxi–xxxv; 2011) and the idea of moral panics being 'rational' (see Hier, 2011).)

In response to this problem of normativity, as well as other problems, several authors have either rejected the concept altogether or have begun to develop a reconceptualization that attempts to overcome this normative assumption (and other limitations, such as the short-term focus on the episode of moral panic) (Hier, 2008; Rohloff & Wright, 2010). However, the attempt to remove the 'political' aspect of moral panic, informed in part by Foucault, has met with some criticism from others (see Critcher, 2008, 2009). It seems that there exists a tension between those who want the concept to retain its political project and those who want to develop a more detached approach to moral panic research that does not carry with it these normative presuppositions.

One way to overcome this apparent divide may be through the application of Norbert Elias's reconceptualization of the problem as a balance between 'involvement' and 'detachment' (Elias, [1987] 2007). Elias was very critical of the intrusion of 'heteronomous valuations' into research and endeavoured to develop sociology into a relatively more autonomous 'science' (Elias, [1970] 2012). Normative, ideological intrusions, such as those outlined earlier by Cohen's extract, could be construed as a type of heteronomous valuation, where a researcher's identification with a particular group (in this case, the 'deviants'), combined with a political project to 'liberate' the particular group, may influence the degree to which the researcher can step back and see the development of, in this case, a 'moral panic' as being more than a short-term irrational aberration.

Even Howard Becker acknowledges that, when we inevitably take sides in social research, 'as our personal and political commitments dictate', we must 'use our theoretical and technical resources to avoid the distortions that might introduce into our work' (Becker, 1967, p. 247). He added that we must also declare our involvement in this way, stating that (if we apply his argument to the case of moral panics) we have studied the panic through the eyes of the folk devils, not through the eyes of the journalists (Becker, 1967).[2] In this sense, Becker is acknowledging that there is no value neutral sociology, yet he is also arguing that we should strive to avoid the biases that the impact of our involvement with our research may have (see Hammersley, 2000, Ch. 3).

Similarly, Elias did not advocate a 'value neutral' sociology, which is something he would have regarded as both an impossible and an undesirable task. Elias argued that one could never be completely involved or completely detached.[3] And as sociology consisted of the study of the interdependent relations between people, a degree of involvement was desirable in order to aid in our understanding of human relations (see Elias, 1956). While an initial 'involvement' in something may spark interest in investigating that particular topic, Elias ([1987] 2007) argued that this initial involvement should be accompanied by an attempt at 'stepping back' through a 'detour via detachment'. The idea being that one can contribute to a more 'reality-congruent' knowledge if one is not too constrained by the short-term aim of achieving some political goal. This does not mean that figurational sociology is apolitical per se.

Maguire summarizes this 'balance' of involvement and detachment: 'Sociologists must, therefore, be both relatively involved *and* detached in order to grasp the basic experience of social life – it is a question of balance.

The sociologist-as-participant must be able to stand back and become the sociologist-as-observer-and-interpreter' (Maguire, 1988, p. 190). Eric Dunning elaborates on this, arguing that, in order to achieve this balance – to be able to stand back and develop a relatively detached approach – sociologists should

> Explore connections and regularities, structures and processes for their own sake. By attempting as dispassionately as possible to contribute to knowledge rather than to help in the achievement of some short-term goal, you will increase your chances of avoiding bias as a result of personal interests or because of your membership of or identification with a particular group or groups.
>
> (Dunning, 1992, p. 253)

This illustrates the difference between how I am approaching this 'moral panic study' of climate change and how moral panic is typically conceived. Following Elias, I wish to understand how such developments have occurred. This does not entail a prior judgement on my part about what I might find (in terms of the 'appropriateness' of reactions to the 'climate crisis'[4]), nor does it involve any overtly political aim. Instead, I wish to contribute to a greater understanding of how such developments have occurred over time, with the overall aim that, by contributing to knowledge, the knowledge garnered can then inform any interventions, with the hope that this would contribute to the development of more 'object-adequate' interventions that may have more intended than unintended consequences (that is, that any interventions may achieve more of what we want them to, culminating in fewer unwanted, unanticipated consequences (see Dunning & Hughes, 2013, Ch. 6)).

However, recent contributions have elaborated on the relationship between values, detachment, and politics in figurational research, which must be taken into consideration. Stephen Dunne provides an overview of the political involvement inherent in figurational sociology (Dunne, 2009), highlighting, amongst other things, Elias's utopian tale (Elias, 1984). Dunning and Hughes discuss the relationship between 'value congruence', 'reality congruence', and 'involvement-detachment'. They argue that Elias believed that researchers 'cannot and *should not* abandon their political interests and concerns' (Dunning & Hughes, 2013, p. 158), referring to the following quote from Elias:

> The problem confronting [social scientists] is not simply to discard [their more individual, political] role in favour of...[a more detached, scientific one]. They cannot cease to take part in, and to be affected by, the social and political affairs of their group and their time. Their own participation and involvement, moreover, is itself one of the conditions for comprehending the problems they try to solve as scientists...

> The problems confronting those who study one or the other aspects of human groups is how to keep their two roles as participant and enquirer clearly and consistently apart, and, as a professional group to establish in their work the undisputed dominance of the latter.
>
> (Elias, cited in Dunning & Hughes, 2013, p. 159)

Indeed, greater political involvement, and the intrusion of greater heteronomous evaluations (a greater degree of value congruence and a greater level of involvement), can in some instances contribute to greater degrees of reality congruence through the searching for and discovery of social processes that, without the same degree of value congruence and involvement, would have been ignored. An example is the concept of moral panic. If it was not for the partisan research and the level of involvement characteristic in the 1960s and 1970s amongst Stan Cohen, Jock Young, Stuart Hall, and other members of the New Deviancy Conference, the concept of moral panic may have never been developed, and the approaches to research characteristic of the time, which shed light on previously neglected areas of research, may have never been utilized. Imagine how different the sociology of deviance would be without *The Drugtakers, Folk Devils and Moral Panics*, and *Policing the Crisis*, to name but a few. Political involvement and partisanship, therefore, can provide insights that might not otherwise be discovered.

This illustrates the necessity for blends of involvement and detachment, and of value congruence and reality congruence. With increasing levels of informalization and 'reflexivity' (Kilminster, 2007), the capacity to utilize greater levels of involvement and value congruence in research, accompanied with a 'detour via detachment' (Elias, [1987] 2007) and 'declared involvement', may increase. It is in this vein that I wish to leave open the possibility for degrees of involvement in moral panic research – to retain the *potential* of the political project.

To summarize, throughout this research I intend to utilize the moral panic concept in a way that differs from the original, and indeed the popular, understanding of the term. I do not intend to use the concept as a debunking, sceptical term that dismisses the reaction to climate change as being an irrational, disproportionate overreaction. Rather, I wish to understand how and to what extent understandings about climate change have developed in relation to the development of the phenomenon of climate change (and associated developments). Throughout, I intend to 'critically' examine reactions, and associated interventions, to this perceived social problem but not with a presupposition that these reactions and interventions are necessarily misguided or misdirected. However, I do intend to eventually assess the adequacy of such interventions, that is, how and to what extent they may contribute to alleviating the potential 'climate crisis'. This approach attends to the normative presupposition of moral panic research that has been the subject of much criticism by several authors. Yet, at the same time, it still allows the potential for a 'political project', where the results of this research may inform interventions that may have more intended than unintended consequences.

## An investigation of processes and interdependent relations

Both moral panic and figurational research seek to ask questions about the processual development by which something has come to pass. For example, Elias explored how some people came to see themselves as more 'civilized' than others (Elias, [1939] 2012). In moral panic research, a 'processual model' (Critcher, 2003) is used to explore how a particular reaction to a perceived social problem has developed. Similarly, with this research I am exploring the processes that have contributed to both the development of anthropogenic climate change *and* the development of understandings about climate change.

The foundations of moral panic theory within symbolic interactionism and labelling theory have ingrained the concept with a focus on relations between people, including *changing* power relations between the 'control culture' and the 'folk devils' (Ben-Yehuda, 2009). Moral panic research sees 'social reality' as constantly in flux – continually contested and forever changing as relations between people change. This is similar to how Elias conceptualizes 'social reality'. Elias was very critical of the notion that one could discover eternal laws about social relations – static laws that are similar to those in the physical sciences. Thinking in terms of *processes, relations*, and *development,* Elias did not regard the 'nature' of 'social reality' as static and unchanging; rather he saw it as a continual process of structured development, resultant from the complex interactions between interdependent players (be they humans, other animals, etc.) (for example, see Elias, [1970] 2012).

While moral panic research has tended to focus on the social construction of reality (where the concept's grounding in symbolic interactionism and labelling theory emphasizes deviance as a *socially constructed* phenomenon), there still exists an element of realism; for example, measuring the 'real' extent of a social problem (and to what extent the reaction was disproportionate to the action/problem), including the extent to which intervention against primary deviance contributed to secondary deviance. This stands in contrast to the mutually exclusive dichotomies that some authors of books on research design/methodology promote. Such authors argue that there are numerous dichotomies involved in research design, where researchers must carefully select which dichotomies they will follow based on their philosophical assumptions about 'social reality'. For example, Crotty outlines what he believes to be a 'divide' between objectivism and subjectivism:

> What would seem problematic is any attempt to be at once objectivist and constructionist (or subjectivist). On the face of it, to say that there is objective meaning and, in the same breath, to say that there is no

objective meaning, certainly does appear to be contradictory...To avoid such discomfort, we will need to be consistently objectivist or consistently constructionist (or subjectivist).

(Crotty, 1998, p. 15)

This extract clearly depicts the core assumption that 'objective' and 'subjective' are mutually exclusive dichotomies. It presumes that *either* one will be searching for true facts *or* one will be exploring people's subjective interpretations or experiences. What this assumption neglects is the *interrelationship* between so-called 'reality' and its 'interpretation'. Though of course, to speak of reality, and the interpretation (or construction) of reality, is to add credence to the notion that 'object' and 'subject' are separate. For example, while much moral panic research may be regarded by some as largely influenced by social constructionism (for example, see Jenkins, 1998), the criterion of disproportionality (where a reaction is deemed to be disproportionate to the 'reality' of the problem) necessitates a degree of 'objectivism' to determine the extent to which claims may be accurate. The example of moral panic therefore highlights the objectivism/subjectivism dichotomy as an unnecessary *false* dichotomy: contra Crotty, there is no need to be 'consistently objectivist' or 'consistently constructionist'.

For this research, I am interested in exploring the interplay between various processes that have contributed to both the development of the phenomenon of 'anthropogenic' climate change and our understanding/perception of it. I am therefore interested in both[5] questions:

1  To explore processes that may have contributed to the development of anthropogenic climate change;
2  To explore how and to what extent anthropogenic climate change has come to be viewed (by some) as a social problem.

These two interrelated questions are being explored with the aim of contributing to knowledge about how such processes are developing – both as an object and a subject – and how 'appropriate' responses to this perceived social problem might be. Thus, the intention is to contribute to a more 'reality-congruent' or 'object-adequate' knowledge. The aim is that the development of more 'reality-congruent' knowledge may inform interventions that may have more intended than unintended consequences, which may then mean that we have greater directed control over the development of the interrelated natural, social, and psychic processes (see Dunning & Hughes, 2013, Ch. 6 and p. 196, on the ratio between intended and unintended developments, and between value congruence and reality congruence).

An important point of departure in much moral panic research is my intended focus on 'natural' processes or, rather, the interrelationship between natural, social, and psychic processes – what Elias terms the 'triad of controls' (Elias, [1970] 2012). As Sutton (2004) argues, through utilizing Elias's 'triad of controls' in sociological research on 'nature, self and society', we can combine what are often separated areas of investigation into one overarching approach, which would include 'exploring the relationships between the natural environment, people's self-identities and the organization of social life' (Sutton, 2004, p. 176). While moral panic research has largely neglected 'natural processes' (though there are exceptions, such as Ungar's (1992, 2001) research on 'real-world events'), this is perhaps in part due to the ideological underpinnings of moral panic, as outlined earlier with the examples derived from Cohen and Critcher. For some moral panic researchers, 'moral' is somehow seen as a separate sphere; for example, Kenneth Thompson argues, 'Sometimes panics about food (e.g. the BSE (Bovine spongiform encephalopathy) scare about infected beef) or health have been confused with panics that relate directly to morals' (Thompson, 1998, p. vii). Such arguments seem to suggest that 'panics about food' cannot contain a moral element (a view echoed by Cohen and Critcher); it is a question of moral panics *versus* risk panics (Ungar, 2001). However, others, such as Hunt and Hier, disagree, arguing that risks can be *moralized* and that moral panics themselves involve risk discourses. A question for exploration could be why are some moral panic researchers so intent on limiting the applicability of the concept? Can this perhaps tell us something about the *function* of the concept for sociologists, and the *motivations* behind (some) moral panic research? A further shift in focus could therefore be on the sociology of moral panic. Several important questions for investigation in this area include why this boxing off of the 'moral'? Is this similar to Marx's reduction of all inequalities being due to the 'economy' (see Elias, [1971] 2009, pp. 10–11)? What is meant by 'moral' (as opposed to 'ethical')? How and to what extent have understandings about what is morality changed? What does 'moral' mean technically? How and to what extent do campaigns utilize 'morality' in their discourse and how has this changed over time? Such questions arise as possible future paths of research following this book: namely the exploration of the sociology of moral panic or the sociogenesis of moral panic.

## The interplay of short-term campaigns and long-term processes

As already mentioned, one way that moral panic research and figurational research can further develop one another is via a synthesis of the two. Moral panic research varies in the degree to which it explores the long-term processes that feed into a given moral panic. As it currently stands, moral panic research tends to focus on short-term processes, to the relative neglect of how long-term processes relate to short-term episodes of moral panics (Rohloff & Wright, 2010).[6] Some authors have criticized the concept on the basis that it does not attend to more long-term developments (and how they relate to a short-term moral panic) (Watney, [1987] 1997). When the time frame for research is extended, the focus is often on the *aftermath* of the panic, not on the antecedents that fed into the panic (Critcher, 2003). A focus on the short term also implies a sort of 'epistemic rupture' that constitutes a revolutionary change in the way (some) people may perceive a particular social problem. In some instances, this short-term focus has also placed greater emphasis on the intentional actions of crusading reformers, to the relative neglect of more long-term unplanned developments that may influence the development of a 'moral panic'.

In contrast, Elias (and other Eliasian influenced research) has been criticized for its relative neglect of what have been termed 'civilizing offensives' – deliberate attempts to bring about changes in behaviour in order to 'civilize' those that are deemed to be 'uncivilized' or less 'civilized' than oneself. Such a criticism may be perhaps unjust for Elias conceptualized social development as being a *combination* of intended and unintended developments:

> ...the interweaving of the planned acts of many people results in a development of the social units they form with each other, unplanned by any of the people who brought them about. But the people who are thus bonded to each other constantly act intentionally, their intentions always arising from and directed towards the developments not planned by them...a dialectical movement between intentional and unintentional social changes.
>
> (Elias, [1980] 2008, p. 32)

Even so, the concept of civilizing offensives has received comparatively less attention than that of more long-term unplanned developments associated with civilizing (and decivilizing) processes (see Dunning & Sheard, [1979] 2005, p. 280). Yet within a figurational approach, conceptually there exists the possibility to explore this relationship between short-term intentional campaigns (which might include moral panics) and more long-term wider social processes. Utilizing this idea, I intend to explore the interrelation between long-term 'blind' social processes and short-term intentional campaigns.

## Methods

This research explores the *long*-term development of climate change as both an actual and a perceived social problem, covering the period from 1800 to the present. In the first part of the analysis, I look at the emergence of concern about climate change in relation to long-term ecological civilizing processes, as well as the emergence of the phenomenon of climate change in relation to civilizing processes, as unintended outcomes of civilization. In the second part, I explore how and to what extent reactions to climate change can be seen as a type of moral panic – these two chapters combined, explore the interplay between civilizing processes and civilizing offensives, of long-term and short-term processes. Following on from this focus on climate change, in the third and final part of the analysis, I undertake a comparative analysis, comparing climate change with several other possible moral panic examples in order to flesh out the complex interplay between civilizing and decivilizing processes and civilizing offensives, thereby contributing to a reformulation of these concepts and the relationship between them.

## Historical documentary analysis parts 1 and 2

For the first stage of the research, I chose to begin around the time of 1800 for several reasons. First, so that I could incorporate the development of changes in understandings about 'nature' and the 'environment', including the development of environmentalism, the ecological sciences, and the antecedents to climate change science. While these developments do not 'begin' in the 1800s – antecedents to environmentalism can be traced back much farther (Coates, 1998; Thomas, 1987) – several key developments did occur throughout the 1800s, including the formation of the first formal environmental organizations (Sutton, 2000). Second, I chose to restrict myself to go back only as far as 1800, so that I could carry out a more in-depth documentary analysis of these last two centuries; had I gone back farther, the research would have become more and more general. Third, I anticipated that two centuries worth of exploration would provide me with a long enough time period to explore long-term unplanned changes in behaviour, such as those explored by Elias in *On the Process of Civilisation*.

For the first and second parts of the research, I wanted to explore the possibility of the development of concern about climate change as being part of (1) a long-term ecological civilizing process and (2) a short-term moral panic. For the first of these two parts, I therefore undertook a 'discourse analysis' of primary documents dating from 1800 to the present. The type of discourse analysis I used was informed by both Eliasian and Foucauldian approaches to 'discourse' and cannot be associated with one particular approach to 'discourse'. It consisted of examining how different 'texts' spoke about particular issues and behaviours, how and to what extent this changed over time, and how and to what extent it related to other developments that were occurring. It also explored the hidden meanings in texts – looking at more explicit and implicit meanings, and at euphemisms within the texts and how these related to other discourses.

The material I analyzed for both parts of the historical documentary analysis included manners books (etiquette books), novels, environmentalist literature, 'green guides', popular science, websites, podcasts, policy documents, governmental and intergovernmental reports, campaigns, magazines, newspapers, documentaries, films, and reality TV shows. However, the second part of the analysis refers primarily to more recent texts, such as podcasts, green guides, websites, reality TV shows, and documentaries.

The majority of primary historical documentation was drawn from UK sources, though I also included some material from other countries, such as the USA, Australia, New Zealand, and Canada as well as multinational material. I chose to focus on the UK to try and provide a more in-depth analysis, while also highlighting more general international trends (at least amongst some countries), with comparisons with the USA, Australia, New Zealand, and Canada. This primary data was supplemented with an analysis of several key secondary sources that explore long-term changes in understandings about 'nature' and 'the natural world'.

Throughout this part of the research, particularly as it is written up in Chapter 5, I analyzed the documents as Elias did in *On the Process of Civilisation* ([1939] 2012) as time-series data. I undertook a diachronic analysis where I looked for what was and what was not present at different times, and how the *meaning* of what was present changed over time. As Dunning and Hughes (2013, p. 150) describe it, Elias likened this type of analysis to thinking about the documents as part of a filmstrip, in process together as a 'movie' rather than as static, isolated 'stills'.

I went into this part of the research with a broad idea of what I was looking for: primarily, changes in understandings about 'nature' and 'the environment'. However, a large part of the research consisted of discovering examples, in the form of exploratory research. For example, I was not intentionally searching for changes in understandings about what constitutes littering and why it is (now) deemed to be unacceptable. While I had the main hypotheses that I wanted to 'test' via empirical analysis (for example, the hypothesis that the development of 'eco-friendly' standards of behaviour is part of a wider 'ecological civilizing process' or that the development of concern about climate change can be explored as a moral panic), the specificities of such hypotheses were not finely tuned prior to the research and therefore necessitated a combination of both 'testing' and 'searching'.

Throughout the documentary analysis, I intended to explore the emergence of new standards of behaviour and new ways of thinking about things, and to then explore how these ideas and behaviours developed and changed over time to reach the present state of both concern about climate change as an *anthropogenic* social problem as well as the contestation over the extent of the problem and what should be done about it. In relation to the contestation over reality, I intended to also explore long-term changes in forms of media as well as changes in the receptivity towards scientific explanations and scientific 'experts'. This also involved analyzing documents that are 'sceptical' about climate change.

One of the reasons I analyzed such a variety of documentation is because I was interested in exploring how different types of texts depict changes in understandings about 'nature' and 'the environment'. For example, what one might read in a manners book from the late nineteenth century may be quite different to what one may find in a novel, which may differ from a letter in a newspaper, which may differ again from a book written by an environmentalist or by a scientist. By analyzing such a wide variety of documentation, I also aimed to gather a representative sample of variant changes that are and were developing in different types of texts. I was also interested in the transferability between ideas from different groups: for example, the transference of concern about climate change from scientists to the general public. Analysing a variety of texts, written by a variety of groups of people in a variety of formats, provides us with the means to explore this transference.

The analysis of the various types of texts was presented in time sequence in Chapter 5 in order to build up a picture of how standards of behaviour have been changing and at what rate and at what frequency (that is, how widespread and how quickly). This involved intermingling different types of texts with one another; highlighting both the time period and the type of text; and situating that within more general trends in changes in communication, changes in the regulation of behaviour, and changes in the governance of social problems.

In Chapter 6, the documentary analysis was presented quite differently. As the focus was less on diachronic themes (as these had been explored in the previous chapter), it instead focussed on demonstrating how and to what extent the analysis relates to moral panic themes, and then using this to reformulate critically both the concept of moral panic and how we go about doing moral panic research. The documents analyzed here largely differ from those analyzed in the majority of moral panic research. Most moral panic research tends to focus on analysis of newspapers and other news media, public opinion polls, legislation, and political debates. For the purposes of this research, I wanted to broaden the scope of 'moral panic media' to include a wide variety of media from popular culture.

In both Chapters 5 and 6, the documents were analyzed with a view that several may be reflecting changes in understanding as well as attempting to *persuade* readers, that is, (some of) these documents may both reflect and affect changes in understandings and changes in behaviour.

Documents and extracts were selected in several ways. Etiquette, manners books, and 'green guides' were sourced from all the items I could find at the British Library and the London School of Economics and Political Science (LSE). The selection of extracts within these and all the other documents was based on themes that emerged from the research process as they broadly related to ecological civilizing processes and/or moral panics. Environmentalist literature and novels were selected from those that were most well known in environmental circles. Podcasts were stumbled across by chance as were the magazines and websites. Documentaries, films, and reality TV shows were actively searched for on the Internet and subsequently viewed.

The advantages of documentary research include the wide availability of the data and the cost-effectiveness of the research (Denscombe, 2007, p. 244); most of these documents I could access for free via the Internet, The British Library, and other libraries (the only costs incurred were minimal: tube rides, photocopying/printing, interlibrary loans, and the occasional purchasing of books and DVDs).

## Comparative moral panic and figurational analysis

Another method of analysis in this research was a comparative analysis of various empirical examples, explored from both moral panic and figurational approaches. The aim was to develop a greater understanding about the various processes involved in moral panics and how they develop, and how civilizing and decivilizing processes and civilizing offensives relate to the development of different potential moral panics. The end result was to utilize this greater understanding to inform reconceptualizations of the relationship between civilizing and decivilizing processes, civilizing processes, and civilizing offensives, and to inform a reformulation of both the moral panic concept and how we undertake moral panic research. While some have compared existing moral panic studies with an 'ideal-type' model of a moral panic (Critcher, 2003) – how they think moral panics *ought* to be in a pure, absolute sense of the term – I think it is more informative to contrast and compare a variety of 'real' examples in order to understand the multiple ways that 'real' processes of moral panics develop (while Critcher (2003) did compare *real* examples of moral panics, he set these against an ideal-type model of moral panic and used them to reformulate this ideal-type model). This will provide us with a more empirically informed and potentially more 'reality-congruent' understanding about the processes of moral panics, thereby, helping us to reformulate a more empirically informed concept as well as inform us about how to undertake 'moral panic research'.

The empirical examples I chose were alcohol, climate change, (illegal) drugs, eating/obesity, terrorism, and tobacco. I chose these specific examples for several reasons. First, they are some of the very few empirical examples that have been examined from both a moral panic approach and a figurational approach (separately). Although with some of the examples, such as tobacco, very little moral panic research has been undertaken. Second, I was interested in exploring those examples that really stretched and tested the concept of moral panic. Both terrorism and illegal drugs are well-researched areas of moral panic, but the others are currently contested and debated, or recognized as examples of 'weak' moral panics (the latter, in the case of alcohol). Additionally, the focus on consumption, overconsumption, and addiction in much of the climate change media contributed to my growing interest in these areas, hence most of the examples in this chapter have come to be associated with problematized consumption and/

or addiction (excluding the case of terrorism, which was primarily included in this chapter due to its status as a relatively 'strong' moral panic).

## Conclusion

This chapter has set out my approach to the research – largely informed by a synthesis of moral panic and figurational approaches, without being completely 'lead' by one or the other. In the next chapter, I discuss the first of my three stages of the research process: a historical documentary analysis of the long-term development of ecological civilizing processes and how this relates to the development of climate change as an actual and perceived social problem.

## Notes

1 Earlier versions of some of the sections from this chapter were written for a chapter in *Moral panic and the politics of anxiety*, see Rohloff (2011b).
2 This is similar in some ways to Baur and Ernst's (2011) assertion, following Elias, that researchers should declare why they are asking their chosen research questions (partiality), and they should also continually reflect on how their motivations for asking those questions influence the research process, such as how they interpret or possibly distort data.
3 Although Elias (1956) did add the exceptions of small babies and perhaps insane people as being completely involved.
4 This is not to ignore the fact that I, like anyone else, have come into this research with *some* preconceived notions about what I might find; the key is to continually critically question and challenge those preconceived notions so that they do not become so fixed that they drive the research too much and close it to other possibilities.
5 That is, 'both' types of questions that are often separated into the epistemologically dichotomous alternatives of objectivism/realism and constructionism.
6 Although some authors, such as Hunt, Hier, and now Critcher, are beginning to address this neglect of the relationship between short-term campaigns and long-term processes via a fusion, of sorts, of moral panic with moral regulation; exploring the relationship between short-term regulatory episodes (i.e. panics) and more long-term projects of moral regulation.

## References

Baur, N., & Ernst, S. (2011). Towards a process-oriented methodology: Modern social science research methods and Norbert Elias's figurational sociology. *Sociological Review, 59*(Supplement s1), 117–139.
Becker, H. S. (1967). Whose side are we on? *Social Problems, 14*, 239–247.
Ben-Yehuda, N. (2009). Foreword: Moral panics—36 years on. *British Journal of Criminology, 49*(1), 1–3.
Coates, P. (1998). *Nature: Western attitudes since ancient times.* Cambridge: Polity Press.
Cohen, S. ([1972] 2002). *Folk devils and moral panics: The creation of the mods and rockers* (3rd ed.). London: Routledge.

88 *On Methodology*

Cohen, S. (2011). Whose side were we on? The undeclared politics of moral panic theory. *Crime, Media, Culture, 7*(3), 237–243.

Critcher, C. (2003). *Moral panics and the media.* Buckingham: Open University Press.

Critcher, C. (2008). Moral panic analysis: Past, present and future. *Sociology Compass, 2*(4), 1127–1144.

Critcher, C. (2009). Widening the focus: Moral panics as moral regulation. *British Journal of Criminology, 49*(1), 17–34.

Crotty, M. (1998). *The foundations of social research: Meaning and perspective in the research process.* Crows Nest: Allen & Unwin.

Denscombe, M. (2007). *The good research guide* (3rd ed.). Maidenhead, Berkshire: Open University Press.

de Young, M. (2004). *The day care ritual abuse moral panic.* Jefferson, NC: McFarland & Company, Inc., Publishers.

Dunne, S. (2009). The politics of figurational sociology. *Sociological Review, 57*(1), 28–57.

Dunning, E. (1992). Figurational sociology and the sociology of sport: Some concluding remarks. In E. Dunning & C. Rojek (Eds.), *Sport and leisure in the civilizing process: Critique and counter-critique* (pp. 221–284). Houndmills, Basingstoke, Hampshire: Macmillan.

Dunning, E., & Hughes, J. (2013). *Norbert Elias and modern sociology: Knowledge, interdependence, power, process.* London: Bloomsbury.

Dunning, E., & Sheard, K. ([1979] 2005). *Barbarians, gentlemen and players: A sociological study of the development of rugby football* (2nd ed.). London: Routledge.

Elias, N. ([1939] 2012). *On the process of civilisation: Sociogenetic and psychogenetic investigations (The Collected Works of Norbert Elias, Vol. 3).* Dublin: University College Dublin Press [Previous editions published as *The civilizing process*].

Elias, N. (1956). Problems of involvement and detachment. *British Journal of Sociology, 7*(3), 226–252.

Elias, N. ([1970] 2012). *What is sociology? (The Collected Works of Norbert Elias, Vol. 5)* Dublin: University College Dublin Press.

Elias, N. ([1971], 2009). Sociology of knowledge: new perspectives. In R. Kilminster & S. Mennell (Eds.), *Essays I: On the sociology of knowledge and the sciences (The Collected Works of Norbert Elias, Vol. 14)* (pp. 1–41). Dublin: University College Dublin Press.

Elias, N. ([1980] 2008). The civilising of parents. In R. Kilminster & S. Mennell (Eds.), *Essays II: On civilising processes, state formation and national identity (The Collected Works of Norbert Elias, Vol. 15)* (pp. 14–40). Dublin: University College Dublin Press.

Elias, N. (1984). Knowledge and power: An interview by Peter Ludes. In N. Stehr & V. Meja (Eds.), *Society and knowledge: Contemporary perspectives in the sociology of knowledge* (pp. 251–291). New Brunswick: Transaction Books.

Elias, N. ([1987] 2007). *Involvement and detachment (The Collected Works of Norbert Elias, Vol. 8).* Dublin: University College Dublin Press.

Garland, D. (2008). On the concept of moral panic. *Crime Media Culture, 4*(1), 9–30.

Hammersley, M. (2000). *Taking sides in social research: Essays on partisanship and bias.* London: Routledge.

Hier, S. P. (2008). Thinking beyond moral panic: Risk, responsibility, and the politics of moralization. *Theoretical Criminology, 12*(2), 173–190.

Hier, S. P. (2011). Introduction: Bringing moral panic studies into focus. In S. P. Hier (Ed.), *Moral panic and the politics of anxiety* (pp. 1–16). London: Routledge.

Jenkins, P. (1998). *Moral panic: Changing concepts of the child molester in modern America.* New Haven: Yale University Press.

Kilminster, R. (2007). *Norbert Elias: Post-philosophical sociology.* London: Routledge.

Maguire, J. (1988). Doing figurational sociology: Some preliminary observations on methodological issues and sensitizing concepts. *Leisure Studies, 7,* 187–193.

Rohloff, A. (2011a). Extending the concept of moral panic: Elias, climate change and civilization. *Sociology, 45*(4), 634–649.

Rohloff, A. (2011b). Shifting the focus? Moral panics as civilizing and decivilizing processes. In S. P. Hier (Ed.), *Moral panic and the politics of anxiety* (pp. 71–85). London: Routledge.

Rohloff, A., & Wright, S. (2010). Moral panic and social theory: Beyond the heuristic. *Current Sociology, 58*(3), 403–419.

Sutton, P. W. (2000). *Explaining environmentalism: In search of a new social movement.* Aldershot: Ashgate.

Sutton, P. W. (2004). *Nature, environment and society.* Houndmills, Basingstoke, Hampshire: Palgrave Macmillan.

Thomas, K. (1987). *Man and the natural world: Changing attitudes in England 1500–1800.* Harmondsworth, Middlesex: Penguin.

Thompson, K. (1998). *Moral panics.* London: Routledge.

Ungar, S. (1992). The rise and (relative) decline of global warming as a social problem. *Sociological Quarterly, 33*(4), 483–501.

Ungar, S. (2001). Moral panic versus the risk society: The implications of the changing sites of social anxiety. *British Journal of Sociology, 52*(2), 271–291.

Watney, S. ([1987] 1997). *Policing desire: Pornography, AIDS and the media* (3rd ed.). London: Cassell.

# 5    Historical analysis (part one)
## Climate change and ecological civilizing processes

## Introduction

Having provided an introduction to the notion of ecological civilizing processes in Chapter 2, I now turn to exploring the extent to which the development of climate change as a perceived social problem can be situated within a wider ecological civilizing process.

Covering the time period from 1800 to the present and focussing on England[1] (while also drawing from examples from other countries), this chapter will explore the extent to which gradual changes in nature-society relations, changes in perceptions about the environment, and changes in behaviour can be characterized as an ecological civilizing process and how these are interspersed with intentional campaigns. In the next chapter, these changes will be linked to more recent developments regarding climate change, combining civilizing offensives with moral panics.

## The aestheticization of 'nature'

In *On the Process of Civilisation*, when discussing art from the Middle Ages (specifically, scenes from the life of a knight in the picture book *Medieval House-Book*, published between 1475 and 1480), Elias observes that in these drawings 'nature' was merely something that was in the background to humans: 'there is nothing in these pictures of the nostalgic mood, the "sentimental" attitude to "nature" that slowly became perceptible not very long afterwards' (Elias, [1939] 2012, p. 200). Not only was there little emotional identification with 'nature' in these drawings; there was also little identification with other people.

Over time, as more and more people (particularly the upper classes) migrated from the country to the town, and as knights came to be increasingly dependent on the court society, perceptions about 'nature' changed. Representations of 'nature' became increasingly more selective, obscuring the less desirable attributes:

> much that really existed in the country, in 'nature', was no longer portrayed. The hill was shown, but not the gallows on it, nor the corpse

hanging from the gallows. The field was shown, but no longer the ragged peasant laboriously driving his horses. Just as everything 'common' or 'vulgar' disappeared from courtly language, so it vanished also from the pictures and drawings intended for the courtly upper class.

(Elias, [1939] 2012, p. 201)[2]

And so, these 'distasteful' aspects of 'nature' came to be increasingly hidden behind the scenes as part of a broader development to make things appear more 'civilized'. Elias links these changes in representations, experiences, and perceptions of 'nature' with broader developments in civilizing processes. For example, the gradual development of the homo-clausus mode of self-experience – in which the self comes to be increasingly perceived to be 'sharply cut off within its own fate, standing opposed to every other self and to the whole world, as if separated from them by an abyss' – facilitated the view of nature as 'landscape' as a visually pleasurable experience (Elias, [1921] 2006, p. 7). An additional way in which Elias links these developments with civilizing processes is by exploring the increasing control over 'nature'.

## Increasing control over 'nature'

An additional long-term change that influenced the development of changes in perceptions about and experiences of nature was the increasing control and pacification of 'nature':

> The manner in which 'nature' was experienced was fundamentally affected, slowly at the end of the Middle Ages and then more quickly from the sixteenth century onwards, by the pacification of larger and larger populated areas. Only then did forests, meadows and mountains gradually cease to be danger zones of the first order, from which anxiety and fear constantly intrude into individual life. And then, as the network of roads became, like social interdependence in general, more dense; as robber-knights and beasts of prey slowly disappeared; as forest and field ceased to be the scene of unbridled passions, of the savage pursuit of man and beast, of wild joy and fear, and as they were moulded by intertwining peaceful activities, the production of goods, trade and transport – so then, to pacified people, a correspondingly pacified nature became visible, and in a new way. It became – in keeping with the mounting significance that the eye attained as the mediator of pleasure with the growing moderation of the affects – to a high degree an object of visual pleasure. In addition, people…grew more sensitive and began to see the open country in a more differentiated way…They took pleasure in the harmony of colour and lines, became open to what is called the beauty of nature; their feelings were aroused by the changing shades and shapes of the clouds and the play of light on the leaves of a tree.

(Elias, [1939] 2012, p. 461)

We can see here how the increasing pacification of nature also contributed to the aestheticization of nature, how, as 'nature' came to be increasingly safer, it became increasingly possible for people to relax in 'nature' and aesthetically enjoy 'seeing' (and smelling, hearing, tasting, and touching) 'nature'. Sutton argues that such developments eventually contributed to the development of changing ecological sensibilities and, later, the development of environmental campaigns and organisations (Sutton, 2000, 2004). As will be discussed later in the chapter, it was this overall increasingly aestheticized engagement with nature that was first expressed as the focus of concern when discourse about littering first emerged, and aesthetic appreciations were also prominent in early concerns about pollution.

## The 'wilderness'

Similar developments occurred in the USA. In the early period of European settlement, during the time of the 'frontier' expansion, the 'wilderness' was seen as both physically dangerous and morally corrupting. The 'wild' 'nature' of it was believed to potentially unleash the 'wildness' in men: 'A more subtle terror than Indians or animals was the opportunity the freedom of wilderness presented for men to behave in a savage or bestial manner' (Nash, [1967] 2001, p. 29). Here, we see not only the low identification with Indians – where they are placed on a par with animals as an additional 'terror' to overcome – but also a metaphor of contagion, where one can 'catch' 'savage' and 'bestial' behaviour simply by living in a 'savage' 'wilderness'. This perhaps relates to in-group and out-group fears that may have existed at the time, with correspondingly very small circles of mutual identification amongst early settlers and particularly between early settlers and Native Americans.

By the early nineteenth century, the American 'wilderness' was still seen as dangerous but only physically so, and it was increasingly regarded as pleasurable and exciting. By this time (and particularly into the early twentieth century), relations with Native Americans were improving as well. As most people now lived in cities or on farms, the 'wilderness' presented a novelty and an escape (Nash, [1967] 2001, pp. 56–57) (similar to the 'countryside' in England). And now, 'wilderness' has shifted from being morally corrupting to morally curing, where 'civilization' is regarded as being problematic and full of restraints and rules; only in the 'wilderness' can one truly be free (Nash, [1967] 2001, p. 65). However, this only represented an ideal, and travellers only ever *visited* the 'wilderness', always returning to 'civilization'.

In this way, we can see how going to the 'wilderness' or going to the 'countryside' came to be a source of 'mimetic excitement' (Elias & Dunning, [1986] 2008), along with other leisure activities. As people came to gain increasing control over the 'wilderness'/'countryside', and increasing control over themselves, it became increasingly possible for them to travel to these places with little or no fear (and, if there was fear, it was a fear to be embraced). Places of 'nature' thus came to be associated with a 'quest for excitement', a controlled decontrolling of restraints on emotions (Elias & Dunning, [1986] 2008), with both self- and social controls. For example, in the 'wilderness', as in the 'countryside', despite this relaxation there were still rules about how to behave and how not to behave – in the 'wilderness', one could never completely escape 'civilization'.

## The contrast between the 'city' and the 'countryside': spatial informalization

In 'the country', manners are different from those required in 'the city'. For example, in the 1868 edition of *The Habits of Good Society*, the author writes, 'While in most cases a rougher and easier mode of dress is both admissible and desirable in the country, there are many occasions of country visiting where a town man finds it difficult to decide' (*The Habits of Good Society: A Handbook of Etiquette for Ladies and Gentlemen*, 1868, p. 136). In this sense, going to the 'country' represents a relaxing of etiquette but not an absence. Rules about what to wear and what not to wear still exist. Yet, as this extract suggests, the spatial 'informalization' that occurs in relation to 'nature', and the relaxation of manners that accompanies it, brings about a confusion and uncertainty about how one should behave. As the extract illustrates, people find it difficult to decide what they *should* wear (similarly, see Hughes, 2010, pp. 44–45, on informalization in the workplace).

In 1897, in *Manners for Men*, we have a comparison of the formal attire of the school 'uniform' with the relaxed 'country suit':

> Dress in the country varies considerably in many matters from that worn in town. A boy's first "country suit" after he leaves school is a great event to him. At Eton and Harrow the style of dress might almost be called a uniform, and the first suit of tweeds marks the emancipation from school-life.
>
> (Humphrey, [1897] 1993, p. 119)

Here, the 'country' is seen as like an emancipation from the town, where the manners and modes of behaviour are increasingly more relaxed, as is evident in the next extract from the early twentieth century.

In 1921, in the following extract from *Cassell's Book of Etiquette*, we can also see the difference in people's emotions when having picnics in 'the country' compared with life in the town or city:

> There are plenty of people who enjoy picnics besides the children for whose benefit they are generally supposed to be arranged. Rural sights and rural sounds, when all nature is alive and gay in the glad summer

time, have a happy and genial effect; then, too, the absence of all state and ceremony, the liberty, the entire change and freedom from etiquette, conduce to gaiety of spirit and mirth. After all, it is the novelty which is the great charm – for the same set of people whom you now see making merry because the salt and the sugar have fraternized on the journey, and who now declare it to be the summit of human felicity to sit in an uncomfortable position upon something never intended to be a seat, beside a table-cloth which, being spread upon an uneven surface, causes everything that should remain perpendicular to assume a horizontal attitude – these same people would grumble loudly did such things occur daily.

(Cassell and Co., 1921, p. 157)

There are several things that we can take from this extract. First, there is the allusion to sex: 'making merry because the salt and sugar have fraternized on the journey', where 'salt' and 'sugar' refer to males and females, and 'causes everything that should remain perpendicular to assume a horizontal attitude', where 'horizontal attitude' refers to sexual relations. While this is written in a cryptic way, where euphemisms are used to disguise the true content of the text, it is also written in a way that is not condemning – the jovial tone of the text makes it appear to be almost acceptable but only in the 'country'; as the author points out, 'these same people would grumble loudly did such things occur daily'.

It is only through an increasing control over natural, social, and psychic processes that this had become possible – as noted earlier in the chapter, the 'wilderness' was seen as terrifying partly because the absence of formal constraints would bring about a 'loss of control' in individuals who ventured there. By the 1920s, however, people were seen to have a greater degree of self-control and were thus seen to be less likely to 'lose control'. However, as already mentioned, manners still remained but in a different format.

Additionally, the tone of the text seems to almost celebrate the informality of manners in rural areas, the 'entire change and freedom from etiquette'. The text depicts how going to rural areas represents an escape, a liberation from the increasingly formalized manners that existed at the time.

The ability of people to travel to the 'countryside' was further aided by the development of technologies, specifically the motor car:

In the past, the picnic was the indulgence largely of country folk, nowadays, thanks to enterprise, the Londoner may hire a private omnibus, go out to some picturesque spot in any of the home counties, or even a far field as the New Forest on one side, or say, Oxford on the other, and come home in the delightful coolness of a summer's evening.

(Cassell and Co., 1921, p. 158)

This contributed to the countryside becoming more and more accessible to more types of people as the motor car and other technologies became more widespread and affordable. Here we still see the visual appreciation of 'nature', where it is described as 'picturesque', and this is juxtaposed with the uncritical appreciation of technology: 'nowadays, thanks to enterprise'. Paradoxically, this same development contributed to environmental problems: for example, the increasing use of motor cars over long distances contributed to increasing pollution and the increase in the building of roads (the latter also necessitated the changing of the 'landscape').

The visual aesthetics of the countryside – and of garden parties in 'the country' – were contrasted with the coldness of the city and town: 'If Fortune favours, there is an abiding charm about such a gathering [Garden Party], even in London or the suburbs, for some of the older houses boast delightful gardens which are in vivid contrast with their stern, forbidding facades' (*Etiquette for Gentlemen: A Guide to the Observances of Good Society*, 1923, p. 102). Here, despite the appreciation of technology noted in the previous extract, we see evidence of an increasingly depressing lifelessness associated with the 'city'. This is contrasted with the life, warmth, and 'charm' of the 'countryside'.

The following extracts recall a point earlier discussed about manners in the 'countryside' compared to those in 'the city'. In 1925, in *Etiquette Up to Date,* the author writes,

> In our fickle climate the success of all outdoor entertainments is more or less at the mercy of the weather, but when it proves kind, the river and countryside offer delightful possibilities, because so much tiresome formality may be dispensed with.
>
> Invitations are often very informal, a riverside hostess frequently giving a general invitation to her friends to "run down and see us any day," though visits have to be more definitely arranged when accommodation is limited.
>
> (Burleigh, 1925, p. 170)

Here, we see that manners in the 'countryside' are less formal than those in the town or city; the 'countryside' is seen as an escape from social mores, from the 'tiresome formality' of life in the city. Yet, as the author of this etiquette book points out, formalities are still required (even if they are less formal), as the following extract also illustrates:

> With the exception of the necessary conventions, life on the river allows of a free-and-easy comradeship, and guests practically entertain themselves with boating, punting, bathing, impromptu concerts or dances by moonlight, motor-boat or motor-car expeditions, up-river trips, long lazy hours in shady backwaters, or the added excitement of a

regatta for which, however, special parties are usually arranged by the hostess, and a rather more formal etiquette and elaborate hospitality may prevail.

(Burleigh, 1925, pp. 170–171)

Here, we see that even in the 'countryside' all is not informal – there are those occasions that are increasingly formalized. We also see reference to both relaxation and excitement, where leisure in the 'country' is seen as an escape from city life in the form of relaxing – 'long lazy hours' – implying that the city is far from relaxing, and exciting – 'the added excitement of a regatta' – implying that the city is not exciting.

In the following extract, the relaxation of dress in the countryside is also evident:

Unlimited scope is offered in the matter of riverside dress, whether one's taste inclines to frilly muslins and organdies or severly perfect linens and white or light-coloured flannels, serges and woollies, gaudily gay colours, soft pastel shades or bizarre effects, but tailored cloth and tweed or elaborate confections and materials are out of place, and the charm of simplicity is perhaps more apparent on the river than any-where else.

(Burleigh, 1925, p. 173)

Here, we see further evidence to suggest that the relaxation of manners re-garding what to wear would have also brought with it confusion over what one *can* wear in the 'countryside' – as the author notes, 'unlimited scope is offered in riverside dress'.

In another extract from the same text, we have an illustration of how, despite these relaxations of manners, there are still rules of how one should behave – one must still exercise a degree of restraint:

Boisterous shouting and laughter or any kind of rowdyism and "horse-play" with needless changing of places and splashing of oars, all betray a lack of breeding that is particularly conspicuous and objectionable on the river, as is also any other want of consideration for one's fellow, such as mooring up close to another boat or punt when there is plenty of room elsewhere along the banks.

(Burleigh, 1925, p. 173)

Despite the fact that the earlier extracts discussed pointed towards an in-creasing security regarding the belief that one could relax the rules in the 'country' as people were seen to have a greater degree of self-control than they had had in the past, this extract suggests that there were still concerns about the degree of self-control people had. The fact that this was written in a manners book in 1925 suggests that it was felt by some, at the time, that there was a risk that people would 'lose control' in the 'countryside', and so they had to be reminded what the (less formal) rules were.

These extracts suggest a *spatial* informalization of manners in the 'countryside', where manners are less strict but require an increasing self-control to manage the divide between acceptable 'country' behaviour and unacceptable 'country' behaviour. This spatial informalization – informalization that is restricted to the 'countryside' – could have contributed to a wider informalizing process. Having to increasingly 'switch' between codes of behaviour when travelling from 'country' to 'city' places increasing demands on people to adjust their behaviour accordingly, to remember where they are, and it is also characteristic of increasingly varied codes of behaviour. As more people were increasingly able to gain more and more access to the 'countryside', this could have contributed to the spread of informalization and its growing development.

It is important to highlight, however, that this contrast between the city and 'the countryside', where the latter is favoured over the former, may have been restricted to countries like England (and America, also in the form of 'the wilderness'). For as Mennell ([1985] 1996) demonstrates, in France this appreciation of 'the countryside' did not occur in the same way; rather, it was quite the opposite, where in France the city and the court society were largely preferred to the 'escape' of 'the countryside', as reflected in the development of cooking in France versus in England.

## The development of 'unnatural' and 'artificial': the idealization of 'natural'

The contrast between 'countryside' and 'city' was related to the development of disgust at 'unnatural' or 'artificial' appearances, where the former came to be seen as 'natural' and the latter as 'artificial'. The following two extracts, from 1883, discuss many don'ts regarding the 'natural' versus 'artificial' presentation of the self:

> Don't use hair-dye. The colour is not like nature, and deceives no one. footnote: Hair and beard dyed black produce a singular effect. They seem to coarsen and vulgarize the lines of the face. Any one who has ever seen an elderly gentleman suddenly abandon his dye, and appear with his grey locks in all their natural beauty, will realize what we mean – for he has seen what appeared to him a rather coarse and sensuous face all at once changed into one of refinement and character.
>
> (Censor., 1883, p. 28)

> Don't supplement the charms of nature by the use of the colour-box. Fresh air, exercise, the morning bath, and proper food, will give to the cheek nature's own tints, and no other have any true beauty.
>
> (Censor., 1883, pp. 91–92)

Here, the use of hair dye and other 'artificial' cosmetics is associated with presenting a 'false' image of self. This perhaps relates to earlier developments regarding sumptuary laws, where laws were developed to restrict consumption according to social status (Hunt, 1995). Presenting an 'artificial' image could have been seen as a form of deception, complicating the ability to determine someone's age, social status, and so on. An additional explanation could be due to the limits of the capabilities of dyes at the time, where they were 'obviously' artificial. In manners books of that time, things like 'obviously' 'false' praise were also criticized. And so, using 'obviously' 'artificial' cosmetics is seen as vulgar too.

In 1936, in *How to be a Good Wife*, we again see a critique of artificial adornments:

> Don't also become one of the blood-red nail brigade. Most men dislike the attempt to improve on nature, especially as it is largely associated with the demi-monde.
>
> (*How to be a Good Wife*, [1936] 2008, p. 28)

In the first extract, the relationship between social status and one's appearance is clearly articulated. The author likens 'artificial' red nail polish with the 'demi-monde', implying that those who adorn themselves in such a way are akin to prostitutes. In contrast to the 'impure' demi-monde (adorned with 'artificial' red nail polish), someone who has a more 'natural' look is seen as more 'pure' and 'innocent'; thereby, 'nature' is seen as 'pure' and 'innocent'.

In another extract from the same text, there is a call to return to nature for its health benefits:

> Don't forget that one of the best doctors in the world is Mother Earth. The trouble is with most of us that we have become too artificial and do not realise that we should gain in health, strength, and efficiency if at least, for a time, we went back to a simpler life. Try the simple, healing power of the countryside rather than the nerve-racking amusements of the fashionable seaside resort.
>
> (*How to be a Good Wife*, [1936] 2008, p. 83)

This latter extract once again draws a contrast between the 'good' countryside and the 'bad', built-up cities (and 'fashionable seaside resort[s]'). Here, there is the perception that 'artificial' things have overwhelmed us – it is not just a few who are dabbling in the 'artificial'. And so, we see a feminine anthropomorphization of 'nature' in the form of 'Mother Earth' who cares for us, heals us, and gives us strength. This further implies that the city and other hectic places (such as seaside resorts), in contrast, are bad for our health.

And while the city, and pollution in the city, did eventually come to be associated with being bad for our health, some of the early concerns about pollution developed for other reasons.

## Pollution

During the seventeenth and eighteenth centuries, growing pollution from increasingly built-up, more populated cities, with growing industries, contributed to the desire for city dwellers to escape to the countryside for some 'fresh air' (Thomas, 1987, pp. 244–246). Prior to this, since the thirteenth century, when a shortage of wood lead to replacing the burning of wood with the burning of sea coal (Coates, 1998, p. 17), people had been complaining about the London air. In 1273, a law to restrict the burning of coal was introduced, and then as industrialization developed, and pollution from coal correspondingly increased, concern about air pollution became increasingly more widespread (Sutton, 2007). As Thomas writes,

> The coal which was burned in the early modern period contained twice as much sulphur as that commonly used today; and its effects were correspondingly lethal. The smoke darkened the air, dirtied clothes, ruined curtains, killed flowers and trees and corroded buildings. By the mid eighteenth century the statues in London of some of the Stuart kings were so black that they looked like chimney sweeps or Africans in royal costume.
>
> (Thomas, 1987, p. 244)

He goes on to argue that it was this pollution and deterioration of the cities that contributed to the appeal of the 'countryside'. And cities were seen to be not just physically polluting but morally polluting as well.

In addition to this industrial pollution, certain sections from manners books highlight the development of growing concern about pollution of smells in general: 'Don't go into the presence of ladies with your breath redolent of wine or spirits, or your beard rank with the odour of tobacco. Smokers should be careful to wash the moustache and beard after smoking' (Censor., 1883, p. 38). Hughes (2003) outlines how such developments restricting the 'polluting' effects of tobacco smoke initially developed for aesthetic reasons and only later came to be medicalized.

In a similar way, technology, particularly cars, also came to be seen to be 'polluting' the 'countryside':

> Cars of all sizes and descriptions which tear along peaceful country roads, through villages and round winding lanes, without slowing down, caring nothing about scaring pedestrians or smothering them with dust and mud, and the danger to children and livestock.
>
> (Burleigh, 1925, p. 165)

Cars which race past others emitting clouds of "exhaust," with its accompanying unpleasant odour.

(Burleigh, 1925, p. 166)

In these two extracts about car pollution, we see that initially the concerns
are primarily aesthetic: disrupting the peace of the 'countryside', smoth-
ering pedestrians with dust and mud, emitting unpleasant odours. An
additional concern mentioned in the first extract is danger to children and
livestock. But this concern for animals is purely an economic one for only
'livestock' is mentioned. Notably, there is no mention of concern for 'the
environment' per se. This concern about car pollution from 1925 is quite
different to today's focus on car pollution contributing to climate change
and to the physical ill health of humans.

Looking at how climate change is discussed today, in terms of carbon
emissions, we can therefore witness a long-term shift from concern with
aesthetics (the aestheticization of 'nature'), to pollution (first aesthetics,
then health), to carbon emissions. Importantly, these shifts do not imply a
shift from one stage to the other, leaving the previous stage behind. Rather,
they represent a widening in the scope of how concerns are framed and
linked, and how current concerns that may on the surface appear to be new
and sudden are connected with and have emerged from a long history of
related concerns.

## Changes in human-animal relations

As is clear from the previous section on car pollution, human-animal relations have changed over time; where once concern for animals was purely
for economic reasons, now there exists more of an emotional identification
with an increasing variety of life so that those creatures that are not eco-
nomically beneficial to humans are still identified with.

In the past, animals were seen as immoral and evil, harbouring evil spirits. Treatises on good manners compared bad manners with animal behaviours (Thomas, 1987, pp. 36–37) (some of these are included in this
chapter in the section on consumption, where people who were relatively
unrestrained in excessive consumption were likened to various animals).
Animals were seen as morally corruptible (similar to how the 'wilderness'
was regarded, as mentioned earlier). And in the nineteenth century, one of
the arguments against vaccines was that the transference of cow fluids into
humans would cause the 'animalization' of people (Thomas, 1987, p. 39).

The development of initial concern about cruelty to animals was less concerned with the welfare of the animals; it was more concerned with how such
behaviour would affect the moral status of the people involved, and how
those people subsequently behaved towards other humans (Coates, 1998,
p. 137). As Franklin observes, animal anti-cruelty legislation[3] enacted from
the early twentieth century was initially targeted at the behaviour of the

working class in an attempt to 'civilize' them (Franklin, 1999, p. 22). The development of animal welfare, then, was initially part of a civilizing offensive directed towards the welfare of humans rather than other animals.

In 1893, an etiquette book depicts how concern about animals came to be linked to the (economic) function they served:

> It is the correct thing to control one's temper in dealing with a horse as well as in other relations of life. If you lose your temper, you spoil the horse's, and you yourself are, of necessity, at a disadvantage.
>
> (M.C., [1893] 1995, p. 179)

In this example, concern with neglect of one's horse was focussed on how the horse's welfare would influence the owner's welfare – the interdependence between the horse and the rider.

Jumping to 1936, in a chapter entitled 'Approval of Animals', readers are advised: 'If you can, lov as many animals as possible and pat and tickle them, especialli pupdogues [puppy dogs] and putzikats [pussy cats], which are very popular in England, whatever they may do. Of course, however, some animals must be disrelished' [the text is next to a drawing of a smiling man, looking down at a dog whose jaw is locked on the man's ankle] (Robertson, [1936] 2001, p. 59). This extract illustrates the growing affection towards *some* animals, noting that others are simply disregarded or perhaps even treated with contempt.

These concerns about animal cruelty initially developed amongst those who were most removed from animal labour and for more economic reasons: treat animals well, and they will perform better. Over time, the reason for this concern shifted to become increasingly dominated by emotional sentiment, concern for the animals for their own sake (rather than for the sake of humans) (Thomas, 1987, pp. 182, 188–190).

From the latter half of the twentieth century onwards, we can see household pets being increasingly treated like humans, as one of the family. Such goods and services formerly the domain of humans included the development of gourmet foods, pet graveyards and obituaries, pet psychologists, and so on (Franklin, 1999, p. 49).

Part of the reason for this shift was related to humans' increasing removal from direct relations with animals (other than pets). Prior to the later nineteenth century, animals were slaughtered and butchered in cities, and were visible to all. Since the beginning of the twentieth century, however, this process has come to be increasingly sequestered to rural areas. Along with a change in location and visibility, the mechanism of slaughter has changed so that workers are increasingly removed from the process: 'Most workers were separated from contact with whole animals and the act of killing was divided between two separate tasks (stunning and bleeding) so that no person was completely responsible for deaths' (Franklin, 1999, p. 41)[4]. As disgust and repugnance towards the killing of animals increased, the visual display of meat shifted towards looking less and less recognizably like part of an animal (Franklin, 1999, p. 42).

However, these developments for mammalian meat differ somewhat to those for seafood. Excluding the exceptions of such creatures as whales and dolphins, seafood is often displayed in supermarkets in its whole form (for example, a whole fish [albeit gutted], a whole *live* crayfish, whole prawns). Hunting is less popular, and seen to be more violent, than fishing. This could be for several reasons. First, mammalian meat is typically red meat (as opposed to the white meat of much seafood), and is therefore bloodier and, one might argue, messier. A piece of fish does not ooze blood the way a joint of beef does, nor does it ooze blood the way a human does. This brings us to our second reason: there is less species distance between mammals and humans than there is between seafood and humans. Lambs, deer, pigs, and cows look more like humans than seafood does – they have four limbs like us, they produce milk for their young like we do. And, until the recent development of the likes of films such as *Finding Nemo* (where the main characters are fish), it tended to be those animals that were biologically closer to us that were anthropomorphized in children's tales. The emotional attachment with these creatures is also limited to their physical proximity to us: you can't cuddle a fish, but you can cuddle a lamb. A fish is cold and slimy; a lamb is warm and fluffy.

## Scientific interest in the study of 'nature' and the democratization of science

Another contribution to changes in human-animal relations, and environmental ideas more generally, comes from developments in the sciences. The science of natural history was initially pursued to further advance human progress and to aid in mastering and managing nature; plants and animals were studied purely to find out if they would advantage humans in any way (for example, as food, medicine, labour) (Thomas, 1987, p. 27). By the eighteenth century, this shifted from a strictly anthropocentric aim, where plants and animals were classified according to their human-serving function, to a more detached understanding, where they were classified according to their structure (Thomas, 1987, p. 66).

From the eighteenth century onwards, as authors published increasingly in English instead of Latin, natural history came to be increasingly popularized and democratized (Thomas, 1987, p. 282). It was no longer restricted to the elite who were educated in Latin; it was now restricted to the literate. In the late eighteenth/early nineteenth century, natural history became an increasingly popular leisure activity: 'Ladies and gentlemen, while strolling along the beach, picked up pebbles and fossils, made notes on the flora and the state of the sky' (Tuan, 1974, p. 125). This popular involvement in 'science for fun' has developed to such an extent that 'citizen scientists' are now used to assist with research. For example, the project 'Planet Hunters' (planethunters.org), which states on its website: 'With your help, we are looking for planets around other stars'. Citizen scientists can then click on 'Start hunting for planets' to begin their search for habitable planets ('Planet Hunters', n.d.).

Returning to the nineteenth century, the development of the ecological sciences was interspersed with campaigns for the preservation of 'nature' reserves. In the mid-nineteenth century, Henry Thoreau[5] and others were arguing for the preservation of nature. In 1832, the Arkansas Hot Springs was proclaimed as a national reservation. In 1864, a national park was established in California. Then in 1872, the Yellowstone region was designated as a preservation, as a public park, and in 1895 a forest reserve was established in New York. However, the rationale for these initial preservations of land was economic, not for the sake of wilderness per se (Nash, [1967] 2001, pp. 102–108). It was only once the idea of conservation became established for economic reasons that it eventually came to be increasingly argued for other reasons, such as ecological ones.

In 1866, Ernst Haeckel first coined the term 'ecology'. He used the word 'oekologie' (ecology) to characterize 'the science of relations between organisms and their environment', emphasizing interdependence and mutual cooperation between species. Prior to 1866, ecological ideas were employed in evolutionary biology, though without using the term 'ecology' (Coates, 1998, p. 142; Worster, 1994). In 1913, the British Ecological Society was formed, with the American one forming two years later (Worster, 1994, pp. 205–206). But it was not until a century later, that the term ecology came to be widespread in popular discourse.

The development of nuclear bomb testing in the 1940s and 1950s brought about increased research into the effects of radiation on the environment. Coupled with general public and scientists' concerns about nuclear radiation, this contributed to the development of the environmental movements in the USA (Worster, 1994, Ch. 16). At the same time, growing control over other areas of life increasingly allowed one the luxury to be concerned about the environment. However, with this growing popularity of and concern about the environment came paradoxical unintended consequences.

By the 1960s and 1970s, wilderness had come to be increasingly popular, with growing numbers of tourism to wilderness reserves (Nash, [1967] 2001, p. 316). Paradoxically, this growing popularity in wilderness tourism has itself endangered wilderness, with reserves having to limit the numbers of visitors, and calls for the education of 'wilderness etiquette' so that those who do visit the wilderness do as little damage as possible (Nash, [1967] 2001, p. 322). Here, the rapid increase in travel to the 'wilderness' has not brought about a rapid enough change in people's self-controls, or at least this is the perception. Therefore, there is a call for increasing regulation of these areas, both formal (restricting numbers) and informal (wilderness etiquette).

## The development of the sciences of climate change

Similar to the role of the ecological sciences in the development of environmentalism, an important part of the development of climate change as a perceived social problem is the development of the sciences that have contributed to the 'discovery of global warming'. Spencer Weart ([2003] 2008) traces this development from the early nineteenth century to the present, noting the struggle for scientists to become concerned about climate change, followed by other groups (including the general public) coming to be concerned. While noting the discoveries of scientists, Weart also traces other developments, including changes in understandings about science, technology, and the environment. Initially, as the science of climate change was developing, most scientists believed that the earth was so robust that humans couldn't possibly have such a worryingly significant impact on climate.

This can be compared with Elias's writings on the initial rejection of the heliocentric theory. Elias ([1987] 2007) argued that the eventual acceptance that the sun, and not the earth, was at the centre of the universe required a greater level of detachment; not only to step back and see things from a distance (from earth, the sun appears to rotate around the earth, but from outside earth...) but also to be open to an idea that 'runs counter to their wishes and self-love' (Elias, [1987] 2007, p. 34), that is, the idea that they are no longer the centre of the universe. In some ways, the idea that we are contributing to climate change (and the implications this has for our way of life) runs counter to ideas of progress. James Lovelock's ([1979] 2000) account of how he came to develop his 'Gaia hypothesis' suggests an additional 'stepping back' – he recounts how he came up with the theory only once he began to visualize earth 'outside', as if he was seeing it as a whole from space.

Conversely, we could argue that a human-centric view of the world has contributed to the very idea of *anthropogenic* climate change. Only a view that sees the influence of humans as being greater than natural processes would allow one to see the possibility of anthropogenic climate change. In this way, the development of the sciences of anthropogenic climate change required both involved and detached thinking.

## Ecological intelligence, Biophilia, and the Land Ethic

Similar to the works by Aldo Leopold ('The Land Ethic') and E. O. Wilson (*Biophilia*) (see Quilley, 2009a, 2009b), Daniel Goleman's *Ecological Intelligence* argues for a new sensibility:

> Ecological intelligence lets us apply what we have learnt about how human activity impinges on ecosystems so as to do less harm and once again to live sustainably in our niche – these days the entire planet.
>
> (Goleman, 2009, p. 43)

Only such an all-encompassing sensibility can let us see the intercon-nections between our actions and their hidden impacts on the planet, our health, and our social systems.

Ecological intelligence melds these cognitive skills with empathy for all life. Just as social and emotional intelligence build on the abili-ties to take other people's perspective, feel with them, and show our concern, ecological intelligence extends this capacity to all natural systems. We display such empathy whenever we feel distress at a sign of the 'pain' of the planet or resolve to make things better. This ex-panded empathy adds to a rational analysis of cause and effect and the motivation to help.

(Goleman, 2009, p. 44)

Here, Goleman is calling for increased mutual identification with all life, with the biosphere as a whole, and for increasing recognition, increasing awareness of the interdependencies between the various forms of life on earth. This is similar to the ecological sciences themselves, out of which both Aldo Leopold's and E.O. Wilson's work emerged. In this way, Gole-man's *Ecological Intelligence* and his other books are similar to manners books, except that instead of a strictly moral proclamation of how one should behave, we have a scientific justification for why one should behave in a particular way: morality thus becomes less explicit as science becomes more explicit.

### *Changing arbiters: from manners books to...*

This shift towards increasingly popularizing these ideas corresponds with a shift in who are the arbiters, what are the texts that dictate socially ac-ceptable behaviour. While in the early twentieth century and before, people may have read manners books for this purpose, increasingly it is a wider variety of texts that people can obtain this information from. And those who are the arbiters can range from scientists to celebrities.

### Consumption: increasing self-restraint

While some of the changes in nature-society relations already explored in this chapter may be developing, in part, as an unplanned process of civiliza-tion, there are also intentional campaigns to bring about a more ecological identity, as reflected in the nineteenth-century and early twentieth-century writings of Henry David Thoreau, amongst others. If we go back to the nineteenth century, we can look at the tandem development of changing references to what might today be termed 'eco-friendly' behaviours in man-ners books, along with corresponding environmentalist literature from the nineteenth and early twentieth centuries.

Throughout the nineteenth century, there are references in manners texts, condemning 'excessive' consumption in eating and drinking as well as 'excessive' clothing and adornments. For example, in 1830, Stanhope writes,

> A man of pleasure, in the vulgar acceptation of that phrase, means only a beastly drunkard, an abandoned rake, a profligate swearer; we should weigh the present enjoyment of our pleasures against the unavoidable consequences of them, and then let our common sense determine the choice. We may enjoy the pleasures of the table and the wine, but stop short of the pains inseparably annexed to an excess in either...Good company are not fond of having a man reeling drunk among them.
>
> (pp. 81–82)

> The more we apply to business, the more we relish our pleasures...But, when I speak of pleasures, I always mean the elegant pleasures of a rational being, and not the brutal ones of a swine.
>
> (Stanhope, 1830, p. 83)

In these extracts, we see those who consume to 'excess' as compared with animals – 'beastly', 'swine'. The notion of losing control when consuming is compared with the perceived lack of control of animals.

We see these same themes in the same year, where Cobbett instructs,

> As to drunkenness and gluttony, generally so called, these are vices so nasty and beastly, that I deem any one capable of indulging in them to be wholly unworthy of my advice.
>
> (Cobbett, [1830] 1926, p. 19)

> But the great security of all is, to eat little, and to drink nothing that intoxicates. He that eats till he is full is little better than a beast; and he that drinks till he is drunk is quite a beast.
>
> (Cobbett, [1830] 1926, p. 27)

Here, we see the notion of the 'slippery slope', where the best thing to do is be seen to be drinking nothing intoxicating, lest one loses control and drinks too much.

In another extract by Cobbett, the focus is on extravagance in dress. Here, rather than losing control in consumption, the concern is with dressing inappropriately. This could be in the form of attracting too much attention due to conspicuous dress or dressing outside (primarily above) one's social status. Much of this concern could be due to changing power relations between the classes and a fear from above about those below.

> Extravagance in dress, in the haunting of playhouses, in horses, in everything else, is to be avoided, and, in youths and young men,

extravagance in dress particularly. This sort of extravagance, this waste of money on the decoration of the body, arises solely from vanity and from vanity of the most contemptible sort. It arises from the notion, that all the people in the street, for instance, will be looking at you as soon as you walk out; and that they will, in a greater or lesser degree, think the better of you on account of your fine dress. Never was notion more false...Dress should be suited to your station: a surgeon or physician should not dress like a carpenter; but there is no reason why a tradesman, a merchant's clerk, or clerk of any kind, or why a shopkeeper, or manufacturer, or even a merchant; no reason at all why any of these should dress in an expensive manner.

(Cobbett, [1830] 1926, pp. 13–14)

In the 1875 edition of *The Habits of Good Society*, the author writes,

but I beg you will not make that odious noise in drinking your soup. It is louder than a dog lapping water, and a cat would be quite genteel to it.

(*The Habits of Good Society*, 1875, p. 259)

So now you have got a plate. Surely you are not taking two on your plate. There is plenty of dinner to come, and one is quite enough.

Fast eating is bad for the digestion, my good sir, and not very good manners either. *Eat slowly.* Have you not heard that Napoleon lost the battle of Leipsic by eating too fast? It is a fact though. His haste caused indigestion, which made him incapable of attending the details about the battle.

(*The Habits of Good Society*, 1875, p. 260)

No man should drink enough wine to make him too easy with the ladies.

(*The Habits of Good Society*, 1875, p. 319)

Drinking much wine is vulgar...all manifest self-indulgence tends to vulgarity.

(*The Habits of Good Society*, p. 328)

Here, we still see concerns about eating and drinking like an animal. And in 1883, in *Don't*:

Don't drink wine or spirits in the morning, or often at other times than at dinner. Don't frequent bar-rooms. Tippling is not only vulgar and disreputable, but injurious to health.

(Censor., 1883, p. 38)

Don't over-trim your gowns or other articles of apparel...Leave excesses of all kinds to the vulgar.

(Censor., 1883, pp. 88–89)

Don't cover your fingers with finger-rings. A few well-chosen rings give elegance and beauty to the hand; a great number disfigure it, while the ostentation of such a display is vulgar.

Don't wear ear-rings that draw down the lobe of the ear. A well-shaped ear is a handsome feature; but an ear misshapen by the weight of its trinkets is a thing not pleasant to behold.

Don't wear diamonds in the morning, or to any extent except upon dress occasions. Don't wear too many trinkets of any kind.

(Censor., 1883, p. 91)

These extracts, similar to the earlier ones, also reflect a notion of temperance in eating, drinking, and dressing.

Around the same time of these temperance themes in etiquette manuals, Thoreau was writing and giving talks about the appreciation of 'nature' and humans' relationship with 'nature'. In 1863, Thoreau was trying to persuade others to think of humans in an ecological sense as part of 'nature'. His essay 'Walking' opens with the following sentence:

I wish to speak a word for Nature, for absolute freedom and wildness, as contrasted with a freedom and culture merely civil – to regard man as an inhabitant, or a part and parcel of Nature, rather than a member of society.

(p. 161)

Here, Thoreau is pointing towards ecological ideas, of seeing the interdependence between humans and the rest of the biosphere. Yet there is also a nostalgic tone to it, similar to that which was present in manners texts' accounts that contrasted the city with the 'countryside'. Thoreau also writes on the separation of man from nature:

I, who cannot stay in my chamber for a single day without acquiring some rust [and when I leave for my walk late in the day], too late to redeem the day...have felt as if I had committed some sin to be atoned for – I confess that I am astonished at the power of endurance, to say nothing of the moral insensibility, of my neighbours who confine themselves to shops and offices the whole day for weeks and months, ay, and almost years.

(1863, p. 165)

Here, again, we see the same themes from manners books: of the idealization of 'nature' in contrast with the everyday 'city' or 'town' life. He adds to this when discussing the transformation of the landscape: 'Nowadays almost all man's improvements, so called, as the building of houses, and the cutting down of the forest and of all large trees, simply deform the landscape, and make it more and more tame and cheap' (Thoreau, 1863, p. 169). The notion of 'landscape' is seen here as being 'natural', as contrasted with the ugly 'artificial' developments. He adds,

> While almost all men feel an attraction drawing them to society, few are attracted strongly to Nature. In their relation to Nature men appear to me for the most part, notwithstanding their arts, lower than the animals...How little appreciation of the beauty of the landscape there is among us.
>
> (Thoreau, 1863, p. 206)

In this extract, we see the beginnings of an increasing identification with non-human life coinciding with a decreasing identification with most other humans, where they are described as being 'lower than the animals'.

In Thoreau's writings, there is not only this idealization/aestheticization of 'Nature', but there are also moments when he refers to the idea of consuming only what is needed – of moderating consumption with self-restraint: 'There is a difference between eating and drinking for strength and from mere gluttony' (Thoreau, 1863, p. 186). Around the time Thoreau wrote this, in manners books there were similar references to restraining consumption, and controlling the way one consumed, such as the examples mentioned earlier. Here, we see tandem developments in both environmental literature and books on general manners and etiquette.

In *Don't*, published in 1883, the author states,

> Don't drink too much wine.
>
> (Censor., 1883, p. 23)

In 1897:

> It is scarcely necessary to remark that drinking too much wine is a very bad phase of ill manners. At one time it was actually fashionable to become intoxicated after dinner, but those days are gone, I am thankful to say. The young man who exceeds in this way is soon made aware of the fact that he has given his hostess dire offence. He is never invited again, or not for a long time.

The wineglass is never drained at a draught in polite society; nor is it considered polite to eat very quickly.

(Humphrey, [1897] 1993, p. 67)

In 1923:

When drinking do not empty the glass at one gulp; it is very vulgar to do so.
*(Etiquette for gentlemen: A Guide to the Observances of Good Society*, 1923, p. 45)

At the conclusion of each course, place your knife and fork side by side on your plate. If you cross them it is taken as a sign that you desire a second helping, and such ought never to be requested at a formal dinner.
*(Etiquette for gentlemen: A Guide to the Observances of Good Society*, 1923, p. 50)

In 1925:

DO NOT
Ask for a second helping of anything at a course lunch or dinner, though at simple family meals of only two or three courses an offer of a second helping of any dish may be accepted. [DO NOT] Take such a large portion of any thing that other guests must go short, or an absurdly small one, but just help yourself moderately.

(Burleigh, 1925, p. 68)

In these latter extracts, it is interesting to observe two absences. There is no direct reference to animals, no explicit comparison between animals and those who consume too much. Likewise, there is no mention of the slippery slope, of fear of losing control. And the phrase 'At one time it was actually fashionable to become intoxicated after dinner, but those days are gone' suggests that becoming intoxicated is increasingly less common. These changes in what is and is not said suggest that there was increasingly less concern about 'excess' consumption of food and alcohol, and less concern about one losing control when consuming these things. The focus, instead, seems to be more on those who are unaware of the rules regarding such conduct.

These same discourses about temperance in relation to eating, drinking, and adorning oneself are to be found in more recent texts on climate change, which will be examined later in this chapter. We can therefore witness the influence of these nineteenth-century temperance ideas on the emergence of a form of 'carbon temperance' in the twentieth and twenty-first centuries.

## Littering: widening circles of identification

While we can see the tandem developments of controlling consumption in both manners books and the writings of Thoreau, it was not until the early twentieth century that Thoreau's and others' writings on ideals of human relationships with 'nature' and the 'environment' appear in manners books.

In the 1868 edition of *The Habits of Good Society*, there is a section on picnics, but there is no mention of litter/trash/rubbish: 'It is of necessity somewhat rough, for these same picnics are the happy occasions when people try to forget that they are highly civilized, but are scarcely ever allowed to do so' (*The Habits of Good Society*, 1868, p. 358). Here, we see further evidence of going to the 'countryside' (in this case for a picnic) as an escape from city life, but there is no concern about how their picnicking will affect the 'countryside'.

It is not until 1921, in the section on excursions and picnics in *Cassell's Book of Etiquette,* that we see the first mention of litter in manners books:

> ['picnic sets'] are cheap, cleanly and portable, but they constitute something that is very untidy if left on the turf of the seashore. Indeed, some owners of private property do not allow picnicking on it on account of the litter and debris left behind. Good manners and consideration for others demand that such unpleasing remnants of the feast should be obliterated, and the simplest and most convenient way of doing this is to dig a hole and bury them.
>
> (p. 161)

And when a landowner gives permission for others to picnic on their land: 'Good manners and gratitude will then take care that no greasy papers or other debris are left behind' (Cassell and Co., 1921, p. 161). In both of these extracts, littering is understood in terms of the blight it has on the landscape. And there is also a consideration for other people, in terms of not wanting to litter on another person's land.

In 1923, in *Etiquette for Gentlemen*, when discussing River Parties, this same consideration is given to other people: 'Paper plates and dishes, if used, should not afterwards be thrown "on the face of the waters," to remain drifting hither and thither to the intense annoyance of other boating parties' (*Etiquette for gentlemen: A Guide to the Observances of Good Society*, p. 100).

And in 1925, in *Etiquette up to Date*:

> Many owners of grounds reaching down to the river have no objection to the mooring of boats along the banks, and some even permit landing at certain places, but all persons availing themselves of such privileges should respect them by refraining from causing any damage or leaving

any litter behind them; indeed, whether it be on public or private property, paper bags, orange and banana skins, used cardboard plates and
boxes, empty bottles and other picnic debris should never be left to
litter up river or countryside beauty spots.

(p. 174)

Here we see again a focus on 'landscape': 'picnic debris should never be left
to litter up river or countryside *beauty spots*'.

In 1933, a children's book discussed 'Untidy People': 'I must not throw
things in the street. Orange peel and banana skins will make people fall.
Paper looks untidy in the street. I can see a bin for it' (*The Happy Child*,
1933, p. 22). Again, the concern here is for the visual effect litter has, and
the effect it has on other people.

In 1936, in a text advising students how to behave in England when at
'pickniks', students are told: 'Never cast a cigarette end into an ambusch,
lest blaze develop. Never relinquisch ods and ends. To permit rubbisch to
repose on the turf is not even the privilege of the best people' (Robertson,
[1936] 2001, p. 14).

In 1949, in a Canadian etiquette book, the following section on picnics
states,

Special hampers for picnics, containing various compartments, are for
sale in the trunk stores. And very much less expensive sets can be made
by using a fibre suitcase and outfitting with cheap enamel or plastic
plates and cutlery. Picnic sets consisting of cardboard plates and dishes,
cups and saucers and tin spoons, cost so little that after being used they
may be disposed of by burying them.

(Pringle, 1949, p. 186)

Here we see two interesting trends. First, the notion of using existing materials (suitcases) to make something else (picnic sets): reusing/recycling
material (albeit not with an ecological rationale). Yet at the same time the
cheapness and wide availability of some materials encourages people to
throw them away and not reuse them. In this same section on picnics, readers are also provided with reasons not to litter – it 'disfigures' the landscape
and 'attracts flies':

Wherever a picnic takes place, whether in the woods, on a public high-
way, or by the water, great care should be taken not to leave any waste
paper, empty cans or bottles about to disfigure the beauty of the landscape and attract flies. Wild flowers are picked only to fade, and if they
are dragged up by the roots, as so often happens, their place knows
them no more. Thus, many beautiful varieties are rapidly disappearing
because of such unthinking carelessness. Cigarette stubs or matches
should be carefully extinguished. Serious forest fires, with loss of life

and property, have been caused by someone dropping down a match he thought was out, or throwing away the butt of a cigarette.

(Pringle, 1949, p. 186)

In this extract flower picking is also condemned, presumably as this also spoils the beauty of the landscape. The concern for the disappearance of certain varieties of flowers may be more due to preservation for beauties sake rather than concern for the biosphere (for example, the impact the removal of one species may have on other species). And again, with concern over cigarette butts causing forest fires, the focus is on the impact on *human* life and *human* property.

These excerpts differ from the way littering is additionally talked about today; they are concerned with how littering will affect other people. But as identification has expanded to an increasing concern about other animals, and to 'nature' and the 'environment' in general, littering is now additionally discussed in terms of the impact it has on animals and on the environment in general. Here we can witness a widening scope of identification – a part of civilizing processes – that encompasses the long-term development of what is now described as 'eco-friendly' behaviours.

This civilizing process was contributed to by civilizing offensives. For example, in 1954, the National Federation of Women's Institutes initiated 'Keep Britain Tidy' in an effort to 'tackle the increasing litter problem' ('Keep Britain Tidy – About Us – Our History').

In a book on the disposal of waste and litter, published in 1970, concern with litter is still restricted to the impact on humans and the visual landscape:

> Assuming that the difficulties with 'land' litter could be overcome, one would still be faced with 'marine' litter, i.e. all the plastics material which, because of their low specific gravity, float on the surface of, or drift half submerged in, rivers, canals, lakes and surrounding seas. Being insoluble in water and entirely inert to marine micro-organisms, waterborne litter is bound to accumulate in time and, when washed up to the water's edge, will drift with wind, tides and currents to inshore waters, harbours and breakwaters where it's unsightly presence can be a hazard to swimmers, anglers, boaters and yachtsmen.
>
> (Staudinger, 1970, p. 87)

It was not until 1985 that litter and harm to animals was mentioned in newspapers. In the *Toronto Star*,

> "I was cutting my third crop of hay when I hit two liquor bottles that shattered into a thousand pieces," says Gray, 44, who worries about his animals eating such dangerous litter.
>
> (Crawford, 1985, November 3)

However, even this first mention in 1985 may relate more to the economic concerns that litter posed to the animals on this person's farm.

In 1988, in *St Petersburg Times* (Florida), in 'Teachers, students plan cleanup of Kings Bay and Shell Island', there appears concern for animals purely for the sake of the animals (and not for any economic reasons):

> There are several reasons beyond aesthetics for cleaning up the water-ways and the island, Miss Merritt said. Plastic products can choke or strangle some animals. One of the worst offenders is monofilament fishing line, which can entangle a bird or animal and cut or choke it. The materials dumped overboard could also add elements to the water that would harm plants and animals. "The key is that anything that you put in the water is going to affect what's there," Miss Merritt said. "You can't just dump things in there and not expect that things will change."
>
> (Behrendt, 1988, October 27)

The use of the phrase 'There are several reasons beyond aesthetics for cleaning up...' suggests an attempt by the author to draw readers' attention beyond merely aesthetics and towards the harm done to animals. This suggests that, at the time the author wrote this piece, the author thought that there was not enough being done towards preventing harm to animals from litter, suggesting that it was not as widespread a concern as the author perhaps wanted it to be.

During the 1980s, research began to uncover the extent to which plastic waste was present in the seas, culminating in the discovery of the 'Great Pacific Garbage Patch', a massive area of plastic waste located in the North Pacific Gyre. An article from the *Independent* in 2008 reflects the growing concern that such litter posed to non-human life:

> According to the UN Environment Programme, plastic debris causes the deaths of more than a million seabirds every year, as well as more than 100,000 marine mammals. Syringes, cigarette lighters and tooth-brushes have been found inside the stomachs of dead seabirds, which mistake them for food.
>
> (Marks, 2008, February 5)

At the beginning of the twenty-first century, Keep Northern Ireland Tidy launched a littering campaign that was directed at youth, highlighting the harm to animals that littering could cause. However, while there is some linkage between littering and harm to animals and the biosphere as a whole, reflecting a widening in identification, the UK government seems to place the focus of littering on the nuisance it poses to other people, including 'littering' as an environmental crime constituting anti-social behaviour (see Directgov, n.d.). So, while we can witness a long-term shift – from concern with humans, to concern with animals, to concern with the environment as a whole – this has not involved a shift where later developments have become more dominant. Rather, it merely represents a widening in the scope of identification and concern but where the majority of concern still remains close to one's self.

## Television shows and eco-etiquette

An additional media involved in the development of ecological sensibilities is television. From 1990 to 1996, the animated series *Captain Planet and the Planeteers* screened in the USA and other countries covering themes such as pollution, recycling, and capitalism. In this series the spirit of Gaia and Captain Planet work with five young people (the Planeteers) to protect the environment from the 'eco-villains', such as 'Sly Sludge', 'Verminous Scum', 'Duke Nukum', 'Hoggish Greedly', and 'Looten Plunder'. At the end of each episode, there is a 'Planeteer Alert', where Captain Planet and the Planeteers educate viewers on different environmental issues and advise them of action they should take:

> We should pass laws to make trading in bear parts illegal.
> We should protect all animals whose habitats are threatened. Kids, write your government representatives. Your letters can save teddy bears and endangered animals around the world. The power is yours.
>
> The best things you can do to help our environment is to get involved.
> Join an environmental group or team up with friends to start your own projects.
> Clean up a park or a beach.
> Organise a recycling programme at school or in your neighbourhood.
> Or plant trees and remember to take care of them.
> It's all part of making our planet healthy again.
> We must all work together to protect the animals, trees, oceans and air.
> The power is yours.
> ('Captain Planet and the Planeteers', 1990–1996, season 4, episode 2)

In this transcript from *Captain Planet*, there is a strong focus on individual action, of individuals working together to improve the planet. The onus is on individuals to organize recycling programmes rather than government-organized initiatives. The only mention of the government is where individuals cannot have much of an influence: the trading in bear parts.

As well as being a form of entertainment, this children's TV show was also a form of education, teaching children about environmental issues, eco-etiquette, and what different types of action they could take to protect the environment. These aims are also present in the more recent eco-makeover reality TV shows, which will be discussed in the following chapter.

## From manners books to 'green guides'

Before 'Captain Planet', guidance on how one should behave in order to protect the environment was already emerging in a genre similar to manners books before it. In 1970 the *Consumers' Guide to the Protection of the Environment* (Holliman, [1970] 1974) was published. This book explored the impact that consumer decisions have on the environment. It argued that increasing production and consumption meant that people were consuming more than what they needed to, and this was having a negative impact on the environment:

> It is certainly not easy for the individual to do much about these more far-reaching effects of our inflated consumption rate. What people *can* control, however, is the extent to which their individual actions contribute to these major collective problems. This is important because up to now it is the escalation of individual *consumption,* more than the increase in our numbers, that has so adversely affected the quality of our environment.
>
> (Holliman, [1970] 1974, p. 13)

> The Consumers Guide looks at several major areas of goods and services and explains simply and clearly the environmental costs of their production, use and disposal. You will find: BACKGROUND INFORMATION – on environmental and consumer problems such as packaging and waste disposal; PRODUCT INFORMATION – specific information on what to buy, selecting alternatives and brand names, what is behind the product or processes and what good or harm it causes; HOW TO EVALUATE – how to measure for yourself what effects the products or processes have on the environment. The Consumers' Guide is not only a handbook but also a strategy for change to a way of life more related to the ability of the environment to support our real needs.
>
> (Holliman, [1970] 1974, back cover)

Similar to the 'how to live green' guides of today, which I will discuss shortly, the *Consumers' Guide to the Protection of the Environment* aimed to inform readers of the environmental impact of different areas of consumption. The environment was regarded as a problem, but it was seen to be a problem that was within the realms of human control (hence the 'guide'). The *Consumer's Guide* provided guidelines on how *individuals* could change their consumer habits to help save the environment. Such tips included 'turn lights off when they are not needed' (Holliman, [1970] 1974, p. 129), and reduce the impact of your car by sharing or hiring vehicles, using car pools, walking, or cycling. However, at this stage, while there was concern about some environmental impacts, littering was still concerned only with humans and aesthetics.

Since the 1970s, there have been a few similar guides, such as *The Green Consumer Guide* in 1988 and *The Young Green Consumer Guide* in 1990. In these guides, there is a focus on how individual actions have a direct impact on the environment:

> Every day of the week, whether we are shopping for simple necessities or for luxury items, for fish fingers or for fur coats, we are making choices that affect the environmental quality of the world we live in. Take a bite out of a hamburger, we are told, and we take a bite out of the world's rain forests. Buy the wrong car and we may end up not only with a large fuel bill, but also with fewer trees and, quite possibly, less intelligent children. Spray a handful of hair gel or a mist of furniture polish from certain aerosols, and you help destroy the planet's atmosphere - increasing everybody's chances of contracting skin cancer.
>
> (Elkington & Hailes, 1988, p. 1)

At the end of this extract, we see that individual behaviour is also connected to harm to others. These early guides focussed on providing readers with information about which brands or products to buy over others. In these guides, we can see a concern with animals and the environment:

> In general, the Green Consumer avoids products which are likely to:
>
> -endanger the health of the consumer or of others
> -cause significant damage to the environment during manufacture, use or disposal
> -consume a disproportionate amount of energy during manufacture, use or disposal
> -cause unnecessary waste, either because of over-packaging or because of an unduly short useful life
> -use materials derived from threatened species or from threatened environments
> -involve the unnecessary use - or cruelty to - animals, whether this be for toxicity testing or for other purposes
> -adversely affect other countries, particularly in the Third World.
>
> (Elkington & Hailes, 1988, p. 5)

In 1990, the same authors published *The Young Green Consumer Guide*. This book emphasized the increasing dangers posed to the earth, and what young people can and must do to help:

> The WORLD needs your help
> From felt tips to rubbish tips, from fizzy drinks to kitchen sinks. Discover how YOU can help save the earth.
>
> (Elkington, Hailes, & Hill et al., 1990, front cover)

Helping to save the Earth
From Manchester to Moscow, from Tokyo to Toronto, young people like you are more aware than ever that our world is under threat.

(Elkington et al., 1990, p. 6)

In 1993, this 'green' or 'ethical consumption' was celebrated with the launch of the 'Buy Nothing Day', an annual challenge for consumers to buy nothing for twenty-four hours.

While these earlier guides, and the development of 'Buy Nothing Day', were directed at consuming (or not consuming) in order to 'help save the earth', many of the more recent 'green guides' are explicitly linked with the climate crisis and contain a greater sense of urgency for change. With growing talk of a potential 'climate crisis', we have witnessed the emergence of guides containing prescriptions on what *you* must do to 'live green', 'save the planet', and 'stop global warming' as well as calls for more formal social controls. For example, in the book, *I Count: Together We Can Stop Climate Chaos: Your Step-By-Step Guide to Climate Bliss*, there is a focus on the individual management of behaviour to decrease individual carbon footprints.

In *I Count*, there are several steps one can go through to try and 'stop climate chaos'. Step 10 is called 'Reject the ridiculous':

On occasion we are all ridiculous.
But this step will help.
It works like this.
Next time you are about to buy something, simply ask yourself if your purchase of that crazy packaged up beef burger is worth planetary chaos, mass starvation and general unpleasantness. Almost magically you will know the answer.
So, repeat after me. I do not need my oranges individually wrapped; I believe their existing skin to be adequate. I do not need to heat the outside of my house with a gas-fired patio heater; I am capable of going inside.

(*I Count: Together We Can Stop Climate Chaos: Your Step-By-Step Guide to Climate Bliss*, 2006, p. 52)

And in another section from *I Count*:

Some habits kind of feel like they're good, but they aren't.
Flying, for instance.
There's no way around this.
Aircraft just pipe greenhouse gases into our upper atmosphere, where they immediately do most damage.
Let's get this in perspective: fly to Athens and to make up for your climate impact you will have to go without heating, cooking,

lighting and all forms of motorised transport for 2 years and 3 months. Which you don't really fancy, do you?
So you have to promise.
I hereby solemnly swear that:
I won't fly when I can take the train or boat.
I will take more holidays in my lovely, comfy UK.
I will use video conference technology.
I will take at least one less flight a year.

> (*I Count: Together We Can Stop Climate Chaos: Your Step-By-Step Guide to Climate Bliss*, 2006, p. 58)

Tamer versions of these guides include *The Rough Guide to Ethical Living* and *The Rough Guide to Green Living*, both very similar books that, like the consumer guides of the 1970s and 1980s, contain information about how to consume responsibly. As the author describes it: '...in the last few years, [ethical living] has come to mean something more specific: adapting our lifestyles and shopping habits with the aim of reducing our negative impact (and increasing our positive impact) on the world's environments, people and animals' (Clark, 2006, p. 3). Here we again see a widening identification – with not just people but also animals and the environment as a whole. In contrast to the earlier green consumer guides, in these two books the concern about impact on the world's environment is focussed very much on climate change and carbon footprints. We thus have a narrowing of the focus of these guides as they come to be attached to a more specific social problem.

Readers of some of these guides are encouraged to carry out audits of their homes with an 'eco-calculator' or 'carbon calculator':

> The impact we are having on the planet is often hard to see. To start, we need to look at the resources we are using, and the waste we are creating in terms of power, water, and fuel...We developed a unique eco calculator...With this we can get an idea of the impact our lives are having on the planet and track the effect of improvements we make.
>
> (*Wa$ted!*, 2007, p. 8)

And in the same book, readers are urged to buy a 'power monitor', which works in a similar way to a speedometer, to track electricity use. This individualized focus on self-monitoring corresponds to a call to increasingly educate oneself about 'hidden' processes (such as what happens to my waste, how much waste do I produce, how much of my electricity bill is from my dryer, and so on). In addition, the self-monitoring encourages an increasingly reflexive self that thinks twice before switching the heater on, before leaving a room with the lights turned on, before driving to work, and so on. One is encouraged to exercise a greater degree of both restraint and foresight, in thinking about how an immediate, short-term action can have a long-term cumulative effect. In this regard, ecology is utilized as a means of regulation, similar to morality and medicine.

In these guides, there is also an emphasis on a perceived trend towards increasing overconsumption. In *How to Live a Low-Carbon Life: The Individual's Guide to Stopping Climate Change*, the author writes, 'As responsible members of prosperous societies, we have a duty to curb our own consumption rather than to rely on ineffectual governments and profit seeking companies' (Goodall, 2007, p. 4). Here there is the perception that not only are individuals failing to regulate their consumption but also that states and corporations are failing to regulate carbon emissions:

> Climate change is the greatest challenge facing humanity: drastic re-duction of carbon emissions is vital if we are to avoid a catastrophe that devastates large parts of the world.
>
> (Goodall, 2007, back cover)

> This book tries to show that individuals – rather than governments or companies – are going to have to be the driving force behind re-ductions in greenhouse gases. We cannot hide behind an unjustified expectation that political or corporate leaders are going to do some-thing for us: the threat from climate change requires each of us to take personal responsibility for reducing our impact on the planet's atmosphere. Individually, of course, we are powerless; but our actions influence those around us. Eventually, private companies will per-ceive a market for low-carbon products, and governments will come to see that real action on climate change is not electorally disastrous. Individuals must provide the leadership that will galvanize the rest of society.
>
> (Goodall, 2007, p. 3)

This focus on bottom-up, individual action, along with a criticism of poli-ticians and corporations, reflects the perceived failure of states and corpo-rations. The themes in these guides relate very much to the development of 'neat capitalism' (Rojek, 2007, Ch. 8), where the guides promote individu-als working with the market (as opposed to the state) to try and improve the environment. This is most evident with Virgin's guide, *The Virgin Green Guide: The Easy Way to Save the Planet and Save £££s* (2007):

> Global warming and environmental issues are front-page news, but a few simple changes to your lifestyle can lead to huge benefits to the health of our planet. The Virgin Green Guide is a practical, no-nonsense and timely guide to help you do your bit for the environment – and save some cash at the same time. Find out how much you could be wasting – from gas and electricity to food and water – and what you can do to stop it.

Virgin's guide epitomizes the corporate social responsibility developments, where big corporations who are contributing to climate change are implementing developments to make it look like they are working with consumers to 'save the planet'.

In other guides, there is a strong metaphor of a diet – where excess consumption is making the earth fat with pollution, and so it and we must go on a diet. The following text is from *The Climate Diet: How You Can Cut Your Carbon, Cut Costs, and Save the Planet* (Harrington, 2008, back cover):

> The atmosphere is getting fat on our carbon and other greenhouse gas emissions and it needs our help. We live in a world of excess, consuming too much of everything – food, clothes, cars, toys, shoes, bricks, and mortar. Our bingeing is often so extreme that it threatens our own health and wellbeing. And we are not the only ones who are getting sick. The Earth, which provides the food, air, water, and land that sustains us, is also under severe pressure. We either take steps to put our personal and planetary systems back into balance or we suffer the consequences. So, what does any unhealthy overweight person do when the doctor tells him or her that they are eating themselves into an early grave? Go on a diet!

This metaphor of diet – a form of 'carbon temperance' similar to the other forms of temperance mentioned earlier (in relation to drinking alcohol, eating food, adorning oneself) – can be compared to the metaphors of addiction that occur throughout many green guides, such as Virgin's guide:

> Sad to say, we've become a nation of shopaholics. Consumerism has run out of control as we buy more products than ever before...these days, people think nothing of buying something because they fancy it rather than because they absolutely need it.
> (*The Virgin Green Guide: The Easy Way to Save the Planet and Save £££s*, 2007, p. 16)

> It's generally the ladies who are tagged with the label 'shopaholic', but more and more men are now compulsive spenders.
> (*The Virgin Green Guide: The Easy Way to Save the Planet and Save £££s*, 2007, p. 17)

This reference to 'addiction', to 'shopaholics', in part removes responsibility from individuals as it is seen to be beyond their control. Additionally, the phrase 'these days' also suggests that moral standards are deteriorating, that life was better in some 'golden age' past. Goodall also contributes to the addiction analogy: 'Speeches and articles contributed by political leaders worldwide conclude that climate change is a serious problem. But the figures reveal that we are as addicted as ever to the consumption of fossil fuels' (Goodall, 2007, p. 4).

The following extract, utilizing the metaphor of 'getting high', also suggests a discourse of addiction, and the comparison with drugs lowers the status of the behaviour:

> A growing number of us are using 'retail therapy' to counter our increasingly stressful and busy lives. Shopping can give us an instant 'high' and buying new things makes us feel good. However, for many, these spending habits are becoming increasingly difficult to manage.
>
> (*The Virgin Green Guide: The Easy Way to Save the Planet and Save £££s*, 2007, p. 17)

This struggle to manage the habit of shopping further contributes to the addiction metaphor, as does the notion of being a slave to the habit: 'Are you a shopping slave? Do you buy things you don't need, use or want? Are you spending more than you can afford? If either of these are the case, you may have a problem' (*The Virgin Green Guide: The Easy Way to Save the Planet and Save £££s*, 2007, p. 17)

And the distinction is drawn between 'normal' shoppers and 'shopaholics' (similar to that between 'normal' drinkers and 'alcoholics'):

> It's not that we should never go shopping again, just because of the temptation to overindulge and splurge, which we all sometimes give in to. But for 'shopaholics' it's a different matter. They are compulsive spenders who act this way most of the time, not just occasionally.
>
> (*The Virgin Green Guide: The Easy Way to Save the Planet and Save £££s*, 2007, p. 18)

There is even a quiz readers can take to find out if they are shopaholics. 'If you answer "yes" to more than five of these questions, your spending may be getting out of control. Try to figure out what triggers your spending sprees' (*The Virgin Green Guide: The Easy Way to Save the Planet and Save £££s*, 2007, pp. 18–19).

The guide then goes on to list the seven deadly sins of shopping: greed, gluttony, lust, wrath, envy, sloth, and pride. The guide then goes on to advise readers on how they should be shopping. And they focus on what individuals can do, while also highlighting the problems of governments and big business:

> Yes, there's a lot of environmental harm that's beyond our control – governments and big businesses have a lot to answer for. But there are an awful lot of us 'ordinary people' out there. And all the little changes we make – like recycling, switching off televisions and using

energy-efficient light bulbs – can be multiplied millions of times over, to make a **real difference**. This book will help you to be a part of that difference. We'll show you how to reduce the impact you have on the environment, both locally and on a global scale. It's easy, it can be fun and, what's more, it can even save you money!

(*The Virgin Green Guide: The Easy Way to Save the Planet and Save £££s*, 2007, p. 1)

Towards the end of the extract, there is also the link between 'carbon temperance' and austerity, where making these changes 'can even save you money'.

In the section 'What kind of waster are you?', readers are asked to tick all of the following descriptions that apply to them:

### Tossers

Do you throw out endless binloads of rubbish without a second thought? If so, you're a tosser! What about all the stuff that could be reduced, reused or recycled? Even if you know your 3Rs, you never apply them.

### Guzzlers

Guzzlers are the big energy wasters. You leave lights blazing away in unoccupied rooms, you've got a glut of kitchen and other household electrical gadgets and run them all day long, and when your TV and video aren't switched on, they're on constant stand-by.

### Belchers

Belchers are the car users, and major polluters in the process. You may even have more that one car and you'd never, ever walk anywhere, let alone think about what damage your fuel is causing.

### Plonkers

Plonkers are large families producing massive overflowing nappy mountains, munching their way through packets and packets of processed food, and binning large quantities of plastic and polystyrene take-away packaging.

### Scrappers

Hey, big spenders! If you can't resist buying the latest trendy new clothes, make-up or shoes, then you're a Scrapper. I bet you never wear or use half the stuff you buy and once the latest TV 'fashion guru' tells you it's no longer hip, it'll go straight in the bin, or waste space cluttering up your wardrobe.

(*The Virgin Green Guide: The Easy Way to Save the Planet and Save £££s*, 2007, pp. 11–12)

Those who score high, with four to five ticks, are described as follows:

> You really are the pits in green terms! You're hot-water hogs; energy bandits through and through, and wanton wasters of energy and resources. But if you pay attention and change your horrible habits you could make a POTENTIAL SAVING of £4,000 a year. Just think what you could spend it on instead of chucking it away – which is literally what you're doing by being so wasteful.
>
> (*The Virgin Green Guide: The Easy Way to Save the Planet and Save £££s*, 2007, pp. 12–13)

The name-calling and deviantization is typical of these guides, most evident in the terms 'eco-criminal' and 'eco-deviant' to be examined in the next chapter. However, some of this name-calling appears almost tongue in cheek, a playful use of the terms rather than a usage that is imbued with hatred and extreme condemnation (even if the sentiment is still there). In this way, deviantization regarding climate change differs to that associated with other social problems.

The illustration of how much money (and carbon emissions) one can save by making changes is also very typical of these guides, exemplified in the notion of the 'carbon audit' and the 'carbon calculator'. This raises the question to what extent some of these guides are more about money, about financial concerns, than they are about ecological concerns.

In *Green is the New Black: How to Change the World with Style*, the focus is on how one can stop climate change without completely sacrificing a life of consumption: 'At the very least, I hope that this book will show you how to choose the handbag and the heels that enhance your life, and contribute least to global warming' (Blanchard, 2007, p. 9). Shopping in itself is not seen as a 'bad' thing, only when it is deemed 'wasteful' and a symptom of 'shopaholism'. In this way, many of these guides are not trying to bring about a revolution but are instead trying to work with the existing system.

Similarly, *The Lazy Environmentalist: Your Guide to Easy, Stylish, Green Living* (Dorfman, 2007) emphasizes how eco-conscious consumerism, even down to death and dying (with eco-burials), can help to save the environment. This focus on how every aspect of our life, along with our death, can be used to control climate change creates a sense that we *do* have control over these processes and that we can make a difference. This once again reflects an egocentric conception of climate change.

In response to this perceived crisis and excess, a wider civilizing offensive is implemented in an attempt to avert the crisis and curb the excess: 'Our excessive use of natural resources – fuelled by population increases and a relentless pursuit of economic growth and material possessions – is causing alarming damage to the environment' (Mann, 2007, p. 6). These green guides are part of that civilizing offensive, and climate change is seen as only a 'sign of the times':

> That's not the only problem. We're close to wiping out much of the planet's marine life. We're destroying rainforests and other wild eco-systems, which is decimating the planet's wildlife and biodiversity. We're turning vast tracts of fertile land into desert by over-farming. We're polluting our waters, soil and air with chemicals that are toxic to plants, animals and ourselves.
> In short, if we don't change – quickly – the future looks grim.
>
> (Mann, 2007, p. 7)

### Signs of crisis

Since 1961, humanity's ecological footprint has tripled while 30 per cent of earth's wildlife and natural ecosystems have been lost. Far from falling, annual global greenhouse emissions have risen 28 per cent since 1990 – and are still rising. 20 per cent of the world's population, mainly in Europe and North America, consume 80 per cent of its natural resources. The average Briton generates as much $CO_2$ in eight days as the average Zambian does in a year. The world's population rose from two billion in 1930 to six billion in 2000 and is predicted to reach nine billion by 2050.

(Mann, 2007, p. 9)

From these green guides readers can develop understandings of how they should behave, similar to the role of manners books before them. A more explicit example of this is found in the guide *It's Easy Being Green*, where the author outlines several 'Green principles': live with less; reduce energy, water, chemicals, waste; use green alternatives. For the author, 'being green' means saving money, being healthier, creating new habits, doing what you can, learning to love nature, being happy with less, and focussing on what you *can* do and not despairing about what you can't (Mann, 2007, pp. 9–13).

These extracts from the green guides, along with all the extracts from manners books discussed in earlier sections of this chapter, suggest that changes in understandings about nature, the environment, and climate change have come about via the interplay between more gradual attempts, via manners books, and via more heightened campaigns to promote changes in behaviour in order to alleviate a perceived crisis (in this case, climate change). The interplay between these processes suggests that the regulation of behaviour may develop via a combination of gradual processes and heightened spurts. However, the extent to which these 'crisis' campaigns *do* affect sudden changes in behaviour has yet to be explored.

## Changes in the regulation of behaviour

On the one hand, the aforementioned 'green guides' point towards a partial phase of reformalization, where the ideals of the likes of Thoreau are still present, but the emergence of the guides indicates a shift towards increasing prescriptions – what behaviour to have, and what not to do, to 'save the planet' and 'stop global warming'. It is almost as if the potential future crises from climate change have engendered a sense that changes in behaviour regarding the environment have not been occurring at a fast-enough rate (or have gone into 'reverse'). And the process of informalization has brought with it fears that a relaxing of controls has brought with it a loss of control, in the form of 'excess' and 'overconsumption'. And so, this perceived social crisis has brought about a phase of reformalization, where (some) nature-society relations are written down in the form of guides containing prescriptions and prohibitions, such as the 'Do something / Do nothing' and 'This good / This bad' sections from *I Count*. However, at the same time, the way these guides are written differs to those manners books of the nineteenth century and earlier. It is as if they are appealing to a more reflexive and self-regulating 'third nature personality'. Some of the extracts are more playful – the name-calling in the Virgin guide. It seems more that there is hope and faith that individuals can change their behaviour, they just need to be educated about why they need to change, with some, but not all, guidelines about how they might go about doing this, with the possibility of picking and choosing what changes to make and what changes not to make.

In a similar way, the development of reality TV shows, such as *Carbon Cops*, *Wasted*, and *No Waste Like Home*, where 'experts' carry out 'carbon audits' of people's homes, and then provide recommendations about how they can change their lifestyle to decrease their carbon footprint, could be seen as a new form of manners/etiquette books. These shows, like other 'lifestyle shows', provide recommendations about how one ought to behave but in a less prescriptive way to manners books of earlier times. In this way, these shows are representative of a wider informalizing of guides on how to live and represent a shift in the way behaviours are regulated.

We can explore how this proliferation of a variety of texts relates to those texts examined by Elias in *On the Process of Civilisation*. Erasmus's 1530 publication, 'On Civility in Boys', was produced at a time when only a select proportion of the population could read, and there were not many other competing texts. There was therefore a dominant discourse on how one should behave that was directed towards those aspiring to become part of the 'good society'. We can view that text as both reflecting and attempting to affect changes in behaviour. Today, however, literacy is more widespread, and there is an increasing variety of multiple types of texts. While manners books are perhaps as not so often read nowadays, we can make the argument that these different texts – newspapers, TV shows, documentaries, 'green guides', films, novels, podcasts, and so on – serve a similar function to manners books of the past. And compared with the time of Erasmus, because there is no single text or type of text to dominate, there is perhaps more contestation over how to behave, and an increasing variety of the types of behaviour that are regarded as acceptable.

## Countervailing trends

In tandem with the aforementioned ecological civilizing process, there are also other trends occurring that have contributed to the development of the phenomenon of climate change. Some of these have developed as unintended outcomes of civilizing processes. Here are just a few of these countervailing trends.

We have already hinted towards some of these earlier in this chapter and other chapters. As mentioned in Chapter 1, anthropogenic climate change can be seen as an unintended outcome of increasing industrialization and increasing population, both of which are intimately tied in with processes of civilization. For example, increasing control over natural processes: increasing control over biomedical processes has contributed to increases in health and longevity; and increasing control over agricultural processes has contributed to increases in food yields. These two examples demonstrate how increasing control over natural processes has contributed to increasing human populations, and thereby the increasing expansion of the anthroposphere (see also Quilley, 2004). In turn, this has contributed to increasing carbon emissions and other greenhouse gases that contribute to climate change.

As populations increased, and as 'rubbish' increasingly came to be dominated by non-biodegradable materials, rubbish and litter increased overall, contributing to concerns about street litter, and more recently ecological concerns associated with especially plastic waste (Quilley, 2009a), such as those outlined earlier concerning non-human animals, the ocean, and space. As two of the 'green guides' mentioned earlier state,

> We're producing three times as much rubbish as we were 20 years ago and a lot of this is because 80% of what we now produce is discarded after a single use [text appears on a photo: background, bags of waste, foreground, empty plastic water bottle].
>
> (*Wa$ted!*, 2007, pp. 24–25)

> We produce and use 20 times more plastic today than we did 50 years ago.
>
> (*The Virgin Green Guide: The Easy Way to Save the Planet and Save £££s*, 2007, p. 2)

The assumption in these extracts is that of a 'throw-away' society, compared with a 'golden-age' past where things were reused and mended, and where people grew and made their own things. It is interesting to note that 'rubbish' is seen as something that is 'dirty' and is hidden behind the scenes – landfills are in remote locations, and jobs associated with rubbish are seen as examples of 'dirty work'. The sequestration of not only rubbish but also the processes involved in the production, transportation, and disposal, of products, has contributed to both a 'not knowing' and a 'not wanting to know'.

The development of increasing networks of interdependence, with more and more people relying on others (such as supermarkets) for their food supplies, has contributed to not only increasing packaging but also transportation has been increasing, along with increases in other associated uses of energy required to store and transport large quantities of food. These developments associated with civilizing processes have further contributed to increasing greenhouse gases in the atmosphere and, thereby, climate change.

Despite the apparent growth of ethical consumption, over the past century battery farming and other intensive farming methods have become more common (with free range less common) (Franklin, 1999, p. 136). This suggests that, if processes are hidden, we can ignore them, focussing our 'ethical' efforts on those things that are visible and less possible to deny. On the one hand, we have greater 'kindness' being shown towards animals in zoos and pets in homes; yet on the other hand we have increasingly intensive farming practices, where animals are treated in increasingly more 'cruel' ways. Perhaps this is because zoos and household pets are 'visible', whereas intensive farming practices are 'hidden' and certain measures are in place to 'remove' even the workers from the more unsavoury aspects of this.

These counter-trends outlined here are but a few of the many counter-trends occurring alongside ecological civilizing processes. Civilizing processes themselves, then, can contribute to both concern about the biosphere and damage towards the biosphere.

## Conclusion

The analysis presented here suggests that there has been at least a partial ecological civilizing process developing, albeit with counter processes occurring that have themselves contributed to the phenomenon of climate change. The gradual, blind development of an ecological civilizing process has affected, and been affected by, more intentional actions by various campaigners and writers throughout the centuries – from the likes of Thoreau and Leopold through to the makers of *Captain Planet*, through to *Virgin* and other producers of 'green guides'. There have been long-term changes in the medium of text that is used to communicate how one should behave, from manners texts to newspaper articles, television shows, 'green guides', and other media that will be discussed in the next chapter. The people who dictate how one should behave have also shifted from the middle class 'good society' and moral figures such as religious leaders, through to scientists, celebrities, and corporations. This more general shift in changes of the arbiters of socially acceptable behaviour is also accompanied by an increasing informalizing of the way that these various media outline prescriptions and proscriptions. In the next chapter, we further expand on these points by exploring how reactions to the perceived crisis of climate change may relate to moral panics, civilizing offensives, and decivilizing processes (that is, how long-term ecological civilizing processes relate to civilizing offensives or moral panics about climate change).

## Notes

1 Some of the developments included in this chapter, which focusses mostly (but not exclusively) on England, may have occurred quite differently in other countries. For example, see Mennell ([1985] 1996) on the different perception of the countryside in France compared with England.
2 It should be noted that this was not the first time such relatively similar (though somewhat different) developments occurred. Coates argues that artwork from ancient Greece and Rome suggests an aesthetic appreciation of 'nature', and the countryside was viewed as an antidote to city life (Coates, 1998, pp. 34–35; for differences in these developments, see Elias, [1921] 2006).
3 This legislation was part of a broader civilizing offensive that included other legislation regulating transport, alcohol consumption, and so on.
4 Such developments in the slaughtering of livestock parallel those developments in the executions of humans, where the process of execution has come to be less visibly violent, those involved are increasingly more physically removed from the act of killing, and the event itself becomes increasingly more private, accessible only to a select audience.
5 Thoreau, author of such books as *Walden and Other Writings* and *Excursions*, was a nineteenth-century writer, poet, environmentalist, philosopher, and naturalist.

## References

Behrendt, B. (1988, October 27). Teachers, students plan cleanup of Kings Bay and Shell Island. *St. Petersburg Times (Florida)*, 1.
Blanchard, T. (2007). *Green is the new black: How to change the world with style*. London: Hodder & Stoughton.
Burleigh, C. (1925). *Etiquette up to date*. London: T. Werner Laurie.
*Captain Planet and the Planeteers*. (1990–1996) [TV Series]. Warner Bros. Television.
Cassell and Co. (1921). *Cassell's book of etiquette: By "a woman of the world"*. London.
Censor. (1883). *Don't: A manual of mistakes and improprieties more or less prevalent in conduct and speech* (3rd ed.). London: Field & Tuer.
Clark, D. (2006). *The rough guide to ethical living*. London: Penguin.

Coates, P. (1998). *Nature: Western attitudes since ancient times.* Cambridge: Polity Press.

Cobbett, W. ([1830] 1926). *Advice to young men and (incidentally) to young women in the middle & higher ranks of life in a series of letters addressed to a youth, a bachelor, a lover, a husband, a father, a citizen or a subject.* London: Peter Davies, Limited.

Crawford, T. (1985, November 3). Ontario's food land: Going, going...We've all got a stake in the dilemma facing urban-fringe farmers. *The Tornto Star,* B1

Directgov. (n.d.). Reporting anti-social behaviour. Retrieved May 1, 2012, from www.direct.gov.uk/en/CrimeJusticeAndTheLaw/Reportingcrimeandantisocialbehaviour/DG_181715

Dorfman, J. (2007). *The lazy environmentalist: Your guide to easy, stylish, green living.* New York: Stewart, Tabori & Chang.

Elias, N. ([1921] 2006). On seeing in nature (E. Jephcott, Trans.). In R. Kilminster (Ed.), *Early writings (The Collected Works of Norbert Elias, Vol. 1)* (pp. 5–21). Dublin: University College Dublin Press.

Elias, N. ([1939] 2012). *On the process of civilisation: Sociogenetic and psychogenetic investigations (The Collected Works of Norbert Elias, Vol. 3).* Dublin: University College Dublin Press [Previous editions published as *The civilizing process*].

Elias, N. ([1987] 2007). *Involvement and detachment (The Collected Works of Norbert Elias, Vol. 8).* Dublin: University College Dublin Press.

Elias, N., & Dunning, E. ([1986] 2008). *Quest for excitement: Sport and leisure in the civilising process (The Collected Works of Norbert Elias, Vol. 7).* Dublin: University College Dublin Press.

Elkington, J., & Hailes, J. (1988). *The green consumer guide: From shampoo to champagne, high-street shopping for a better environment.* London: Victor Gollancz Ltd.

Elkington, J., Hailes, J., & with Douglas Hill. (1990). *The young green consumer guide.* London: Victor Gollancz Ltd.

*Etiquette for gentlemen: A guide to the observances of good society.* (1923). London: Ward, Lock & Co., Limited.

Franklin, A. (1999). *Animals and modern cultures: A sociology of human-animal relations in modernity.* London: Sage.

Goleman, D. (2009). *Ecological intelligence: How knowing the hidden impact of what we buy can change everything.* New York: Broadway Books.

Goodall, C. (2007). *How to live a low-carbon life: The individual's guide to stopping climate change.* London: Earthscan.

Harrington, J. (2008). *The climate diet: How you can cut carbon, cut costs, and save the planet.* London: Earthscan.

Holliman, J. ([1970] 1974). *Consumers' guide to the protection of the environment* (2nd (revised and reset) ed.). London: Pan Books.

*How to be a good wife.* ([1936] 2008). Oxford: Bodleian Library (Originally published as *Do's and don'ts for wives*, by Universal Publications Ltd).

Hughes, J. (2003). *Learning to smoke: Tobacco use in the West.* Chicago: University of Chicago Press.

Hughes, J. (2010). Emotional intelligence: Elias, Foucault, and the reflexive emotional self. *Foucault Studies, 8,* 28–52.

Humphrey, M. ([1897] 1993). *Manners for men.* Kent: Pryor publications.

Hunt, A. (1995). Moralizing luxury: The discourses of the governance of consumption. *Journal of Historical Sociology, 8*(4), 352–374.

*I count: Together we can stop climate chaos: Your step-by-step guide to climate bliss.* (2006). London: Penguin.

Keep Britain Tidy – About Us – Our History. Retrieved November 24, 2011, from www.keepbritaintidy.org/AboutUs/OurHistory/Default.aspx

Keep Northern Ireland Tidy (Producer). (n.d., 2011, November 24) Litter kills. Poster retrieved November 24, 2011, from www.tidynorthernireland.org/campaigns/youth-litter/index.php

Lovelock, J. ([1979] 2000). *Gaia: A new look at life on earth.* Oxford: Oxford University Press.

Ludgate, S. (Director). (2005). *No waste like home* [TV Series]. United Kingdom: BBC.

Mann, M. (2007). *It's easy being green.* Chichester, West Sussex: Summersdale.

Marks, K. (2008, February 5). The world's rubbish dump: A tip that stretches from Hawaii to Japan. *The Independent.* Retrieved October 2, 2009, from www.independent.co.uk/environment/the-worlds-rubbish-dump-a-garbage-tip-that-stretches-from-hawaii-to-japan-778016.html

M.C. ([1893] 1995). *Everybody's book of correct conduct, being the etiquette of every-day life.* Kent: Pryor publications.

Mennell, S. ([1985] 1996). *All manners of food: Eating and taste in England and France from the Middle Ages to the present* (2nd ed.). Urbana: University of Illinois Press.

Meyrick, S., & Cousins, S. (Director). (2007). *Carbon cops* [DVD]. Australia: ABC (Australian Broadcasting Corporation).

Nash, R. F. ([1967] 2001). *Wilderness and the American mind* (4th ed.). New Haven: Yale University Press.

Planet Hunters. (n.d.). Retrieved May 1, 2012, from www.planethunters.org/

Pringle, G. (1949). *Etiquette in Canada: The blue book of Canadian social usage* (2nd ed.). Toronto: McClelland & Stewart, Limited.

Quilley, S. (2004). Social development as trophic expansion: Food systems, prosthetic ecology and the arrow of history. *Amsterdams Sociologisch Tijdschrift, 31*(3), 321–347.

Quilley, S. (2009a). 'Biophilia' as an 'Ecological Civilising Process': The Sociogenesis and Psychogenesis of Litterlouts and Recycling Eco-Citizens (Working Paper).

Quilley, S. (2009b). The Land Ethic as an ecological civilizing process: Aldo Leopold, Norbert Elias, and environmental philosophy. *Environmental Ethics, 31*(2), 115–134.

Robertson, A. ([1936] 2001). *How to do and say in England: A trim kompaktikum for students of Englisch talk and society behaviourism.* London: Prion Books, Ltd.

Rojek, C. (2007). *Cultural studies.* Cambridge: Polity Press.

Stanhope, P. D. (1830). *Lord Chesterfield's advice to his son on men and manners: The principles of politeness and the art of acquiring a knowledge of the world, are laid down in an easy and familiar manner, to which are added, a selection of de la Rochefaucault's maxims.* London: Bloomsbury.

Staudinger, J. J. P. (1970). *Disposal of waste and litter.* London: Society of chemical industry.

Sutton, P. W. (2000). *Explaining environmentalism: In search of a new social movement.* Aldershot: Ashgate.

Sutton, P. W. (2004). *Nature, environment and society.* Houndmills, Basingstoke, Hampshire: Palgrave Macmillan.

Sutton, P. W. (2007). *The environment: A sociological introduction.* Cambridge: Polity Press.

*The habits of good society: A handbook of etiquette for ladies and gentlemen.* (1868). London: Cassell, Petter, and Caplin.

*The habits of good society: A handbook of etiquette for ladies and gentlemen: With thoughts, hints, and anecdotes concerning social observances; nice points of taste and good manners; and the art of making one's-self agreeable.* (1875). (New ed.). London: Virtue & Co., Limited.

*The happy child.* (1933). Exeter: Wheaton & Co., Ltd.

*The Virgin green guide: The easy way to save the planet and save £££s.* (2007). London: Virgin Books.

Thomas, K. (1987). *Man and the natural world: Changing attitudes in England 1500–1800.* Harmondsworth, Middlesex: Penguin.

Thoreau, H. D. (1863). *Excursions.* Boston: Ticknor and Fields.

Tuan, Y.-F. (1974). *Topophilia: A study of environmental perception, attitudes, and values.* London: Prentice-Hall.

Wallis, T., & Pringle, L. (Director). (2007). *Wa$ted!* [DVD]. New Zealand: Fumes NZ Ltd.

*Wa$ted!* (2007). Auckland: Random House.

Weart, S. R. ([2003] 2008). *The discovery of global warming* (Revised and expanded ed.). Cambridge: Harvard University Press.

Worster, D. (1994). *Nature's economy: A history of ecological ideas* (2nd ed.). Cambridge: Cambridge University Press.

# 6 Historical analysis (part two)

## Climate change and moral panics[1]

## Introduction

In the previous chapter, we explored how the development of concern about climate change can be seen as part of a broader ecological civilizing process, including such developments as increasing identification with animals, plants, and the biosphere as a whole, and increasing awareness of the interdependencies between different natural processes. In this chapter, we turn to exploring the development of climate change campaigns as a reaction to the perception that ecological civilizing processes either are not occurring at a fast-enough rate (to counter other processes) or have gone into reverse. Combining the concept of moral panic with the notion of civilizing offensives, this chapter explores the extent to which reactions to climate change can be considered to be moral panics and how this relates to the previously explored ecological civilizing processes.

Following this discussion of moral panics, the question of folk devils is raised, during which the relationship between climate change campaigners and sceptics is explored. This then leads into a discussion of the relationship between panic and denial. I then examine the media and moral panic, exploring how changes in the production and dissemination of knowledge (including changes in media technologies) may influence the development of concern about and regulation of social problems, thereby influencing the development of moral panics and, therefore, informing how we conceptualize moral panic and how we go about moral panic research.

## The emergence of concern

One of Goode and Ben-Yehuda's ([1994] 2009) five elements or criteria of moral panic includes the notion of concern, where (some) people come to be increasingly concerned about the behaviour of a group of people or about particular events that are occurring. This is what Critcher (2003) terms the 'emergence' of the problem – where the problem comes to be recognized as such and is perceived to be a threat to the moral and social order.

We can trace the emergence of concern about climate change in several ways; one is through inferring concern from newspaper coverage. Boykoff and Roberts (2007, p. 36) have shown how coverage of climate change has steadily increased since 1988, with a rapid increase from 2004 onwards.

An additional way to infer concern is by examining the publication of the 'green guides' that were mentioned in the previous chapter. In January 2008, when I entered two small bookshops in Sydney, Australia, I discovered what I now call 'green guides' – 26 of them. These included books about climate change, how to 'live green', and how to 'stop global warming'. Soon after this, I ventured to bookshops in other countries, finding numerous copies of this seemingly new genre of publication.

Since 1990 there has been an increase in these types of guides on how to live green, suggesting a sudden concern about eco-friendly behaviour and climate change (the guides reflecting and/or generating concern about climate change). This coincides with the aftermath of 'the greenhouse summer of '88', a summer of severe heat and drought during which climate change campaigners and the media increasingly came to link the 'strange weather' to climate change (Ungar, 1992). That same year, the United Nations (UN) created the Intergovernmental Panel on Climate Change (IPCC).

Popular interest in climate change further increased in the early 2000s and especially after the disaster of Hurricane Katrina and the release of the Al Gore-presented climate change documentary *An Inconvenient Truth* (Guggenheim, 2006). While *An Inconvenient Truth* received a great deal of attention at the time, it is only one of many, representative of a wider discourse surrounding climate change, as represented in other 'texts', such as other 'eco-documentaries'; popular books about climate change; guides on 'how to live green', 'save the planet', and 'stop global warming'; 'eco-makeover' lifestyle reality TV shows; and manners podcasts dedicated to 'green living'. For example, a *Scientific American* podcast episode, 'Anesthesiologists Can Help Cut Climate Change', suggests that climate change should be on the mind of anaesthesiologists 'because the gasses used to knock you out contribute to global warming'. The presenter describes a study undertaken on three common gases used by anaesthesiologists, noting how two of the three gases have a significantly lower carbon footprint: 'if a choice can be safely made, anesthesiologists should go with the one that's *kindest* to the climate' (*Scientific American -60-Second Science*, 2010, December 6). Here, we see that concern about the effects of climate change, and how we should modify our actions accordingly, is present in a variety of areas, amongst a variety of groups (including, in this case, medical professionals).

Discourses about climate change also include the 'new catastrophism' (Urry, 2011), predicting catastrophic consequences of 'high-carbon' lifestyles. As already mentioned, there exists the perception that what have been termed ecological civilizing processes either are not developing at a fast-enough rate (to counter other processes) or have gone into reverse. Such discourses are present in the 'green guides' explored in the previous chapter and in other texts to be explored here. Importantly, however, these discourses are not uniform in that there is no overall consensus about climate change in *popular* media.

## Consensus about climate change

An additional criterion of Goode and Ben-Yehuda ([1994] 2009) is that there is consensus amongst a group of people (not necessarily the whole population) that there is a problem. It is relatively easy to prove that a degree of consensus exists within the community of those engaged in climate science. Naomi Oreskes (2004), in a paper subtitled 'the scientific consensus on global warming', reports findings from an analysis of peer-reviewed journal articles on 'global climate change'. Her results found no study that disagreed with the apparent scientific consensus on the reality of anthropogenic climate change. However, this consensus does not extend to the entire population. As will be discussed later in this chapter, there are those who believe or at least claim to believe that (a) the threat of anthropogenic climate change is not as great as is believed; (b) it is happening but so slowly that we will be able to address it, so we need not be concerned; (c) it is happening, but it is not caused by humans; or (d) the global climate is not changing. It is this disagreement about different aspects of climate change that may have contributed to the increasing moralization of the issue.

## Increasing moralization and responsibilization

One important characteristic of moral panics is that they are *moral* panics. But for some moral panic researchers, 'moral' is somehow seen as a separate sphere: for example, Kenneth Thompson argues, 'Sometimes panics about food (e.g. the bovine spongiform encephalopathy (BSE) scare about infected beef) or health have been confused with panics that relate directly to morals' (Thompson, 1998, p. vii). Such a stance suggests that 'panics about food' cannot contain a moral element; it is a question of moral panics *versus* risk panics (Ungar, 2001). In his introduction to the third edition of *Folk Devils and Moral Panics*, Stan Cohen describes how technical risks can be transformed into moral panics when the risk 'becomes perceived as *primarily* moral rather than technical (the moral irresponsibility for taking this risk)' (Cohen, [1972] 2002, p. xxxvi). While climate change has been informed by the science of climate change, and carries with it elements of a technical risk, I wish to argue that it has become increasingly moralized over time.

### Eco-documentaries

An example of this increasing moralization is the award-winning climate change documentary *An Inconvenient Truth* (Guggenheim, 2006). In a previous paper, I analyzed the documentary, demonstrating the moral panic themes that were present and how they might relate to wider social processes (Rohloff, 2011). I saw the documentary when it was first released in theatres in 2006 and was immediately struck by how moralized the 'risk' of climate change was throughout it; I remember leaving the theatre contemplating whether or not this could indeed be a prime case to explore from a moral panic perspective (it then formed the basis of my Honours dissertation, which was eventually rewritten into the aforementioned paper). Examples of the moralization throughout the documentary include the following quotes from Al Gore:

> the moral imperative to make big changes is inescapable
>
> Ultimately, this is really not a political issue so much as a moral issue. If we allow [the projected carbon dioxide (CO2) concentrations after 50 years of unrestricted fossil fuel burning] to happen, it is deeply unethical.
>
> this is what is at stake, our ability to live on planet earth, to have a future as a civilization. I believe this is a moral issue. It is your time to seize this issue. It is our time to rise again to secure our future.
>
> (Guggenheim, 2006)

If we refer back to Cohen, the 'moral irresponsibility of taking this risk' becomes further apparent when Gore compares the development of the science of climate change and a lack of action with initial responses to the scientific literature linking tobacco smoking with lung cancer. In the case of tobacco, Gore argues that the slow response resulted in the deaths of many, implying that a slow or inadequate response to climate change could have devastating consequences. He also draws comparisons between the storm brewing in Nazi Germany and the storm brewing in the form of Hurricane Katrina (for further analysis of the documentary, see Rohloff, 2011).

### Podcasts and blogs

Similarly, in an episode of *Make-It-Green-Girl: Quick and Dirty Tips for An Earth Friendly Life,* titled 'Dry Clean Dilemma' (2008, September 18), the presenter discusses the problem of 'eco-guilt' associated with dry cleaning, urging listeners to choose dry cleaners that use 'environmentally friendly' solvents. This 'eco-guilt' is manifested clearly in *The Guardian* blog 'Ask Leo & Lucy: Your Green Questions Answered' (guardian.co.uk/environment/series/ask-leo-lucy), where readers submit questions such as 'Can I use perfume and be green?', 'Do dimmer switches really save energy when lighting a room?', 'What is the most eco-friendly alcoholic drink?', 'What's the best form of carbon offsetting?', 'How green is your pension?', and so on. While some of these questions are about 'living green' and being 'kind to the environment' in general, many relate back to climate change and carbon footprints.

## 'Green guides'

An additional source of information on 'green' questions is the recent proliferation of 'green guides' mentioned earlier. As seen in the extracts presented in Chapter 5, these texts typically contain prescriptions and pro-scriptions on how one should modify their behaviour in order to combat climate change. One of the themes from these texts, the diet metaphor, contrasts excess eating or drinking with excess consumption in general (i.e. a 'high-carbon' lifestyle). This draws parallels with other wider discourses and practices for moderating one's behaviour and is perhaps an attempt to establish a moderation of 'carbon consumption' as a status aspiration (for example, see Aarts, Goudsblom, Schmidt, & Spier, 1995). Many of these same themes from the 'green guides' are also present in other media, such as eco-makeover lifestyle reality TV shows.

## Eco-makeover lifestyle reality TV shows

A further type of media is the 'eco-makeover' lifestyle reality TV show. In these shows, which have been made in many countries around the world, such as *Wa$ted* (New Zealand) (Wallis & Pringle, 2007), *Carbon Cops* (Australia) (Meyrick & Cousins, 2007), and *No Waste Like Home* (UK) (Ludgate, 2005), 'experts' go into people's homes, workplaces, etc., and carry out a carbon audit. In some of these 'eco-makeover' shows, 'partic-ipants' are described as 'eco-criminals' and their actions as 'eco-crimes'. There occurs a 'naming and shaming' process in some of these shows, where the 'eco-deviance' is exposed, and attempts are made to transform this into 'eco-friendly' practices (see also Lewis, 2008). Throughout, various sugges-tions appear to the audience (anyone who might be watching the show) about what they can do (or should do) to cut down their own carbon emissions.

The transference between 'ethical living' and 'green living', often tied to climate change, further highlights the morality of climate change discourse and the processes of moral regulation occurring in relation to climate change.

# The 'climate crisis': a symptom of wider problems

This highlights the 'moral dimension' of climate change discourse, but this deviance is also seen to be symptomatic of other problems (Garland, 2008). This is what Cohen refers to as 'it's not only this' ([1972] 2002, p. 39), where other issues come to be associated with the prime issue of concern. With the case of climate change, it is not only the natural crisis but also the social crisis of our relationship with the environment, including patterns of consumption. The 'climate crisis', as with other moral panics, is not simply a crisis about the changing climate. It is also a crisis about overconsump-tion, industrialization, capitalism, and how we see ourselves in relation to each other, other animals, and the biosphere as a whole.

Related to this is the notion of the issue being seen as a 'sign of the times' (Cohen, [1972] 2002, p. 46). As early as the 1970s, the antecedents of to-day's 'green guides' were drawing attention to environmental problems as being a sign that people's values were wrong, and that environmental prob-lems are a symptom of this; for example, as Jonathan Holliman wrote in the *Consumer's Guide to The Protection of the Environment*, 'Certainly the state of the environment is the clearest indication that some of our cher-ished values may be wrong' (Holliman, [1970] 1974, p. 13).

More recently, in the green guides of today, we can see examples of how climate change is seen as a symptom of several deeper problems, such as overconsumption and capitalism. The diet metaphors mentioned in the previous chapter, along with the metaphor of addiction, suggest that con-sumption has gotten out of control. The development of initiatives such as 'Freecycle'[2] (uk.freecycle.org) and 'Buy Nothing Day'[3] (buynothingday.co.uk), along with the emergence of groups such as 'Freegans'[4,5] (freegan.info), is indicative of perceptions that capitalism itself is a problem. This is most clearly represented in notions of how to transform capitalism towards a 'green' capitalism or how to replace capitalism with an entirely different system.

There thus exists the perception of *moral decline*, hence the perceived need for these guides, documentaries, TV shows, and so on. Similar to manners books of the past, these 'green' documents implicitly entail a sense of looking down to those who are not 'ethical consumers', and a corre-sponding looking up to those who are (as epitomized in the 'eco-celebrity'). Having explored the *moral* dimension of climate change discourse, we now turn to the *panic* dimension.

## Disproportionality

Disproportionality – the *panic* part of moral panic – is potentially a prob-lematic criterion for climate change for in some people's minds it implies that the reaction is an overreaction, and is therefore inappropriate and un-just. Refuting Ungar's contention that disproportionality is not an essential feature of moral panic, Goode and Ben-Yehuda argue that 'the very word "panic" *implies* disproportion' ([1994] 2009, p. 82). However, it depends how we define 'panic' and how we define 'disproportionality'. Goode and Ben-Yehuda also mention several different indicators of disproportion, one of which is 'changes over time'. They argue that

> if the attention paid to a given condition at one point in time is vastly greater than that paid to it during a previous or later time, without any corresponding increase in objective seriousness, then, once again, the criterion of disproportion may be said to have been met.
>
> (Goode & Ben-Yehuda, [1994] 2009, p. 46)

It is a slightly modified version of this that I wish to utilize in relation to climate change. I wish to conceptualize disproportionality in two ways. First, by exploring the change in the degree of attention paid to a given issue, what sort of attention is paid to it in what way, and how this changes over time. Put in another way, we can explore the relation over time between changes in (a) public awareness of the problem, (b) 'media' and other coverage or attention paid to the problem, and (c) the actual incidence of the problem.

The second way that I wish to reconceptualize disproportionality is in terms of degrees of 'reality congruence' and 'value congruence'. By this I mean we should assess, through empirical research, the accuracy and appropriateness of representations of the issue, and attempts to regulate the issue, that is, assessing the degree to which regulatory attempts are likely to have more intended than unintended, and integrative rather than disintegrative consequences, as well as exploring the values behind different representations. This will be further explicated in Chapter 8 (the concluding chapter) where, following this theoretical-empirical research, I discuss to what extent moral panic, as a concept, still remains useful; the purpose of the concept, including how it should be used; and how moral panic research should be undertaken.

## Volatility

A related criterion to disproportionality is volatility. However, for the purposes of this chapter, I will ignore volatility. In their book, Goode and Ben-Yehuda contradict themselves about the meaning of this term. At the beginning of the section on volatility, they state that 'moral panics are *volatile*; they erupt fairly suddenly…and, nearly as suddenly, subside' and 'the fever pitch that characterizes a society during the course of a moral panic is not typically sustainable over a long stretch of time' (Goode & Ben-Yehuda, [1994] 2009, p. 41). At the end of that section, however, they then go on to point out that 'The satanic witch craze gripped Europe for nearly three centuries. The fact that certain concerns are long-lasting does not mean they are not panics, though' (Goode & Ben-Yehuda, [1994] 2009, p. 43). This latter quote seems to negate the necessity and validity of 'volatility' as a criterion for moral panic. However, we can still think about volatility in relation to civilizing offensives – how gradual long-term civilizing processes may be accelerated by a civilizing spurt.

## Civilizing offensives, decivilizing processes, and moral panics

The campaigns surrounding climate change – books, guides, documentaries, reality TV shows, and other media mentioned earlier – that seek to both educate people and bring about changes in behaviour can be conceptualized as a civilizing offensive: campaigns to 'civilize' the self and/ or the other in an attempt to develop a civilizing spurt. In this way, moral panics in general can be seen as civilizing offensives. However, depending on how the historical social processes have been developing in relation to any particular example, different types of civilizing offensives may accompany moral panics: from 'civilizing' all of us, in the case of climate change; to 'civilizing' some, making 'them' more like 'us'; to more exclusionary campaigns that seek to make society more 'civilized' by excluding those that are deemed by some to be too 'uncivilized'.

Perhaps civilizing processes themselves have contributed to decivilizing consequences in the form of what Urry calls a 'capitalism of excess' and overconsumption. On the one hand we can witness certain trends towards increasing moderation and self-control (changes in long-term patterns of eating (Mennell, [1985] 1996) and smoking (Hughes, 2003)), and on the other we can see the growing emergence of multiple sites of excess consumption, and the increasing 'freedom to become "addicted", to be emotionally and/or physically dependent upon excessive consumption of certain products and services of global capitalism, legal, illegal or semi-legal' (Urry, 2010, p. 204).

Here, consumption associated with climate change may share some similarities with the consumption of tobacco. As a counter to the notion of 'consumer gluttony', excessive consumption may in part be being used as a means of self-control, akin to the use of tobacco, and perhaps in some ways alcohol, and as a means to try and control one's emotions (for example, consider the concept of 'retail therapy' – shopping to 'improve' one's mood). The notion of 'ethical consumerism' or 'green consumerism' is an additional way that consumption (albeit not excess consumption) can be used as a means of control, as a means to try and control environmental and ethical developments.

Additionally, the notion of travelling to sites of 'excess consumption' shares some similarities with the notion of travelling to 'the countryside'. In the previous chapter I outlined how, when one travelled to 'the countryside', there was a relaxation of manners, a spatial informalization, and a 'quest for excitement'. Similarly, for these places of 'excess consumption' that Urry writes of, people also have to travel to these sites, and there is also a relaxation of rules – the same rules do not apply in these 'places of excess' as they do elsewhere. In that respect, like 'the countryside', 'places of excess' represent an emancipation from everyday life.

These decivilizing consequences may be contributing to the detriment of the environment and social life as a whole (see also Ampudia de Haro, 2008), including the development of anthropogenic climate change. To counter this, climate change campaigns could potentially be utilized as 'good' moral panics or civilizing offensives, to bring about a civilizing 'spurt' or an acceleration in ecological civilizing processes. However, the notion of 'good' moral panics is not so straightforward in several ways.

First, from whose perspective is the moral panic 'good'? For example, from past moral panics that have been deemed 'bad' by researchers, the moral entrepreneurs involved in those quite often probably regarded their campaigns as 'good' (not that they would have called them good *moral panics*). Second, while attempting to do 'good' (again a problematic use of the word), these campaigns also have the potential to have decivilizing consequences: for example, if 'good' and 'bad' behaviours developed into 'good' and 'bad' people. We can already witness this to a certain extent with the notion of 'eco-criminals' and 'eco-deviants' mentioned earlier, two labels that featured in eco-makeover lifestyle reality TV shows. So, potentially, moral panics over climate change could be regarded as both civilizing and decivilizing processes, with the possibility of contributing to the development of deviance and deviants, crime, and criminals. The extent to which these deviants will become integrated or sequestered is uncertain. This takes us into a discussion about 'folk devils'.

## Folk devils and hostility

Goode and Ben-Yehuda, in *Moral Panics: The Social Construction of Deviance*, argue that

> threatening, dangerous or risky conditions...[such as] nuclear energy, swine flu, *E. coli*, global warming, the shrinking ozone layer...and so on....may cause anxiety, concern, or fear but in the absence of folk devils or evildoers do not touch off *moral* panics.
>
> ([1994] 2009, p. 42)

They acknowledge that some have argued that we should look at such issues in relation to moral panic, but Goode and Ben-Yehuda disagree. The question is why do they and others disagree? Can this tell us something about the function of moral panic research, and the political and ideological influences on the researcher? There is not space here to answer such questions. Instead, in this chapter I wish to illustrate how folk devils may be being formed in relation to climate change, how these folk devils differ from folk devils from other more 'classic' moral panics, and what implications this has.

As with manners books of the past, in today's 'green guides' and other climate change-related media, there are dictums of how one should and should not behave (see Chapter 5 for examples). Within these various texts, the implication is that if you 'do nothing' or do 'bad' things, you are a 'bad' person. This is epitomized in the *Virgin Green Guide*'s name-calling and deviantization of 'eco deviants' mentioned in the previous chapter. And in some of the eco-makeover lifestyle reality TV shows, this is further evident. For example, in *Wa$ted*, people whose behaviour is regarded by the producers as 'bad' are shown in a mug style shot, with the label 'guilty' emblazoned across the screen. The very development of the terms 'eco-deviant' and 'eco-criminal' is further evidence to suggest that there is certainly a deviantization process occurring, but to what extent this equates to folk devils is unclear.

A more likely candidate for the label of folk devil is the 'climate change sceptic' or the 'climate change denier'. The more pejorative term, 'climate change denier', is a prevalent term: a search carried out in Nexis UK on 6 June 2018, for the phrase 'climate change denier' in 'anywhere', retrieved more than 3,000 results; a google search for the same phrase retrieved about 693,000 results. So strongly established is this label, it sometimes does not take much to be termed a 'sceptic' or 'denier'. I had the unfortunate experience once, of being labelled a 'climate change sceptic', and my research a piece of 'climate change denial'. And this was simply because I was exploring climate change from a (reformulated) moral panic approach. As well as telling us something about moral panic, this example (along with many others) demonstrates how quick some people can be to label others as 'deniers', with the associated stereotypical assumptions that it carries. The comparison of those who dispute the reality of anthropogenic climate change, or the urgency of it, with holocaust deniers adds an additional emotive, demonizing characteristic to these folk devils – associating them, implicitly, with neo-Nazis.

However, despite the relative popularity of the term 'climate change denier', and other potential folk devils associated with climate change, this example contrasts with some of the classic examples of moral panic – panics over youth, working class, and other marginalized groups. Climate change provides us with new types of folk devils: (1) 'climate sceptics/deniers'; (2) big corporations (including, but not limited to, the energy industry); (3) governments; (4) the affluent, SUV-driving, 'gas-guzzling' consumer with a large carbon footprint; and (5) the extremely rich who consume to 'excess' in sites of 'excess consumption' (in relation to the latter, see Urry, 2010). As the power ratios between these new types of folk devils and the 'control culture' is less 'unbalanced' than power ratios between more marginalized groups and the control culture, we witness a different type of governance. On the one hand, we witness an increase in the development of non-governmental interventions – the campaigning of environmental organizations, celebrities, and scientists; the increasing occurrence of 'activism' and participation in protests and demonstrations; and the emergence of 'neat capitalism' (Rojek, 2007, Ch.8), 'ethical consumerism', and 'green consumerism'. At the same time, however, as well as these notional (or difficult to regulate) folk devils, there is also a call upon everyone to regulate and reassess their own behaviour, and their own contributions to climate change. These trends towards a critique of current practices of consumption and the 'guides' (books, reality TV shows, documentaries, podcasts, etc.) that have been produced to try and provide a means for people to change their own behaviour, 'save the planet', and 'stop global warming' are similar to manners books, etiquette books, and environmental literature of the past, but they also differ from the extent that they are connected with a perceived 'crisis'.

And while this general trend towards 'self-governance' is directed towards everyone, as mentioned earlier, we can also witness the emergence of 'eco-deviance' and 'eco-crime'. Similar to issues such as smoking and drinking, one's own behaviour can affect the 'well-being' of many others (Hier, 2008, 2011). With the example of climate change, the choices of one person are related to the impact on the whole world, most explicitly in the case of the individual carbon footprint. Therefore, it may be the case that these deviant behaviours associated with climate change come to be increasingly established; the gap between the 'eco-friendly' and the 'eco-deviant' may widen, and a more established, more marginalized folk devil may eventually emerge. These divides may become further entrenched as climate change continues to accelerate, and natural and social crises increasingly develop as an outcome of this.

## Panic and denial

There is also the flipside of this 'moral panic': 'denial'. As witnessed in the aftermath of 'Climategate', as well as the development of so-called 'climate change sceptics' or 'climate change deniers', along with existing research interviewing people about their thoughts about climate change, the growing concern with 'exaggeration and distortion' in the media, combined with multiple media sources (McRobbie & Thornton, 1995), suggests that generating both concern and changes in behaviour can prove difficult in some cases. Paradoxically, moral panics themselves may contribute to the denial of social problems as the general public grows increasingly more sceptical and cynical about the media. It is in this regard that moral panic research can be tremendously informative: in assessing past and current campaigns and interventions in terms of how adequate, appropriate, and successful they may be, that is, whether they will have more intended than unintended outcomes.

As with other moral panics, there has been contestation over the reality of the social problem of climate change, with sceptics critiquing advocates, and advocates, in turn, responding to sceptics. There is even now an iPhone application called 'Our Climate' that one can use to 'discredit' climate change sceptic arguments (Cook, 2010, August 6). There are also numerous blogs dedicated to addressing and debunking 'climate change denial' as well as numerous books. This exchange and battle between advocates and sceptics, along with increasing scepticism regarding the media, relates to how changes in the production and dissemination of knowledge affect the development of moral panics (and the denial of them).

## The media and moral panic: long-term changes in the production and dissemination of knowledge

Since the concept of moral panic was developed by Stan Cohen and Jock Young in their PhD theses in the late 1960s and early 1970s, there have been tremendous developments in media and communications, including the development of the Internet, blogs, Twitter, Facebook and other social networking sites, Skype, SMS (Short Message System) text messaging, smartphones with applications and cameras, online newspapers with comments sections, podcasts, YouTube, and others. Building on McRobbie and Thornton's argument about 'multi-mediated social worlds' (1995), these 'new media' platforms have all contributed to the rapid exchange of information, the increasing ease with which 'citizen journalists' produce and disseminate their own interpretations of events and issues, and therefore the growing potential (in some cases but not all) to contest dominant narratives. Although some argue that professional and elite journalism 'institutions still break and frame a large proportion of the news stories circulating through the online sphere and this is unlikely to change in the foreseeable future' (Goode, 2009, p. 1291). Additionally, for some issues that are firmly entrenched, it may be more difficult and less likely that dissenting voices would be communicated and listened to; with others, it may be more likely.

Along with these changes in technology that have facilitated the potential for a degree of increasing democratization of knowledge, there has also been a gradual shift in the types of media that have been utilized and how they have been utilized. While much moral panic research has focussed on news media – newspapers, television news – throughout this research I have attempted to broaden that scope, to explore how and the extent to which other types of media, other types of documents, contribute to moral panics. Not just newspapers but also manners books, environmentalist literature, science books, novels, 'green guides', television shows, documentaries, and films have all contributed to media representations of climate change, 'nature', and 'the environment'. They have contributed to the formulation of 'good' and 'bad' behaviours, and 'good' and 'bad' people. Within these texts, as mentioned in the previous chapter, the arbiters of 'good' and 'bad' have changed to include celebrities, amongst others.

As with other social problems, celebrities are increasingly used to support climate change campaigns and 'green living'. They are used as an authority, as in the case of documentaries – for example, *The 11th Hour* (Conners & Conners-Petersen, 2007), produced and narrated by Leonardo DiCaprio; the National Geographic documentary *Six Degrees Could Change the World* (Bowman, 2007), narrated by Alec Baldwin; the PBS documentary, *Global Warming: The Signs and the Science* (Taylor, 2005), hosted and narrated by Alanis Morissette; and *An Inconvenient Truth* (Guggenheim,

2006), presented by Al Gore. Celebrities are also used as a status aspiration, in the case of 'green living' and 'ethical living'. For example, in 2006 *Vanity Fair* began releasing an annual 'green issue' of their magazine[5]. The magazine covers featured 'eco-celebrities': Julia Roberts, Al Gore, George Clooney, Robert F, Kennedy Jr., Leonardo DiCaprio, and Madonna. Just as celebrities became models of what to buy and what to wear (think of the women's magazines that show photos of celebrities in their outfits and where you can buy look-alike outfits at affordable prices), some celebrities are now becoming models of how to live 'eco-friendly' lives. Some are like moral entrepreneurs of previous times. They are like the 'good society', the 'court society' that other people aspire to be like and to be part of.

## Conclusion: climate change moral panics?

I wish to suggest that climate change campaigns – including the previously mentioned green guides – have similarities with moral panics but some differences as well. Certainly, I do not wish to suggest that climate change campaigns are moral panics in the classic understanding of the term; I do not wish to suggest that this reaction to climate change is necessarily an irrational overreaction. Instead, I wish to utilize a reformulation of the moral panic concept, one that does not carry the same normative assumptions of the original model.

Situating the concept within Elias's theory of civilizing processes, I wish to argue that moral panics can be conceptualized as perceived social crises, where there is a perceived failure in the civilizing of the 'self' and/or the 'other', in long-term civilizing processes. In the case of climate change, it is not only the natural crisis but also the social crisis of our relationship with the environment, including patterns of consumption. The campaigns surrounding climate change – books, guides, documentaries, reality TV shows, and other media – that seek to both educate people and bring about changes in behaviour can be conceptualized as a civilizing offensive: campaigns to 'civilize' the self and/or the other. In this way, moral panics in general can perhaps be seen as civilizing offensives. However, depending on how the historical social processes have been developing in relation to any particular example, different types of civilizing offensives may accompany moral panics: from 'civilizing' all of us, in the case of climate change; to 'civilizing' some, making 'them' more like 'us'; to more exclusionary campaigns that seek to make society more 'civilized' by excluding those that are deemed by some to be too 'uncivilized'.

In Chapter 7, I take this analysis further by comparing this example of climate change to several other examples, in order to further develop my reformulation of moral panic and civilizing processes, and to reassess the relationship between civilizing offensives and civilizing processes.

## Notes

1  An earlier version of this chapter was written for the *Ashgate Companion to Moral Panics*, see Rohloff (2013).
2  'Freecycle' is similar to eBay, except that items are 'gifted' rather than sold, the aim being to reduce the number of products that are sent to landfills by instead reusing them.
3  'Buy Nothing Day' is an annual, international day when people are urged to protest against consumerism by not buying anything for the whole day.
4  According to their website, 'The word freegan is compounded from "free" and "vegan". Vegans are people who avoid products from animal sources or products tested on animals in an effort to avoid harming animals. Freegans take this a step further by recognizing that in a complex, industrial, mass-production economy driven by profit, abuses of humans, animals, and the earth abound at all levels of production (from acquisition to raw materials to production to transportation) and in just about every product we buy'. Freegans therefore avoid buying products and services wherever they can.
5  These 'annual green issues' were subsequently abandoned in 2009.

## References

Aarts, W., Goudsblom, J., Schmidt, K., & Spier, F. (1995). *Toward a morality of moderation: Report for the Dutch national research programme on global air pollution and climate change.* Amsterdam: Amsterdam School for Social Science Research.

Ampudia de Haro, F. (2008). *Discussing decivilisation: Some theoretical remarks.* Paper presented at the First ISA Forum of Sociology: Sociological Research and Public Debate.

Bowman, R. (Director). (2007). *Six degrees could change the world.* [DVD]. United States: National Geographic.

Boykoff, M. T., & Roberts, J. T. (2007). Media coverage of climate change: Current trends, strengths, weaknesses. *Human Development Report 2007/2008: Fighting climate change: Human solidarity in a divided world*: Occasional Paper 2007/3, Human Development Report Office.

Cohen, S. ([1972] 2002). *Folk devils and moral panics: The creation of the mods and rockers* (3rd ed.). London: Routledge.

Conners, N., & Conners-Petersen, L. (Director). (2007). *The 11th hour* [Motion Picture]. United States: Warner Independent Pictures.

Cook, J. (2010, August 6). Climate change denial? There's an app for that. *Guardian.* Retrieved August 6, 2010, from www.guardian.co.uk/environment/blog/2010/aug/06/iphone-climate-denial-app.

Critcher, C. (2003). *Moral panics and the media.* Buckingham: Open University Press.

Garland, D. (2008). On the concept of moral panic. *Crime Media Culture, 4*(1), 9–30.

Goode, E., & Ben-Yehuda, N. ([1994] 2009). *Moral panics: The social construction of deviance* (2nd ed.). Chichester: Wiley-Blackwell.

Goode, L. (2009). Social news, citizen journalism and democracy. *New Media & Society, 11*(8), 1287–1305.

Guggenheim, D. (Director). (2006). *An inconvenient truth: A global warning* [Motion Picture]. United States: Paramount Pictures.

Hier, S. P. (2008). Thinking beyond moral panic: Risk, responsibility, and the politics of moralization. *Theoretical Criminology, 12*(2), 173–190.

Hier, S. P. (2011). Tightening the focus: Moral panic, moral regulation and liberal government. *British Journal of Sociology, 62*(3), 523–541.

Holliman, J. ([1970] 1974). *Consumers' guide to the protection of the environment* (2nd (revised and reset) ed.). London: Pan Books.

Hughes, J. (2003). *Learning to smoke: Tobacco use in the West.* Chicago, IL: University of Chicago Press.

Lewis, T. (2008). Transforming citizens? Green politics and ethical consumption on lifestyle television. *Continuum, 22*(2), 227–240.

Ludgate, S. (Director). (2005). *No waste like home* [TV Series]. United Kingdom: BBC.

Oreskes, N. (2004). Beyond the ivory tower: The scientific consensus on climate change. *Science, 306*(5702), 1686.

Rohloff, A. (2011). Extending the concept of moral panic: Elias, climate change and civilization. *Sociology, 45*(4), 634–649.

Rohloff, A. (2013). Moral panics over the environment? "Climate crisis" and the moral panics model. In C. Krinsky (Ed.), *The Ashgate Companion to Moral Panics* (pp. 401–414). Abingdon: Routledge.

*Make-It-Green-Girl: Quick and Dirty Tips for an Earth Friendly Life.* (2008, September 18). Dry clean dilemma [Podcast], episode 20.

McRobbie, A., & Thornton, S. L. (1995). Rethinking 'moral panic' for multi-mediated social worlds. *British Journal of Sociology, 46*(4), 559–574.

Mennell, S. ([1985] 1996). *All manners of food: Eating and taste in England and France from the middle ages to the present* (2nd ed.). Urbana, IL: University of Illinois Press.

Meyrick, S., & Cousins, S. (Director). (2007). *Carbon cops* [DVD]. Australia: ABC (Australian Broadcasting Corporation).

Rojek, C. (2007). *Cultural studies.* Cambridge: Polity Press.

*Scientific American – 60-Second Science.* (2010, December 6). Anesthesiologists can help cut climate change [Podcast].

Taylor, M. (Director). (2005). *Global warming: The signs and the science* [DVD]. United States: PBS.

Thompson, K. (1998). *Moral panics.* London: Routledge.

Ungar, S. (1992). The rise and (relative) decline of global warming as a social problem. *Sociological Quarterly, 33*(4), 483–501.

Ungar, S. (2001). Moral panic versus the risk society: The implications of the changing sites of social anxiety. *British Journal of Sociology, 52*(2), 271–291.

Urry, J. (2010). Consuming the Planet to Excess. *Theory, Culture & Society, 27*(2–3), 191–212.

Urry, J. (2011). *Climate change and society.* Cambridge: Polity Press.

Wallis, T., & Pringle, L. (Director). (2007). *Wa$ted!* [DVD]. New Zealand: Fumes NZ Ltd.

# 7 Moral panics as civilizing and decivilizing processes

## A comparative analysis[1]

### Introduction

Having demonstrated in Chapters 5 and 6 how climate change can be explored from both a figurational and a moral panic approach, this chapter goes on to compare several case studies: alcohol, climate change, (illegal) drugs, eating/obesity, terrorism, and tobacco. It will draw from existing research on these examples, research on both moral panic studies and figurational sociology.

The aim of this comparative analysis is twofold. First, to identify the complex, countervailing trends that occur before, during, and after a moral panic, highlighting the complexity of moral panics and therefore dismissing the notion that they are mere 'bad' (or 'good') aberrations. This will aid in the theoretical-conceptual-empirical development of moral panic. Second, to use these case studies to raise some questions about how we conceptualize civilizing and decivilizing processes and civilizing offensives.

By combining this comparative analysis with a discussion of Elias, Foucault, and the concept of moral panic, this chapter will identify several areas where we can further the development of the work of Norbert Elias and figurational sociology. These areas are the relationship between civilizing and decivilizing processes, the relationship between intended and unintended developments, the relationship between short-term and long-term processes, and the role of knowledge in civilizing processes.

### Moral panics

Before we go on to compare these examples, let us first explore the extent to which (some of the) reactions to them might be regarded as moral panics.

#### Alcohol

A small number of moral panic scholars have examined alcohol, specifically the 'gin craze' of the eighteenth century and recent concerns about 'binge drinking' (see Critcher, 2008, 2011a, 2011b; Yeomans, 2009). In 2003, the

New Labour government declared that 'binge drinking' was a serious social problem. Chas Critcher's analysis of several British newspapers illustrates a process of stereotyping people who binge drink, labelling the males as violent or criminals and the females as 'potentially risking their health and/ or sexual integrity' (Critcher, 2008, p. 169). However, he adds that 'binge drinkers' do not make 'impressive folk devils' for they do not induce the same feeling that one will be a likely victim of the 'binge drinker' the way that other folk devils, such as paedophiles and muggers, do. And aside from politicians and journalists, there is little in the way of public outcry and moralization (Critcher, 2008, p. 169).

However, campaigns by health authorities in numerous countries and voluntary organizations such as MADD (Mothers Against Drunk Driving[2]), along with the activities of groups, such as HSM (Hello Sunday Morning[3]), suggest that there is a degree of concern about alcohol and 'binge drinking'. Hier (2008) observes how this moralizing at the individual level, of drinking responsibly and avoiding the risks associated with the self, goes hand in hand with moralizing at the collective level, directed towards the potential (or actual) 'irresponsible' drinker – the 'binge drinker' whose actions, while under the influence of alcohol, are harmful to others. The notion of 'passive drinking' captures the collective moralizing well.

'Passive drinking' has been used in the popular media to refer to the practice of inhaling alcohol vapour or fumes[4] (see Bruce-Briggs, 1988, April 25; Stepney, 1993, December 28). But it has most recently been used by Sir Liam Donaldson, Chief Medical Officer in the UK, to refer to the direct and indirect effects that people's drinking of alcohol has on others – what he terms 'the collateral damage from alcohol' (Donaldson, 2009, pp. 16–23). Comparing alcohol with tobacco (and 'passive smoking'), Donaldson defines 'passive drinking' as 'the consequences of one person's drinking on another's well-being'; these consequences can include 'harm to the unborn fetus, acts of drunken violence, vandalism, sexual assault and child abuse, and a huge health burden carried by both the NHS (National Health Service) and friends and family who care for those damaged by alcohol' (Donaldson, 2009, p. 17). This further extends the responsibility of the 'drinker' to 'the rest of us'.

Critcher does observe, however, the changes in policing, with 'heavier on-the-spot fines, increased arrests for drunkenness and more extensive investigation of under age selling', some of which are related to the Anti-Social Behaviour Act. He concludes that while rhetoric about binge drinking shares similarities with issues such as terrorism, the two threats do not compare: 'binge drinking is a fairly mild moral panic' (Critcher, 2008, p. 170). In contrast, the 'gin craze' is regarded by Critcher as being a much more fully fledged moral panic (Critcher, 2011b), 'one of the first truly modern moral panics in Britain' (Critcher, 2011c, p. 259). The reasons for this difference will be explored later in this chapter.

## Climate change

As already suggested in Chapter 6, several different reactions to climate change can be conceptualized as moral panics. First, we have reactions of concern about 'runaway climate change', urging governments, corporations, and individuals to develop more 'green', 'ethical', moderate ways of living and thus reduce carbon emissions (Cohen, 2011; Rohloff, 2011a). Second are the reactions of climate change 'sceptics' to such campaigns, some of which claim that climate change campaigners and scientists are conspiring to distort and exaggerate the evidence for climate change (Ungar, 2011). And then there is a third possible moral panic: the reaction of campaigners to sceptics, where sceptics themselves become folk devils in the form of climate change 'deniers' (Cohen, 2011). Within these different moral panics, we may have a variety of folk devils: the affluent, SUV-driving, 'gas-guzzling' consumer with a large carbon footprint; big corporations; the extremely rich who 'binge' consume in new 'places of excess'; and climate change 'sceptics'/'deniers'.

## (Illegal) Drugs

In the first published moral panic study, Jock Young (1971a, 1971b) explored the moral panic surrounding marijuana smokers in Notting Hill. Young focussed in particular on the role of the police and how media coverage of the 'drugtakers' influenced police perceptions about them and their policing practices. He argued that the media's amplification and stereotyping of the drugtakers and their activities, combined with the change in policing, contributed to the marginalization of the drugtaker and an amplification of deviance. Since Young's groundbreaking study, several authors have explored moral panics around other (illegal) drugs, such as mephedrone, LSD, and ecstasy (Collins, 2013; Goode, 2008; Hier, 2002).

## Eating/obesity

In the edited collection *Alcohol, Tobacco and Obesity: Morality, Mortality and the New Public Health* (Bell, McNaughton, & Salmon, 2011), several contributors explore the 'obesity panic'. Conversely, Critcher argues that concerns about obesity differ from those around binge drinking – the former, he contends, is less likely to generate a moral panic: 'Binge drinking affects public order; obesity affects the economics of productivity and of health care. Excessive drinkers and those who supply them can be legally prosecuted. Nobody can be taken to court for being fat' (Critcher, 2009, p. 25). Critcher further compares obesity with child abuse and drugtaking:

> Child abuse is evil; some drug taking is evil; foreigners might be evil; obesity is not and never can be evil. Evil represents a challenge to the moral order of such magnitude that it must be identified, named, cast out.
>
> (Critcher, 2009, p. 27)

Here, Critcher seems to be arguing that 'evil' is an extreme example of 'immoral', where something comes to be seen as so immoral that it is perceived to be evil and comes to be personified in 'evil' people – an extreme type of folk devil.

However, we can see at least some evidence to suggest that obesity is being likened to one of Critcher's 'evils': child abuse. LeBesco refers us to a case in the USA, where a mother was charged with the medical neglect of her 555-pound son (LeBesco, 2011, p. 33). LeBosco illustrates that, since the early 1990s, we have witnessed a rapid increase in media coverage of obesity: 'a search for the phrase "obesity epidemic" in the general news of major newspapers in English-speaking countries shows an explosion of interest, from just one hit in 1993 to 770 in 2004' (LeBesco, 2011, p. 35). Campos et al. provide further evidence of moral panic-type media discourse: 'A content analysis of 221 press articles...found that over half employed alarming metaphors such as "time bomb"' (Campos, Saguy, Ernsberger, Oliver, & Gaesser, 2006, p. 58). This suggests that obesity is coming to be increasingly moralized, with a growing concern for the perceived rapid increase in incidences of obesity.

One of the issues with exploring obesity from a moral panic perspective is that by using the phrase 'moral panic' we may be implying that the social problem of obesity does not exist or is not important. This is most evident with the example of tobacco smoking, which we will look at shortly.

### Terrorism

Several authors have explored terrorism from a moral panic framework – indeed, it is probably the most 'obvious' moral panic example I will be looking at in this chapter. Kappeler and Kappeler (2004) illustrate how the rhetoric themes in the political discourse following 9/11 are conducive to dehumanizing terrorists and others viewed as the enemy, and to the construction of a folk devil. Rothe and Muzzatti (2004) further explore the relationship between the increased media and popular culture coverage of terrorism and changing patterns of behaviour amongst Americans – increased displays of patriotism, attacks on mosques, increase in hate crimes – as well as changes in the justice system – (non-public) military trials for suspected terrorists, with no counsel, no proof of guilt beyond a reasonable doubt, and no right of appeal.

Interestingly, Altheide (2009) observes that terrorism was only recently linked to moral panic in academia; in the immediate aftermath of 9/11, moral panic researchers tended to refrain from linking reactions to 9/11 with moral panic. This, Altheide argues, is because many people in the USA and the UK regard terrorism as a legitimate concern. This suggests that only illegitimate concerns can be moral panics. The problem here, again, is one of normativity and value judgements: who decides if concern about a given social problem is legitimate or illegitimate? And why can we not have moral panics about legitimate issues? Stan Cohen ([1972] 2002, 2011) would certainly argue that we can – and perhaps that we should – have moral panics about legitimate issues.

## Tobacco

A subject that, to date, most moral panic researchers have avoided is tobacco smoking. The 'moral panic' entry on *RationalWiki*[5] argues that there are some issues which do cause panic but are 'amoral in nature'. These include 'Global warming; Health dangers from trans fatty acids, obesity and cigarette smoking; Overpopulation; Embryonic stem cell research' (RationalWiki, 2012, 31 January). The author(s) of this *Rational-Wiki* entry seem to be arguing here that smoking tobacco and the other issues mentioned do not involve any moralization and are not seen as threats to the moral order.

Some authors disagree about this lack of moralization. Alan Hunt (2011) argues that tobacco smoking, and other issues, have gone through a process of 'medico-moralization'. He gives the example of secondary or passive smoking, where 'smoking is no longer a choice about personal health, but rather a form of harm imposed on others' (Hunt, 2011, p. 65). While Hunt prefers the concept of moral regulation to moral panic (due to the latter's normative connotations), he does argue that smoking has gone through a process of increasing moralization; indeed, he prefers the concept of 'moralization' to that of 'moral order' or even 'moral regulation' for moralization encourages researchers to focus on *processes* of moralizing (and further argues that it should be used in combination with Foucault's concept of problematization – how and why certain things become a problem) (Hunt, 2011, p. 66). Yet authors such as Critcher (2009) still maintain that reactions to issues such as smoking are not moral panics as smokers do not pose the same kind of threat to the moral order as other groups, such as asylum seekers (akin to his arguments about obesity). This again raises questions about *degrees*: what degree of threat equates to a moral panic? This is an important question, and perhaps instead of focussing on whether or not a given reaction to a perceived problem *is* a moral panic, we can instead use the concept of moral panic (along with other concepts and theories) to develop a greater understanding of the processes involved and thereby develop a more informed understanding about how to direct policy, education, and so on.

The strongest assertion that reactions to passive smoking constitute a moral panic occurs in an episode of an Online Classroom TV podcast titled 'Smoking as a Moral Panic' (2009, 20 May). Host Steve Taylor argues that the moral panic about passive smoking is similar to classic panics, such as those around the Mods and Rockers, and drugtakers, where claims about the problem are false or exaggerated. He goes on to compare tobacco with alcohol, arguing that the harm from 'passive drinking' is greater than that from 'passive smoking' but that the power relations between smokers versus drinkers of alcohol are great as smokers are a minority, and drinkers are a majority (2009, 20 May). While his argument about claims being false or exaggerated may not be accurate, his observation of power relations is interesting. However, he does not go on to explore how it has come to pass that tobacco smoking has declined (in numbers of smokers), whereas alcohol drinking has remained widespread. For this, we can turn to figurational research.

## Moral panics as decivilizing processes

As already argued in Chapters 1 and 3, and elsewhere (see Rohloff, 2008; Rohloff & Wright, 2010), moral panics could be seen as a type of decivilizing episode. We have already explored in Chapter 6 how this might apply to climate change; let us now compare this with other variant examples.

Some of the reactions to alcohol consumption can be conceptualized as partial decivilizing processes. During moral panics about both gin and binge drinking, we have witnessed the introduction of new legislation aimed at increasing social controls – a shift towards increasing social constraint, with perceived decreasing self-constraint (as people are believed to have less self-control over their consumption of alcohol, hence the call for increased social control).

Research also suggests that there has been a shift in modes of knowledge. Yeomans argues the reaction to the Licensing Act 2003 (and the alleged impact it would have on 'binge drinking') 'appears irrational and disproportionate to the level of threat actually posed' (Yeomans, 2009, para. 2.6). Presumably, Yeomans would suggest this could apply to all moral panics about alcohol that have occurred since the first 'gin panic' in the eighteenth century. Such comments suggest an increasing incalculability of the dangers posed by alcohol, or at least an increase in the fantasy-content and a decrease in the reality-congruence of knowledge about alcohol consumption.

In *The Drugtakers* (Young, 1971a), based on research undertaken in the late 1960s with a group of marijuana smokers living in Notting Hill, Jock Young observed a process occurring whereby the population in England was continually changing, and while there was increasing heterogeneity, this *appeared* to be happening at too fast a pace for some people to be able to adjust to. There was no longer the homogenous population to dictate patterns of behaviour; there was ongoing resistance to established ways of behaving, which resulted in the development of subcultures such as bohemianism. There existed the perception that informal social controls (and self-controls) were failing to regulate the behaviour of particular groups (such as the 'drugtakers'), so social control was left largely in the hands of formal agencies, such as the police.

Young focusses particularly on the police for their isolated position and how this plays a role in deviancy amplification. He argues that 'drug taking' begins as a minor actual problem. Via the media's effect, the problem is amplified, and so comes to be perceived as being greater than what it actually is. This perception contributes to police action, which makes the real problem greater, contributing to developments such as increased marginalization of the drugtaker from the rest of society and the progression onto other drugs and other crimes (as unintended outcomes) (Young, 1971a; see also Becker, [1963] 1991, for earlier research on this). If we follow Young's argument, the intentional interventions by the police are contributing to the kinds of things they are trying to prevent: the escalation of occasional marijuana use, the development of heroin use, other crimes, etc. And so it becomes a self-fulfilling prophecy, where perceived decivilizing processes contribute to actual decivilizing processes.

The drugtaker is seen as a threat to the moral standards of both the policeman and the regular criminal; drugtakers are seen as something different altogether, as Young quotes one policeman:

> I tell you, there's something about users that bugs me. I don't know what exactly. You want me to be frank? OK. Well, I can't stand them; I mean I *really* can't stand them. Why? Because they bother me personally. They're *dirty*, that's what they are, filthy. They make my skin crawl. It's funny but I don't get that reaction to ordinary criminals. You pinch a burglar or a pickpocket and you understand each other; you know how it is, you stand around yacking, maybe even crack a few jokes. But Jesus, these guys, they're a danger. You know what I mean, they're like Commies or some of those CORE people. There are some people you can feel sorry for. You know, you go out and pick up some poor chump of a paper hanger [bad-cheque writer] and he's just a drunk and life's got him all bugged. You can understand a poor guy like that. It's different with anybody who'd used drugs.
>
> (policeman, quoted in Young, 1971a, p. 173)

Here, we can see a process of dehumanization – where 'they' (the drugtakers) come to be seen increasingly less like the rest of 'us'.

Young noted how the drugtaker was a visible target to police, with his long hair, unusual style of dress, all of which made him exceedingly visible (Young, 1971a, p. 174). This visibility, along with the power ratios between the police and the media on the one hand, and the drugtakers on the other, meant that the drugtaker was comparatively easy to typify as a folk devil (as compared to the example of climate change).

The media are often our main source of information about events and about people that we have no direct involvement with. But, as Young argues, news has to be 'newsworthy', so the mass media 'selects events which are *atypical*, presents them in a *stereotypical* fashion, and contrasts them against a backcloth of normality which is *overtypical*' (Young, 1971a, p. 179). This further contributes to the notion of a 'deviant them' and a 'good us'; contrasting the 'bad' with the 'good', the 'wrong' with the 'right'.

This is similar in some ways to manners books but in a different format; such media coverage further contributes to the establishment of what is considered acceptable behaviour. How stories are played out in the news could be seen to function as 'moral' narratives in the same way as the much more explicit prescriptive manners books of the past. We can also see similarities with Elias & Scotson's *The Established and the Outsiders* ([1965] 2008), regarding how 'praise gossip' and 'blame gossip' further contribute to amplify divisions between groups, to further contribute to misperceptions about the reality of what all of these people are really like. Instead of showing a complex picture of a variety of people who do and do not smoke marijuana, for example, we are instead presented with polar opposites that are stereotyped and presented as representative of all.

In contrast, it is less clear how reactions to obesity entail decivilizing trends, although the phenomenon of obesity itself may be seen as a partial decivilizing process. It may be too early yet to say, but some developments in the USA, for example, suggest an increasing involvement of the state in the regulation and punishment of those who are obese or are seen to have contributed to someone's obesity (see LeBesco, 2011). The processes of individualization and process reduction – whereby individuals come to be increasingly blamed for obesity (Campos et al., 2006), based on their alleged individual choices (whether it is the individual choices of said person, or the individual choices of their parent or guardian) – do seem to be contributing to misperceptions about obesity and a concomitant decrease in tolerance towards those viewed as 'obese' (or being responsible for obesity).

One might argue that the incidence of obesity is a symptom of decivilizing – where a rapid increasing availability of food has gone hand in hand with a decrease in self-control over eating, or at least self-control has not increased at a fast-enough rate to keep pace with the increasing availability of food. Hughes (2004, November) suggests that with increasing control over natural, social and psychic processes that have enabled the development of stable survival units, the growth of agriculture, and the production of surplus food supplies, we have also witnessed a change in the makeup of the food that we produce – meat has more fat, fruit and vegetables are selectively bred and cultivated to produce goods that are higher in carbohydrates, carbohydrates have come to be increasingly refined, and so on. These developments, he argues, have outpaced the rate of biological evolution: when humans and their ancestors were hunting and foraging, they typically did not have frequent access to large quantities of high carbohydrate food sources – honey being one rare and no doubt infrequent source of high carbohydrates – and the biological processes involved in the intake of high carbohydrate food sources did (and still do) contribute to a greater desire for higher calorie foods (for example, see Page et al., 2011). And so, the changes in the types of food we have access to have gone hand in hand with the development of what Hughes terms the 'infantilization of taste', where there is a trend away from 'sophisticated and nuanced cuisine' towards 'sweet, salty hits that both satiate and leave one unfulfilled', exemplified in the McDonald's burger (Hughes, 2004, November). This 'infantilization of taste', and responses to it, could be seen as a decivilizing outcome of civilizing processes. But this also appears to be occurring alongside civilizing trends, as will be discussed later in this chapter.

It is fairly easy to see how some reactions to terrorism are moral panics and decivilizing processes. The word 'terrorism' itself is used to dehumanize and stigmatize a group, and to delegitimize their actions (Dunning, 2016). Kappeler and Kappeler's analysis of political discourse following 9/11 clearly demonstrates this process, where terrorism is constructed as a threat to civilization, and terrorists are likened to evil barbarians that slither like serpents and are associated with a host of other crimes, such as drugs, kidnapping, robbery, extortion, corruption, and so on (Kappeler & Kappeler, 2004). Those who question this rhetoric, or the actions of those who are on the 'hunt' for these terrorists, are also regarded as aiding 'the enemy'. Any counter discourses are thereby silenced.

This process of dehumanization facilitates the development of increasingly cruel measures and an increase in violence. Welch provides an excellent overview of the human rights violations that have occurred post 9/11, such as those that developed from the USA Patriot Act of 2001 (Welch, 2004). Rothe and Muzzatti demonstrate the increase in violence: attacks on mosques, graffiti such as 'bomb the terrorists', and an increase in hate crimes towards those who look like the current stereotype of a terrorist (Rothe & Muzzatti, 2004).

However, the moral panic literature on terrorism, which highlights the decivilizing trends involved in reactions to terrorism, neglects exploring how the process of terrorism itself develops; for that, we must look elsewhere (for example, see Vertigans, 2011).

The relative absence of moral panic research on tobacco smoking provides us with little evidence for exploring the decivilizing trends in reactions to tobacco smoking. However, throughout the history of tobacco use in the West, we can see episodes where tobacco came to be increasingly problematized and moralized by some (see Bell, 2011; Hughes, 2003). During *some* of these episodes, we can witness an increasing uncertainty about the dangers associated with tobacco, fuelled by the media. For example, in the late nineteenth/early twentieth century, there were growing concerns about mental health issues developing as a result of tobacco. And, indeed, smoking itself was seen to be linked with insanity, with a woman in 1900 being committed to a psychiatric unit because she smoked cigarettes (Hughes, 2003). Newspaper headlines, for example, 'Cigarettes Made Him a Lunatic!' and 'Crazed by Cigarettes' (cited in Hughes, 2003, p. 101), potentially reflected and affected increasing incalculability of the dangers of tobacco smoking[6]. At this stage, however, more research is required to explore the possible moral panics about tobacco and the decivilizing and civilizing trends that may be involved. In a later section of this chapter, we will explore how civilizing offensives may be a useful concept in exploring possible moral panics about tobacco and other issues.

## How civilizing processes contribute to moral panics

I wish to argue that it is not simply the case that all moral panics are merely decivilizing processes, and not all moral panics necessarily fit this 'classic' model of moral panics as decivilizing processes. Indeed, as Elias himself would no doubt have argued, civilizing and decivilizing processes (and, thereby, moral panics) are much more complex than this. Potentially, civilizing processes may contribute to the emergence of moral panics (and moral panics may, in turn, feed back into civilizing processes).

As we saw in the earlier account of *The Drugtakers*, one characteristic of civilizing processes – increasing heterogeneity – in part could be said to have contributed to the development of the moral panic about drugtakers. Perhaps the degree of heterogeneity increased at such a rapid rate that people's personality make-ups did not have time to adjust to these changes. Their response, therefore, took the form of a moral panic, containing decivilizing symptoms, and with attempts to 'reformalize' the process of 'informalization' (on informalization and reformalization, see Wouters, 2007). Along with stereotypes of drug users, the popular understanding of drugtaking as a means to *lose control* can be seen to exemplify fears associated with informalization; fears that a shift towards more informal codes, with behaviours that were once seen as 'bad' now being accepted, will result in a decrease in self-control and a growth in immorality. These fears then contribute to the development of attempts to *maintain control* in the form of increasing social controls over those who are seen to be most at risk – processes of reformalization. In this way, some moral panics can also be seen not just in relation to civilizing and decivilizing processes but also to informalizing and reformalizing processes.

Increasing division of labour and functional democratization, also symptoms of civilizing processes, similarly contributed to the moral panic about drugtaking and the decivilizing trends that accompanied it. As we saw earlier, the police, along with members of the public, had little direct access to the issues and the people involved (i.e. drugtakers and drugtaking). This meant that they were reliant on highly mediated sources of information – media portrayals, rumour, and so on. This mediated knowledge facilitated the distortion of the reality of the social problem, contributing to increasing the fantasy-content and decreasing the reality-congruence of knowledge about drugtakers.

Within the three possible climate change moral panics, civilizing processes may be giving rise to decivilizing trends in several ways, particularly in the area of knowledge. The long-term civilizing trend of the monopolization of scientific knowledge through increasing specialization within scientific establishments (where knowledge becomes less and less accessible to those outside the specialism) has contributed to what Ungar (2000) calls a 'knowledge-ignorance paradox'. While everyone potentially has access to this knowledge, to be able to have readily full access to it they have to learn the language of that specialism and how to interpret its knowledge. Due to the time it would take to 'learn the language' of each specialism and due to the sheer number that exist, there is a relative illiteracy between areas of knowledge. And so, people come increasingly to rely upon mediated, popular, simplified versions of knowledge, as we saw in the example of the drugtakers. For climate change, the numbers of different disciplines that are contributing to the science of climate change further complicate this as it is difficult for even one specialist to grasp all the areas of expertise required to understand all the different methods that contribute to what we know (and what we do not know) about climate change. And so, the monopolization of knowledge by scientific establishments coincides with a de-monopolization of knowledge via the public sphere – popular, mediated versions of scientific knowledge that scientific establishments may have little control over (Rohloff, 2011a). In this way, the civilizing trend of increased division of labour in science has contributed to the development of mediated knowledge, facilitating the campaigns by both climate change advocates and climate change sceptics, and allowing for increasing uncertainty about the relative dangers of climate change.

In a different way, civilizing processes may be contributing to moral panics about alcohol use. Critcher (2011b) identifies several processes that contributed to the 'gin craze'. He notes how, from the late seventeenth to early eighteenth centuries, England had a surplus of grain, which was, in turn, used to make alcohol. At the same time, the government passed laws to encourage the production of spirits in England (and prohibited imports). This contributed to a great increase in the production and consumption of gin. Many of those involved (in both drinking and selling gin) were female. It thus contributed to shifting power relations between males and females. However, by providing employment for women, it was seen at the time to be wrongfully taking them away from their domestic duties. Gin soon came to be seen as the source of all things evil and was targeted as a problem drink (while people were encouraged to instead drink alternatives such as beer). Subsequently, the government passed eight acts of parliament, including ones to increase taxes and licensing fees. Later, poor harvests resulted in a ban on using grain for distilling alcohol (Critcher, 2011b).

We can see, then, how rapid changes in the power relations between men and women, changes towards more equal relations, were responded to with increasing social controls and an increase in the fantasy-content (and decrease in the reality-congruence) of knowledge about gin drinking. It could also be the case that the sudden wide availability of gin happened at such a fast rate that people did not have time to gradually adjust and develop self-restraint towards the consumption of gin.

In contrast to these moral panic approaches, Gerritsen (2000), in his study of the regulation of alcohol (and opiates), uses Elias to highlight some of the long-term processes that have contributed to the development of different ways alcohol is regulated, consumed, and perceived. We might extend Gerritsen's work to explore how these long-term processes he identifies feed into various moral panics about alcohol. During the nineteenth century, as the temperance movement was developing, Gerritsen notes how at the same time industrialization was changing workers' jobs. Many people, who had previously worked on the land, were increasingly required to work in factories where they had to adjust to a new way of working: 'they had to learn more controlled and more predictable patterns of behaviour; the mechanized and factory-based production methods made this indispensable' (Gerritsen, 2000, p. 144). This regulation of people's personalities at work transferred to their lives outside work as well, and so they came to be more disciplined in all areas of their lives. This is just one example of how one aspect of civilizing processes contributed to changing standards of behaviour, thereby contributing to concerns about the amount of alcohol people were consuming and how alcohol affected their behaviour. And so, we can see how civilizing processes can contribute to moral panics – and possible decivilizing trends – about alcohol.

Looking at the time period from the Middle Ages to the present, Stephen Mennell (1987) provides an argument for viewing changes in appetite as paralleling long-term civilizing processes. The civilizing of appetite, including increasing self-restraint on appetite and a shift in focus from quantity to quality of food, was made possible by the increasing security of food supplies. This security of food supplies was only made possible by civilizing processes such as increasing state control over violence and taxation, the development of a commercial economy, increasing division of labour, and increasing extension of trade. As food became more widely available more often, increasing competition between the classes contributed to growing anxieties and fear from 'those below', which resulted in the development of the sumptuary laws (Mennell, 1987). [Could this be an example of a moral panic? Alan Hunt certainly looks at the process as an example of moral regulation (Hunt, 1995).] These sumptuary laws restricted what one could eat and what one could wear, in an attempt to prevent lower classes from emulating the upper classes. In this sense, civilizing processes may have contributed to a process of moral regulation, and a period of panic, perhaps it can even be described as a moral panic.

The civilizing of appetite itself could be seen to be contributing to the emergence of concern about obesity. The development from the mid-eighteenth century onwards of favouring quality of food over quantity and using more refined and delicate styles of eating, with small, delicate, costly dishes, have in the long term coincided with an increasing awareness and anxiety about overeating and obesity (Mennell, 1987). It is similar to Elias's argument about child abuse: with long-term changes in relations between children and their parents that have gone alongside civilizing processes, we have seen a growing development of concern about children (Elias, [1980] 2008). This explains why, today, a majority of people are concerned about child abuse, and indeed what constitutes child abuse is forever expanding as standards of behaviour rise, and those actions that were formerly tolerated are now regarded as a form of abuse.

We can see, in part, how standards of etiquette and the associated quest for distinction may have contributed to campaigns to reduce or alter tobacco use. Etiquette manuals and manners books are filled with instructions on how to smoke. Before the increasing medicalization of tobacco, etiquette dictated how one consumed tobacco. And in terms of what we now call 'passive smoking', only gradually were these arguments that were originally based on aesthetics transformed into medical arguments concerned with the dangers posed to one's health (Hughes, 2003). This is not to say, necessarily, that these changes in etiquette corresponded, at times, to moral panics. Due to the absence of moral panic research on this topic, all we can say at this stage is that there might have been moral panics about tobacco, and then investigate further. We can say, however, that the civilizing of tobacco smoking – how the long-term changes in tobacco use paralleled a civilizing process, similar to changes in appetite – may have facilitated the development of moral panics about passive smoking (if, indeed, there have been moral panics about passive smoking; perhaps, instead, we might say the increasing moralization of tobacco smoking).

## How moral panics contribute to civilizing processes

In contrast to seeing moral panics as simply decivilizing trends, we could also conceptualize them as civilizing offensives or civilizing spurts that may further the development of civilizing processes.

In the last section about alcohol, we explored how civilizing processes such as industrialization, and the changes in behaviour accompanying it, contributed to a moral panic about alcohol use. We can argue that this particular moral panic (which occurred during the temperance movement) may have contributed, in the long term, to increasing self-restraint.

Similarly, moral panics about climate change, at least those that are seeking to highlight the dangers of climate change and bring about change before it is too late, can be regarded as civilizing offensives. Many aspects of climate change campaigns share similarities with campaigns about alcohol, tobacco, and obesity. All of these forms of consumption – eating, drinking, and smoking – have experienced long-term changes towards increasing moderation, as discussed earlier (Hughes, 2003; Mennell, 1987). Likewise, there now exist many guides on 'living green' or stopping climate change that urge consumers to decrease their overall consumption; stop 'bingeing'; and overcome their addictions to consuming, shopping, and fossil fuels.

Climate change moral panics can thus be seen as civilizing spurts, as attempts to accelerate the development of 'ecological civilizing processes'.

For the example of the drugtakers, it is less clear how that particular moral panic may have contributed to civilizing processes in the long term. Nevertheless, the moral indignation directed at the drugtakers can perhaps be understood as a civilizing offensive that is rationalized in the rhetoric of humanitarianism. A rhetoric of 'saving' or 'bettering' these people is used to mask the 'moral or material conflicts behind the mantle of humanitarianism' (Young, 1971a, p. 99). This is perhaps similar to Robert van Krieken's (1999) argument that civilizing offensives may be carried out in the name of civilization but may contain within them decivilizing symptoms.

Stephen Mennell notes how the incidence of obesity is most prevalent in (a) the poorest people within the world's more affluent societies and (b) the privileged few in the Third World. This, he argues, is due to several reasons. First, there needs to be an abundant supply of food for people to be able to eat enough on a regular basis in order to be classified as obese. Second, he argues 'clinical evidence suggests that psychological pressures to overeat are often rooted in past hunger, perhaps in a previous generation' (Mennell, 1987, p. 397). Perhaps, with the rapid increase in supply of food to people who, until comparatively recently, had a less stable supply of food, the 'civilizing of appetite' has not had a chance to develop at a fast-enough rate. Could moral panics about obesity function as a civilizing spurt to further the civilizing of appetite? Perhaps. But they may also have unintended decivilizing consequences as so many moral panics have.

Perhaps, some of the outrage directed at the decivilizing trends (such as torture and other cruel activities mentioned earlier) that have developed with current moral panics about terrorism will feed into a growing desire to 'civilize' the world and prevent such cruel measures from occurring. Andrew Linklater (2007) argues that the war on terror not only highlights decivilizing aspects but also illustrates a global civilizing process, reflected in the global condemnation of the torture that has occurred. Perhaps, such episodes of moral panic (and the associated decivilizing trends), leading unintentionally to the condemnation of those activities, will contribute, in the long term, to increasing civilized self-restraints.

Some of the different campaigns directed at tobacco may have contributed to civilizing processes (if not, then they may have merely reflected them). It is interesting to note that in a recent study, people who were successful in quitting smoking were most often motivated by health (Aarts, Goudsblom, Schmidt, & Spier, 1995). But once again, as already mentioned in the previous sections on tobacco, more research is required on this topic. However, I would suggest that some of the developments for alcohol, obesity, and climate change could be very similar to those for tobacco as they all focus on consumption and moderation; the 'civilizing of appetite' (Mennell, 1987) certainly shares some similarities with the civilizing of tobacco use (Hughes, 2003).

The examples discussed in this chapter highlight the complexity of moral panics, of civilizing offensives, and of civilizing and decivilizing processes. How can this inform our understanding of moral panic? How can it aid our theoretical-conceptual-methodological development of moral panic? First, let us utilize the aforementioned analysis to inform our understandings about 'good' and 'bad' moral panics.

## Good and bad moral panics

What implications does the previous comparative analysis have for the tendency to normatively judge moral panics as being 'bad' events? The following two extracts are taken from Stan Cohen's Introduction to the third edition of *Folk Devils and Moral Panics* in a section titled 'Good and Bad Moral Panics?':

> It is obviously true that the uses of the [moral panic] concept to expose disproportionality and exaggeration have come from within a left liberal consensus. The empirical project is concentrated on (if not reserved for) cases where the moral outrage appears driven by conservative or reactionary forces...the point [of moral panic research] was to expose social reaction not just as over-reaction in some quantitative sense, but first, as *tendentious* (that is, slanted in a particular ideological direction) and second, as *misplaced* or *displaced* (that is, aimed – whether deliberately or thoughtlessly – at a target which was not the 'real' problem).
>
> (Cohen, [1972] 2002, p. xxxi)

> Perhaps we could purposely *recreate* the conditions that made the Mods and Rockers panic so successful (exaggeration, sensitization, symbolization, prediction, etc.) and thereby overcome the barriers of denial, passivity and indifference that prevent a full acknowledgement of human cruelty and suffering.
>
> (Cohen, [1972] 2002, p. xxxiii)

The first extract clearly illustrates the assumption – the presupposition – that moral panics are seen as 'bad'. However, while they are deemed to be 'bad' in the eyes of the researcher, no doubt in some instances those involved in the panic thought that they were doing 'good' (their intentions may have been good, but they may have had unintended outcomes). This illustrates the necessity for moral panic researchers to look beyond the 'conservative' examples that are typical of the classic moral panics; no doubt the political context of the 1960s/1970s contributed to a particular research focus that has left a legacy where the 'political project' (Critcher, 2009) of moral panic research remains a prime focus, thereby limiting the application, exploration, and development of the concept of moral panic (see Garland, 2008; Rohloff & Wright, 2010).

In stark contrast to this, in the second extract earlier, Cohen suggests the possibility of purposefully engineering moral panics, to overcome the denial of atrocities (linking in with his work on the flipside of panic: denial; see Cohen, 2001). One could say that Cohen's idea of a good moral panic is similar to the idea of a civilizing offensive or a civilizing spurt. However, I wish to suggest that even Cohen's hypothetical 'good' panics could have unintended, disintegrative, decivilizing outcomes; given certain conditions, rather than merely bringing attention to atrocities and overcoming denial, the 'good' panic may contribute to further cruelty and suffering[7]. Furthermore, if the 'good' panic is still not well informed, it may lead to further denial; communicating emotion and fear, rather than enabling, may instead be disabling (for example, in relation to climate change, see O'Neill & Nicholson-Cole, 2009).

One of the important contributions of Cohen's suggestion of 'good' and 'bad' moral panics is as a heuristic device. As we have seen, moral panic has largely been conceptualized in negative terms, as a 'bad' episode that needs remedying and even debunking. The introduction of the term 'good moral panic' may help to shift the focus of moral panic studies towards those examples that in the past have largely been neglected (climate change, tobacco smoking, obesity, and so on) as campaigns surrounding those issues are increasingly supported by moral panic researchers (see Cohen, 2011, for a discussion on the changing relationship between researchers and the campaigns they are investigating), and where the notion of debunking would not necessarily apply. This expansion of the selection of real-type examples for analysis would then more widely inform the conceptualization of the ideal-type process of moral panic (on the relationship between real type and ideal type in moral panic analysis, see Wright, 2011).

While the notion of 'good' moral panic is useful as a heuristic device, we need to be wary of the dichotomy of bad and good moral panics, or moral panics as *either* decivilizing processes *or* civilizing spurts. As we have seen earlier, moral panics are much more complex than this.

## Moral panics as civilizing and decivilizing processes

As argued elsewhere (Rohloff, 2011b; Rohloff & Wright, 2010), one way to overcome this dichotomy – of good or bad, of civilizing or decivilizing – is to utilize a figurational approach to moral panic studies. This would involve efforts to reduce the intrusion of 'heteronomous valuations' (Elias, [1970] 2012) into moral panic research and remove the normative presupposition that a particular reaction to a given issue is an inappropriate reaction in need of debunking. Such a method would require a detour via detachment and a subsequent secondary involvement (Elias, [1987] 2007) to allow for the possibility of intervention after the research has been completed (for example, to suggest more adequate responses to perceived problems). Combining this with a figurational approach that focusses on long-term developments, exploring gradual processes that influence the development of panics, can also help to overcome the inherent bias within moral panic studies (this is already happening, to a certain extent, with some researchers incorporating moral regulation approaches (for example, see Hier, 2008; Hunt, 2011)).

As well as employing these methods, we can combine all that we have learned from the aforementioned comparative discussion to focus on exploring both civilizing and decivilizing trends, to conceptualize moral panics as civilizing offensives with both civilizing and decivilizing implications. Such an approach can take account of the interplay of complex civilizing and decivilizing processes that are developing before, during, and after moral panics, thereby avoiding the dichotomy of 'good' or 'bad' moral panics.

We can take climate change and broader environmental and animal rights campaigns as an example. As outlined earlier, moral panic research has explored the role of information and knowledge in climate change – both in campaigns by those who are demanding action to mitigate climate change and in campaigns by climate change sceptics. Ungar in particular explores what he terms 'strong' and 'weak' disproportionality; the former referring to claims by sceptics that scientists are distorting and exaggerating, the latter referring to climate campaigners focussing on claims that represent the direst threats (Ungar, 2011). In relation to the argument that climate change campaigns represent civilizing offensives to further civilizing processes (Rohloff, 2011a), there has been some figurational research that has argued that the development of ecological sensibilities could be seen as a type of civilizing process (Quilley, 2009; Schmidt, 1993). The development of the phenomenon of climate change may, in part, have been contributed to by certain outcomes of processes of civilization, where decivilizing consequences have resulted in the form of *excess* capitalism and *over*consumption, to the relative detriment of the environment and social life as a whole (see Ampudia de Haro, 2008). Moral panics about climate change (excluding those instigated by sceptics) might be used as a civilizing offensive to bring about a civilizing 'spurt'.

While we might be tempted to classify such a moral panic as a civilizing offensive with civilizing effects, we must consider its possible decivilizing trends as well. One has already been mentioned: the strong and weak disproportionality, contributing to increasingly incalculability of danger. Another decivilizing disintegrative process could occur via the development of 'good' and 'bad' behaviours into 'good' and 'bad' people. This is already occurring, through the emergence of such terms as 'eco-friendly', 'eco-criminal', and 'eco-deviant'. Potentially, if standards of behaviour increased to such an extent, those who do not behave in an eco-friendly enough manner might come to be seen as a great enough threat to the planet and, thereby, every person. Then, mutual identification between the 'eco-friendly' and the 'eco-deviant' may decrease, contributing to changes in the way these groups interact. Such a process is already happening, to a limited extent, with a minority of animal rights and environmental activists who prioritize animal/environmental rights over the rights of people they see to be threatening certain animals and environments. Here, increasing mutual identification with animals and the environment is accompanied with a decreasing mutual identification with some other people (for example, see Quilley, 2009, p. 133). And so, we see civilizing processes occurring alongside decivilizing processes. Consequently, moral panics over climate change could be regarded as having both, potentially, civilizing and decivilizing implications.

## Elias and Foucault: on (de)civilizing processes and moral panics

Having outlined how moral panics can be explored as instances of civilizing offensives with both civilizing and decivilizing potential, we now turn to bring an additional approach into the discussion – Foucault's – to further rethink the notions of civilizing and decivilizing processes, intended and unintended developments, short- and long-term processes, and the role of knowledge in processes of civilization.

Before we turn to Foucault, let us first recap on what combining Elias's theory of civilizing processes and the concept of moral panic can suggest about civilizing and decivilizing processes. To date, decivilizing processes have been conceptualized as civilizing processes in reverse (Mennell, 1990), occurring where there is an increase in actual danger and a decrease in the calculability of danger. Conversely, as we have seen earlier, some moral panics occur where there is only a perceived, and not necessarily an actual, increase in danger. This suggests that we may need to expand how we conceptualize decivilizing processes, taking into consideration both realities and perceptions, and the interplay between the two. An additional issue arises when we ask the question: is this particular episode civilizing or decivilizing? Is this even an important question? Does it increase the likelihood of falling into a dichotomous trap (as with good and bad moral panics)? Should we instead be exploring both the civilizing and decivilizing trends that are occurring in any given period of time that we are studying, without concerning ourselves with which ones are dominant? But if we *do* want to, how do we quantifiably assess the dominance of civilizing processes over decivilizing processes, or vice versa? The question of the relationship between civilizing and decivilizing processes will be further explored in Chapter 8.

An additional question we can draw out of the combination between moral panics and de/civilizing processes research is of the relationship between intended and unintended developments. As argued elsewhere (Rohloff & Wright, 2010), some researchers have conceptualized moral panics as intentional developments (while others have characterized them as unintentional). It is well recognized that, while Elias acknowledged that people 'act intentionally, their intentions always arise from and [are] directed towards developments not planned by them' (Elias, [1980] 2008, p. 32). Elias is thus regarded as focussing on unplanned developments (even though his 'process model' 'encompasses at its nucleus a dialectical movement between intentional and unintentional social changes' (Elias, [1980] 2008, p. 32)). Foucault, on the other hand, is seen to focus on planned action (Binkley, Dolan, Ernst, & Wouters, 2010, pp. 75–6). Combining approaches from Foucault and Elias, as exemplified in moral panic research, may help to overcome this division between intended and unintended developments. If we utilize the concept of civilizing offensive, we can devote more space to exploring the relatively neglected area of the relationship between processes and offensives, between the unplanned and the planned. As Dunning and Sheard ([1979] 2005, p. 280) and van Krieken (1990, p. 366) argue, this is an area of relative neglect in figurational research.

Inextricably tied into planned action and unplanned developments is the relationship between short- and long-term processes. Moral panic research has tended to focus on the short term, implying (perhaps in a Foucauldian way) the occurrence of an epistemic rupture. All of a sudden, a problem is identified, and we have a moral panic. This focus on sudden, abrupt change is similar to Foucault's focus on ruptures, discontinuities, breaks, and so on (Binkley et al., 2010; Foucault, [1969] 2002). This contrasts with Elias's attention to the long term. Similar to the aforementioned, if we combine the work of Foucault and Elias, in the case of moral panics (and other examples), we can explore the interrelation between short-term and long-term processes, thereby developing a more encompassing method for sociological research.

### The role of knowledge in civilizing (and decivilizing) processes

As already outlined in the case studies discussed earlier, the role of knowledge in civilizing and decivilizing processes (and moral panics) should be of central focus. Research on decivilizing (and dyscivilizing) processes in particular tends to focus on the role of violence – on its monopolization and de-monopolization by a central state authority (for example, see de Swaan, 2001; Fletcher, 1997; Mennell, 1990). However, as the cases discussed earlier suggest, as does the development of moral panics more generally, the monopolization and de-monopolization of knowledge can also play a prominent role in the development of decivilizing processes.

Increased reliance upon expert knowledge – the expertization and monopolization of knowledge – leads to increased interdependencies, characteristic of civilizing processes, but this can also contribute to decivilizing trends. For example, with a moral panic, where claims may be exaggerated, distorted, or even invented, danger may come to be perceived as greater than it actually is[8]. Thus, as with the monopolization of violence, the monopolization of knowledge may also entail the potential for 'dyscivilizing processes' (de Swaan, 2001), as may be the case with 'elite engineered' (Goode & Ben-Yehuda, [1994] 2009) moral panics.

Conversely, the growth in alternative media and the advent of the Internet have increasingly enabled the possibility for alternative claims and counter-claims, thereby reducing the monopolization of knowledge in some cases. The decrease in monopolization may then contribute to danger becoming increasingly incalculable (who's knowledge, or claims, do we believe?). This rise in the incalculability of danger may then contribute to rising fears and anxieties, which may then be expressed as moral panics. And so, the de-monopolization of knowledge, as with violence, may contribute to deciv-ilizing processes. However, the de-monopolization of knowledge may also assist in the prevention of moral panics and, when they do occur, foreshorten the process of moral panics; for, in 'multi-mediated social worlds', dissenting voices may be readily voiced and heard (McRobbie & Thornton, 1995).

## Conclusion

This chapter has compared several moral panic case studies – alcohol, climate change, drugtaking, eating/obesity, terrorism, and tobacco – to analyze and flesh out the civilizing and decivilizing processes that occur before, during, and after moral panics. The analysis has furthered the de-velopment of moral panic research by highlighting that panics are much more complex processes than what many researchers tend to recognize. In doing so, I have attempted to address the issue with moral panics being conceptualized dichotomously as either bad or good moral panics (while acknowledging the usefulness of this as a heuristic).

For figurational research, the aforementioned discussion has contributed to efforts to further develop theorizing and research on the relationship between civilizing and decivilizing processes, questioning how we concep-tualize and quantify these processes. In drawing attention to the relatively neglected role of knowledge, I have highlighted an additional area of re-search to pursue, one that may contribute to how we conceptualize the development of processes of civilization.

The comparison between Elias, Foucault, and moral panic highlights the value of figurational researchers engaging with non-Eliasian concepts and theories. Through combining these three areas of research, we can begin to explore the relatively neglected areas of the relationship between short- and long-term processes, and intended and unintended developments, and possibly much more.

In the next and final chapter, I return to the research aims that were introduced in Chapter 1. I suggest how the research findings can inform understanding about climate change. I build upon the discussion presented here and in Chapter 4, of how moral panic should be conceptualized and how moral panic research should be undertaken. Following on from this comparative chapter, I then discuss the relationship between civilizing pro-cesses and civilizing offensives and answer some of the questions posed earlier about decivilizing processes.

## Notes

1 An earlier version of this chapter was written for the figurational sociology special issue of the journal *Política y Sociedad / Politics and Society*, see Rohloff (2013).
2 madd.org.
3 hellosundaymorning.com.au.
4 This is akin to the notion of 'secondary smoke': non-smokers inhaling the smoke of smokers.
5 rationalwiki.org/wiki/Moral_panic.
6 This uncertainty of the dangers gradually decreased with developments in research on tobacco.
7 For example, while some might argue that drugs are 'bad' and in need of regulation, Spierenburg (2008, pp. 216–8) notes how the criminalization of drugs has gone hand in hand with an increase in violence and organized crime, and the spread of drug addiction – unintended outcomes, similar to those that developed during the prohibition era.
8 Although this is not necessarily always the case, as can be seen with the example of climate change (Rohloff, 2011a).

## References

Aarts, W., Goudsblom, J., Schmidt, K., & Spier, F. (1995). *Toward a morality of moderation: Report for the Dutch national research programme on global air pollution and climate change*. Amsterdam: Amsterdam School for Social Science Research.

Altheide, D. L. (2009). Moral panic: From sociological concept to public discourse. *Crime Media Culture, 5*(1), 79–99.

Ampudia de Haro, F. (2008). *Discussing decivilisation: Some theoretical remarks*. Paper presented at the First ISA Forum of Sociology: Sociological Research and Public Debate.

Becker, H. S. ([1963] 1991). *Outsiders: Studies in the sociology of deviance*. New York: Free Press.

Bell, K. (2011). Legislating abjection? Second-hand smoke, tobacco-control policy and the public's health. In K. Bell, D. McNaughton, & A. Salmon (Eds.), *Alcohol, tobacco and obesity: Morality, mortality and the new public health* (pp. 73–89). London: Routledge.

Bell, K., McNaughton, D., & Salmon, A. (Eds.). (2011). *Alcohol, tobacco and obesity: Morality, mortality and the new public health*. London: Routledge.

Binkley, S., Dolan, P., Ernst, S., & Wouters, C. (2010). The planned and the unplanned: A roundtable discussion on the legacies of Michel Focuault and Norbert Elias. *Foucault Studies, 8*, 53–77.

Bruce-Briggs, B. (1988, April 25). The health police are blowing smoke: Bolstered by bad science, the war on passive smoking is a trial run for a larger program of social manipulation. *Fortune [CNN Money]*. Retrieved April 20, 2012, from money. cnn.com/magazines/fortune/fortune_ archive/1988/04/25/70438/index.htm.

Campos, P., Saguy, A., Ernsberger, P., Oliver, E., & Gaesser, G. (2006). The epidemiology of overweight and obesity: Public health crisis or moral panic? *International Journal of Epidemiology, 35*, 55–60.

Cohen, S. (2001). *States of denial: Knowing about atrocities and suffering*. Cambridge: Polity Press.

Cohen, S. ([1972] 2002). *Folk devils and moral panics: The creation of the mods and rockers* (3rd ed.). London: Routledge.

Cohen, S. (2011). Whose side were we on? The undeclared politics of moral panic theory. *Crime, Media, Culture, 7*(3), 237–243.

Collins, J. (2013). Moral panics, governmentality and the media: A comparative approach to the analysis of illegal drug use in the news. In C. Critcher, J. Hughes, J. Petley, & A. Rohloff (Eds.), *Moral panics in the contemporary world* (pp. 125–144). London: Bloomsbury Academic.

Critcher, C. (2008). Moral panics and newspaper coverage of binge drinking. In B. Franklin (Ed.), *Pulling newspapers apart* (pp. 162–171). London: Routledge.

Critcher, C. (2009). Widening the focus: Moral panics as moral regulation. *British Journal of Criminology, 49*(1), 17–34.

Critcher, C. (2011a). Double measures: The moral regulation of alcohol consumption, past and present. In P. Bramham & S. Wagg (Eds.), *The new politics of leisure and pleasure* (pp. 32–44). Basingstoke: Palgrave Macmillan.

Critcher, C. (2011b). Drunken antics: The gin craze, binge drinking and the political economy of moral regulation. In S. Hier (Ed.), *Moral panic and the politics of anxiety* (pp. 171–189). London: Routledge.

Critcher, C. (2011c). For a political economy of moral panics. *Crime, Media, Culture, 7*(3), 259–275.

de Swaan, A. (2001). Dyscivilization, mass extermination and the state. *Theory, Culture & Society, 18*(2–3), 265–276.

Donaldson, L. (2009). *150 years of the annual report of the chief medical officer: On the state of public health 2008.* London: Department of Health.

Dunning, M. (2016). 'Established and outsiders': Brutalisation processes and the development of 'jihadist terrorists'. *Historical Social Research, 41*(3), 31–53.

Dunning, E., & Sheard, K. ([1979] 2005). *Barbarians, gentlemen and players: A sociological study of the development of rugby football* (2nd ed.). London: Routledge.

Elias, N. ([1970] 2012). *What is sociology? (The collected works of Norbert Elias, Vol. 5).* Dublin: University College Dublin Press.

Elias, N. ([1980] 2008). The civilising of parents. In R. Kilminster & S. Mennell (Eds.), *Essays II: On civilising processes, state formation and national identity (The collected works of Norbert Elias, Vol. 15)* (pp. 14–40). Dublin: University College Dublin Press.

Elias, N. ([1987] 2007). *Involvement and detachment (The collected works of Norbert Elias, Vol. 8).* Dublin: University College Dublin Press.

Elias, N., & Scotson, J. L. ([1965] 2008). *The established and the outsiders (The collected works of Norbert Elias, Vol. 4).* Dublin: University College Dublin Press.

Fletcher, J. (1997). *Violence and civilization: An introduction to the work of Norbert Elias.* Cambridge: Polity Press.

Foucault, M. ([1969] 2002). *Archaeology of knowledge.* London: Routledge.

Garland, D. (2008). On the concept of moral panic. *Crime Media Culture, 4*(1), 9–30.

Gerritsen, J.-W. (2000). *The control of fuddle and flash: A sociological history of the regulation of alcohol and opiates.* Leiden: Brill.

Goode, E. (2008). Moral panics and disproportionality: The case of LSD use in the sixties. *Deviant Behavior, 29,* 533–543.

Goode, E., & Ben-Yehuda, N. ([1994] 2009). *Moral panics: The social construction of deviance* (2nd ed.). Chichester: Wiley-Blackwell.

Hier, S. P. (2002). Raves, risks and the ecstasy panic: A case study in the subversive nature of moral regulation. *Canadian Journal of Sociology/Cahiers canadiens de sociologie, 27*(1), 33–57.

Hier, S. P. (2008). Thinking beyond moral panic: Risk, responsibility, and the politics of moralization. *Theoretical Criminology, 12*(2), 173–190.

Hughes, J. (2003). *Learning to smoke: Tobacco use in the West.* Chicago, IL: University of Chicago Press.

Hughes, J. (2004, November). Personal correspondence that the author has permitted me to cite.

Hunt, A. (1995). Moralizing luxury: The discourses of the governance of consumption. *Journal of Historical Sociology, 8*(4), 352–374.

Hunt, A. (2011). Fractious rivals? Moral panics and moral regulation. In S. P. Hier (Ed.), *Moral Panic and the Politics of Anxiety* (pp. 53–70). London: Routledge.

Kappeler, V. E., & Kappeler, A. E. (2004). Speaking of evil and terrorism: The political and ideological construction of a moral panic. *Sociology of Crime, Law and Deviance, 5*, 175–197.

LeBesco, K. (2011). Neoliberalism, public health and the moral perils of fatness. In K. Bell, D. McNaughton & A. Salmon (Eds.), *Alcohol, Tobacco and Obesity: Morality, Mortality and the New Public Health* (pp. 33–46). London: Routledge.

Linklater, A. (2007). Torture and civilisation. *International Relations, 21*(1), 111–118.

McRobbie, A., & Thornton, S. L. (1995). Rethinking 'moral panic' for multi-mediated social worlds. *British Journal of Sociology, 46*(4), 559–574.

Mennell, S. (1987). On the civilizing of appetite. *Theory, Culture & Society, 4*, 373–403.

Mennell, S. (1990). Decivilising processes: Theoretical significance and some lines of research. *International Sociology, 5*(2), 205–223.

O'Neill, S., & Nicholson-Cole, S. (2009). "Fear won't do it": Promoting positive engagement with climate change through visual and iconic representations. *Science Communication, 30*(3), 355–379.

Online Classroom TV. (2009, 20 May). Smoking as a moral panic [Podcast]. Retrieved April 20, 2011, from http://onlineclassroom.tv/ sociology/podcast/ smoking_as_a_moral_panic.

Page, K. A., Seo, D., Belfort-DeAguiar, R., Lacadie, C., Dzuira, J., Naik, S., et al. (2011). Circulating glucose levels modulate neural control of desire for high-calorie foods in humans. *Journal of Clinical Investigation, 121*(10), 4161–4169.

Quilley, S. (2009). The land ethic as an ecological civilizing process: Aldo Leopold, Norbert Elias, and environmental philosophy. *Environmental Ethics, 31*(2), 115–134.

RationalWiki. (2012, 31 January). Moral panic. Retrieved March 2, 2012, from http://rationalwiki.org/wiki/Moral_panic.

Rohloff, A. (2008). Moral panics as decivilising processes: Towards an Eliasian approach. *New Zealand Sociology, 23*(1), 66–76.

Rohloff, A. (2011a). Extending the concept of moral panic: Elias, climate change and civilization. *Sociology, 45*(4), 634–649.

Rohloff, A. (2011b). Shifting the focus? Moral panics as civilizing and decivilizing processes. In S. P. Hier (Ed.), *Moral panic and the politics of anxiety* (pp. 71–85). London: Routledge.

Rohloff, A. (2013) Moral panics as civilizing and decivilizing processes? A comparative analysis. *Política y Sociedad, 50*(2), 483–500.

Rohloff, A., & Wright, S. (2010). Moral panic and social theory: Beyond the heuristic. *Current Sociology, 58*(3), 403–419.

Rothe, D., & Muzzatti, S. L. (2004). Enemies everywhere: Terrorism, moral panic, and US civil society. *Critical Criminology, 12*, 327–350.

Schmidt, C. (1993). On economization and ecologization as civilizing processes. *Environmental Values, 2*(1), 33–46.

Spierenburg, P. (2008). *A history of murder: Personal violence in Europe from the Middle Ages to the present.* Cambridge: Polity Press.

Stepney, R. (1993, December 28). Health: Drunk? But not a drop passed my lips: Did you know that you can get tipsy simply by breathing in the fumes from other people's booze? Rob Stepney looks at the risks and possibilities of passive drinking. *The Independent.* Retrieved April 20, 2012, from www.independent.co.uk/life-style/health-and-families/health-news/health-drunk-but-not-a-drop-passed-my-lips-did-you-know-that-you-can-get-tipsy-simply-by-breathing-in-the-fumes-from-other-peoples-booze-rob-stepney-looks-at-the-risks-and-possibilities-of-passive-drinking-1469632.html.

Ungar, S. (2000). Knowledge, ignorance and the popular culture: Climate change versus the ozone hole. *Public Understanding of Science, 9*(3), 297–312.

Ungar, S. (2011). The artful creation of global moral panic: Climatic folk devils, environmental evangelicals, and the coming catastrophe. In S. P. Hier (Ed.), *Moral Panic and the Politics of Anxiety* (pp. 190–207). London: Routledge.

van Krieken, R. (1990). The organization of the soul: Elias and Foucault on discipline and the self. *Archives Europeenes de Sociologie/European Journal of Sociology, 31*(2), 353–371.

van Krieken, R. (1999). The barbarism of civilization: Cultural genocide and the 'stolen generations'. *British Journal of Sociology, 50*(2), 297–315.

Vertigans, S. (2011). *The sociology of terrorism: People, places and processes.* London: Routledge.

Welch, M. (2004). Trampling human rights in the war on terror: Implications to the sociology of denial. *Critical Criminology, 12*(1), 1–20.

Wouters, C. (2007). *Informalization: Manners and emotions since 1890.* London: Sage.

Wright, S. (2011). *Angel faces, killer kids and appetites for excess: Reapproaching moral panic.* Unpublished doctoral dissertation, Victoria University of Wellington, Wellington, New Zealand.

Yeomans, H. (2009). Revisiting a moral panic: Ascetic protestanstism, attitudes to alcohol and the implementation of the Licensing Act 2003. *Sociological Research Online, 14*(2). Retrieved March 11, 2011, from www.socresonline.org.uk/14/2/6.html.

Young, J. (1971a). *The drugtakers: The social meaning of drug use.* London: Paladin.

Young, J. (1971b). The role of the police as amplifiers of deviancy, negotiators of reality and translators of fantasy: Some consequences of our present system of drug control as seen in Notting Hill. In S. Cohen (Ed.), *Images of deviance* (pp. 27–61). Middlesex: Penguin.

# 8 Conclusion

## Introduction

Throughout this book, I have explored how and to what extent climate change has developed as a perceived social problem. This has involved exploring this development as part of an ecological civilizing process, and as part of a moral panic, in the long term and the short term. The central aims of this research were fourfold: (1) to utilize the research findings to develop conclusions about how the governance of climate change has been developing and how it might or ought to develop in the future; (2) to use the process of research to assess critically the value of the concept of moral panic, concluding with how we can improve both the concept of moral panic and the approach to doing moral panic research; (3) to use the various stages of this research – those focussing on climate change, drawing upon moral panic, and utilizing comparative analysis – to develop a more adequate understanding of the relationship between civilizing processes, civilizing offensives, and decivilizing processes; and (4) to reconceptualize decivilizing processes. I will go through my conclusions about these four aims in turn later.

## The past, present, and future of climate change governance

As demonstrated in Chapter 5, the development of concern about climate change, along with the individual regulation of climate change, is intimately connected with a long-term ecological civilizing process and a more general civilizing process. The discourses present within various media that have been produced to try and affect the development of ecological sensibilities, and changes in behaviour regarding climate change, share similarities with the discourses from manners and etiquette books from before climate change became a 'popular', mainstream topic. In understanding how they link into more long-term developments, future creators of popular media and policy can tap into these changing sensibilities and try to direct them from within.

Importantly, those who dictate how we should and should not behave, and those who we seek to emulate, are changing. The shift from authors of manners texts and the middle class to celebrities, scientists, and others highlights the need to utilize these 'new arbiters' but in a way that does not elicit scepticism.

The documentary analysis suggests that the individual governance of climate change, through various popular media and campaigns, must be combined with social controls and incentives from various formal institutions, including local and national governments. While the individual regulation from popular media and other people does appear to be having some effect, it can be only partial, resulting in people focussing on a few things that make them feel good (as if they are doing something to help the environment) while neglecting others that may be contributing to climate change.

In this way, the individualized responsibilization of climate change may serve as a distraction from instigating broader, structural changes in society that would be necessary to alleviate climate change. These personal, individual changes serve as a form of emotional satisfaction to alleviate concerns about climate change, concerns that one is not acting to stop it.

Furthermore, the urgency of climate change necessitates more formal interventions in order to accelerate the development of this ecological civilizing process, to create an ecological civilizing spurt. This could be achieved through more partnerships between the new arbiters of behavioural standards, governments, and corporations. However, this would need to be accompanied by structural transformations, engineered intentionally by people, but the question remains, unfortunately, to what extent are we adequately informed to be able to make such massive interventions, and how could they practically be achieved? Such questions would constitute an entire research project and would require the input of scientists from a wide variety of disciplines – not just the social sciences. As such, they will have to wait for a subsequent piece of research.

## The contribution to climate change research

One way in which this book has contributed to climate change research is through its focus on exploring the interplay between short-term and long-term processes, and intentional actions and unintended consequences. In *On the Process of Civilization*, one of the examples Elias ([1939] 2012) explored in changing manners was 'on blowing one's nose'. The intentional campaigns (or civilizing offensives) to change the way people blew their noses, along with other specific campaigns, fed into unintended consequences, such as an increasing internalization of restraints in general, with regard to bodily functions, emotional expression, the expression of violent impulses, and so forth. Nonetheless, nose-blowing campaigns were successful to the extent that they did affect changes in the way people blew their noses. And so, short-term campaigns can have both intended and unintended consequences.

We can apply this same notion to the example of climate change and to the theoretical-empirical research discussed in the previous chapters. From

Chapter 5, which explored the long-term development of ecological sensibilities, it appears that *ecological* concerns about littering have developed, to a certain extent, as the unintended outcome of civilizing processes – there is the growing pacification of 'nature' that contributes to the growing aestheticization of 'nature', which, in turn, contributes to aesthetic concerns about littering, which then, in combination with increasing mutual identification with other animals and other forms of life (and indeed the biosphere as a whole), contributes to growing ecological concerns about littering. Throughout this gradual long-term process, there is the interweaving of many part-processes, as explored in Chapter 5, which includes intentional civilizing offensives. In order to predict the extent to which a given civilizing offensive will have intended relative to unintended consequences, it is necessary to understand the related historical trajectories that have developed thus far and how they relate to the social problem in question (in this case, climate change). In doing so, campaigners and policymakers may have a greater chance of tapping into those themes that are already developing and perhaps of accelerating them.

As well as exploring these time frames, this research has done something no other climate change research has done to date – it has combined the analysis of the aforementioned civilizing processes and civilizing offensives with an analysis of moral panics. The concept of moral panic has been a useful tool to explore the unintended consequences of climate change campaigns (or civilizing offensives). For example, as was discussed in Chapters 6, some climate change campaigns, instead of causing panic and inducing positive behavioural change, are having the unintended consequence of inducing denial and avoidance in some people – the opposite of what was intended, potentially contributing to an increase in the problem. Another potential unintended consequence can occur through the scapegoating of so-called 'eco-deviants', 'climate change deniers', and so forth. Directing blame at these groups may deflect attention away from the necessary structural and general lifestyle changes that would realistically be required were anthropogenic climate change to be adequately addressed.

## The future of the concept of moral panic

Throughout this research, I have demonstrated how complex moral panics are, with the discussion in Chapter 3, the analysis of climate change in Chapter 6, and the comparative moral panic (and figurational) analysis in Chapter 7. Having demonstrated that previous conceptualizations of moral panics do not allow researchers to explore their complexity, I now wish to turn to explicating how I think the concept should be used and how one should go about doing moral panic research.

Primarily, moral panic should not be used as merely a taxonomic tool to say, for example, this is a moral panic, that is not a moral panic; this is a successful moral panic, that is a failed moral panic; this is a strong moral panic, that is a weak moral panic; and so on. While the concept of moral panic may be used outside of academia in this way, as a descriptive term to dismiss a reaction to a social problem, we as researchers should strive to use the concept in a much more sociological and 'detached' way.

Instead, moral panic should be used as an investigative tool, as a sensitizing device to assist in the exploration of an empirical example. Herbert Blumer ([1969] 1998, Chapter 8) provides an argument about the nature of concepts, which can be applied to the current status of moral panics. He delineates between two types of concepts: 'definitive concepts' and 'sensitizing concepts'. To date, moral panic has largely been used as a definitive concept. Blumer defines definitive concepts as follows:

> What is common to a class of objects, by the aid of a clear definition in terms of attributes or fixed benchmarks. This definition [of the concept], or the benchmarks, serve as a means of clearly identifying the individual instance of the class and the make-up of that instance that is covered by the concept.
>
> (Blumer, [1969] 1998, pp. 147–48)

This is similar to what Goode and Ben-Yehuda ([1994] 2009) often referred to as criteria of moral panic, where moral panics, according to them, must have folk devils and must be comprised of the following five criteria: concern, hostility, consensus, disproportion, and volatility. In contrast to this, we can instead use moral panic as a sensitizing concept:

> A sensitizing concept lacks such specification of attributes or benchmarks and consequently it does not enable the user to move directly to the instance and its relevant content. Instead, it gives the user a general sense of reference and guidance in approaching empirical instances. Whereas definitive concepts provide prescriptions of what to see, sensitizing concepts merely suggest directions along which to look.
>
> (Blumer, [1969] 1998, p. 148)

Using concepts as sensitizing devices rather than definitive devices allows the concepts to grow and develop for it allows the input of empirical data to influence how we think about moral panic – a sensitizing concept is characterized by a much more even relationship between the concept and empirical data.

To undertake moral panic research in this way – by using it as a sensitizing concept – one still has to provide guidelines and suggestions about what sort of things to look for. These guidelines and suggestions can be developed and continuously redeveloped in relation to empirical analyses (including Cohen's original formulation of the concept). For now, let me propose some guidelines for what could be explored. We can break the concept of moral panic up into various different processes and explore how and the extent to which something is moralized, how and the extent to which there is concern about an issue, the degree of 'reality congruence' of the representations of the problem and how these representations develop, and the power relations between those who are seen to be the 'problem' and those who are trying to 'control' the problem. This is just a selection of the many processes and relations that can be explored. Importantly, rather than seeing these guidelines as 'criteria', they are merely suggestions of areas that might be explored. The presence or absence of them is irrelevant for deciding if a given phenomenon is a moral panic. In fact, by approaching research in this way that question becomes irrelevant.

However, we cannot ignore the political origins of the concept of moral panic, and the likelihood that many who have undertaken moral panic research in the past and will undertake moral panic research in the future contain a political element in their research. As mentioned in earlier chapters (see in particular, Chapters 3 and 4), I do not wish to remove politics from research. Rather, I wish to propose a different way to approach politics in moral panic research. Instead of deciding at the outset that the empirical example one is about to investigate as a moral panic is a 'bad' thing that must be debunked to liberate those who are suffering as a result of this moral panic, researchers must strive to be aware of their preconceived ideas and work hard at focussing their passion on the research process itself, rather than on their prior political involvements. They should strive to make their research as autonomous from their personal valuations as possible, thus being open to accept the results of the research, despite what these might mean to their prior political commitments. As outlined in Chapters 3 and 4, following this 'detour via detachment', researchers can then practice a form of secondary involvement but only *after* the research is complete. This could be comprised of intervening in, or communicating with, policy, education, media, and so on to try and affect more adequate representations, regulation, and so on of a given problem.

If reconceptualized in this manner, the usefulness of the concept of moral panic is reinforced in several ways. First, it provides some direction about what to look for, what to investigate (as explicated earlier). Second, moral panic emerged as a political concept. This political aspect can be retained, though it must be redrawn as proposed earlier. Third (and to summarize), the point of moral panic research is to understand how 'moral panics' have been and are developing, and to redraw the part-processes in order to improve their adequacy.

As mentioned in Chapter 6, redrawing these part-processes can be achieved through utilizing a reconceptualization of disproportionality. First, by exploring the change in the degree of attention paid to a given issue, what sort of attention is paid to it and in what way, and how and to what extent this changes over time. Second, by exploring the degrees of 'reality congruence' and 'value congruence', that is, the accuracy and appropriateness of representations of the issue, and attempts to regulate the issue (including assessing the degree to which regulatory attempts are likely to have more intended than unintended, and integrative rather than disintegrative consequences, as well as exploring the values behind different representations).

These changes that I have proposed here for how we think about the role of the concept of moral panic, how one should undertake moral panic research, and how the political purpose of research can be redrawn facilitates the ongoing development of the concept of moral panic. It was initially developed in the 1960s and 1970s, but the political landscape has changed since then, and there have been major developments and changes in the media. Using moral panic as a sensitizing concept, and using it in a similar way to how I have proposed here, allows for the potential ongoing development of the concept of moral panic, thereby its continuing relevance and longevity.

## The contribution to moral panic research

To summarize, this research has contributed to moral panic studies in many ways. To date, no one has synthesized moral panic and figurational sociology through a detailed empirical analysis (a few authors have referred to my first few articles on Elias and moral panic in their own articles that have discussed empirical examples, but these have not been detailed, lengthy research projects such as the one presented here). The value of synthesizing these two bodies of research has been evident in several ways. As with the contribution to climate change research, the focus on exploring the interplay between various different levels and time frames of analysis is unique to moral panic studies. Prior to this, moral panic research has been very short-term focussed. The utilization of civilizing and decivilizing processes and civilizing offensives in comparing several different empirical examples in Chapter 7 provided a more complex insight into the values in moral panic. Specifically, it demonstrated how a conceptualization of moral panics as 'good' or 'bad' was highly problematic, considering the complex integrative and disintegrative, and intended and unintended developments that occur. This complexity of moral panics provided a further demonstration for why it is necessary to remove the normative presupposition and to exercise greater levels of detachment in research. The empirical analysis of climate change provided an additional rationale for this – the results reported in Chapter 6 demonstrate how, while we might think that climate change moral panics would be a 'good' thing (to address the social problem of anthropogenic climate change), they might have many unwanted, unintended consequences, such as the denial and avoidance of the issue of climate change, the creation of scapegoats, and a focus on ways of addressing climate change that may not adequately resolve the problem (for example, focussing on individual lifestyles in 'green guides', while neglecting structural changes).

## On the relationship between figurational sociology and other approaches to research

Throughout this study, I have attempted to draw comparisons between Elias's arguments and those of other social theorists, between figurational sociology and other approaches to research. There were two main reasons for doing this. First, to assist with the critical reassessment of the various concepts and theories I was primarily using. Second, to demonstrate the similarities and differences between these theories and approaches in order to stimulate dialogue *with* different theories and approaches, by working with them (rather than against them). These comparisons, including those with Beck, Foucault, and Urry, have shed some light on how, for example, we might consider the relationship between intended and unintended developments and between gradual and sudden change. These are useful to consider when concerning the relationship between civilizing processes and civilizing offensives.

## The relationship between civilizing processes and civilizing offensives

In Chapter 5, I primarily explored the development of climate change in relation to ecological civilizing processes – gradual, unintended developments. Indeed, some of the contributing factors to the actual phenomenon of climate change have occurred, in part, as unintended consequences of civilizing processes. Within these gradual, unplanned developments, however, it was clear that there were deliberate, intentional, ecological civilizing offensives launched to try and bring about more rapid changes in sensibilities. This was further examined in Chapter 6, where I looked at climate change in relation to moral panics.

In assessing how moral panics relate to civilizing offensives and processes, and to intended and unintended developments, I argued that we could utilize the concept of moral panic in order to assess the reality congruence and value congruence of the representations and regulation of social problems. By doing so, I proposed, we could explore the extent to which a given moral panic could have more intended than unintended consequences. And so, it is not merely the case that short-term, sudden change is intentional (i.e. moral panics) and that long-term, gradual change is unintentional.

All of this suggests that social processes involve a blend of civilizing offensives and civilizing processes, of intended and unintended developments, and of sudden and gradual changes. Future research should focus on exploring these blends in various empirical examples.

## Conceptualizing decivilizing processes

This research has suggested two ways in which decivilizing processes can be approached anew, and it has also raised some questions about the very concept of decivilizing. As argued throughout, notions of decivilizing need to not just focus on the monopolization and demonopolization of violence but to consider other factors that contribute to decivilizing processes. I have focussed on the monopolization and demonopolization (and democratization) of knowledge, but future research could explore additional areas.

I have also argued that various symptoms or criteria of decivilizing processes, as proposed by Mennell and Fletcher, need not to actually occur initially, but the mere perception that they are occurring can lead to the development of actual symptoms/criteria. In other words, perceived decivilizing can lead to actual decivilizing.

In addition, and in accordance with the likes of van Krieken, Pratt, and Vertigans, in exploring moral panics I have examined decivilizing as *partial* decivilizing, or as part-processes occurring in tandem with civilizing processes. This further suggests that civilizing and decivilizing processes should be conceptualized as a blend, as degrees of civilizing and decivilizing.

However, several questions still remain. Should decivilizing be conceptualized as a reversal? Does that make it a more normative concept? Do we even need the term decivilizing? I wish to suggest that we might want to consider exploring some of the examples discussed here – both my own and others' – without using the concept of decivilizing. This could help to avoid normative charges associated with both civilizing and decivilizing processes; a simplification of the dynamic shifts occurring within civilizing processes; and a slip into dichotomous, normative thinking. Instead of using the concept of decivilizing, we can explore the degrees of different part-processes and relations, how the degree of these different part-processes shift, and how this relates to other part-processes (for example, exploring shifts in the degree of the state monopolization of violence and how this relates to the degree of emotional identification with different groups, and so on). In this way, we do not need to classify part-processes or whole processes as either civilizing or decivilizing. We could even perhaps not speak of decivilizing processes. Only through research, however, can we determine how and to what extent we might be able to proceed without the concept of decivilizing processes.

## The contribution to figurational research

This study has contributed to figurational research by further testing and developing the concept of ecological civilizing processes. It has added to the concept by exploring it in relation to multiple time frames of analysis (as mentioned earlier) and by examining it in relation to the concept of moral panic. It has suggested that both long-term unplanned ecological civilizing processes are developing, and that short-term ecological civilizing offensives may be contributing to these to a certain extent. However, the question remains whether these developments will occur at fast enough rates to adequately address anthropogenic climate change.

In exploring these different time frames, including the relationship between the planned and the unplanned, this research has gone some way to addressing the lack of research on civilizing offensives and the interplay between offensives and processes. By combining this with the concept of moral panic, the attention given in research to offensives increases.

An additional relative area of neglect is the problematic relationship between civilizing and decivilizing processes. While several important works have been written on this, it is still unclear precisely how we should conceptualize this relation. It is notable that many figurational researchers do not actually use the term 'decivilizing' or 'decivilization'. This therefore suggests that we could, perhaps, undertake research without it. As I have suggested earlier in this chapter, and in Chapter 7, the notion of civilizing in contrast to decivilizing has strong normative connotations, akin to 'good' and 'bad' panics. In collapsing both of these dichotomies, this research intends to contribute to the relative decrease in normative judgements made in both figurational and moral panic research, thereby hopefully decreasing the normative charges that are made towards these fields of study.

## Limitations of the study and suggestions for future research

As with any piece of research, this study had several limitations, some of which I will outline here. One of the limitations was time: I would have liked to have had the time to have analyzed more and a greater variety of historical documents. I had initially intended to explore, in detail, the development of the natural sciences, including popular science, and how these processual changes related to those that were occurring in manners books. While I did briefly touch upon this, future research should examine this in more detail. Further research should also address a greater variety of documents that are sceptical about climate change.

Additionally, future research could carry out biographical interviews that explore interviewees life stories with the purpose of exploring individual ecological civilizing processes and provide greater insight into ecological developments within a person's lifetime, including the shift from external restraint to the internalization of standards of behaviour as 'second nature'.

Another possible and associated line of research is photo diaries. It might prove insightful to utilize these by asking participants to photograph things they associate with 'nature' and 'the environment', things they enjoy related to these, and things they regard as being 'eco-friendly' or 'eco-deviance'.

Having identified potential lines of research, I will outline here those that I consider to be immediate priorities. It is important to further develop a reformulation of the moral panic concept in the context of an analysis of the development of moral panics. This will involve looking at the development of the concept in both sociological (and related) literature and the popular/ media usage of the concept.

First, trace the development of the concept (including the antecedents to the concept) in academia. This will involve looking at what topics have been the foci of moral panics research at different times and the frequency of these topics. It will also imply looking at the frequency of moral panics studies per year and examine definitions of moral panics in sociology (and criminology, media studies, and related disciplines) dictionaries, encyclo-paedias, and textbooks.

The concept of moral panic has also become widespread in popular culture, being employed by the general public and even the media themselves. The term is used in popular discourse sometimes as a way to dismiss reac-tions, including media stories, as being 'just' a moral panic. It is therefore important to trace the development of moral panic in popular culture. This will involve looking at the frequency of usage of the term over time, and in relation to what particular examples, as well as the *function* of the employ-ment of the term. Throughout this analysis, we can ask the question as to whether or not a concept that has a particular meaning in popular culture can still be used in a slightly different way in academia; for example, just as the term 'civilization' (as a process) is employed by Elias in a different way to the everyday usage of the term.

### Comparative figurational moral panic analysis of problematized consumption

Some of the discourse surrounding climate change focusses on consump-tion, with references to overconsumption and excess consumption, requir-ing 'dieting', and comparisons to addiction, drug addiction, shopaholics, and so on. This rather fuzzy usage raises questions of how a large-scale comparative study of various forms of consumption that have been prob-lematized at particular times in particular places can help to inform understandings about addiction and 'problem' consumption. Building upon what has already been developed in the comparative chapter of this book, future research could utilize both moral panic and figurational ap-proaches to develop a large-scale piece of comparative historical research that explores the historical and biographical developments of how vari-ous forms of consumption are perceived, regulated, and consumed in a variety of Western and non-Western nations, and how this has changed and developed over time. This would also feed into understandings about the relations discussed in this conclusion: between civilizing offensives and civilizing processes, between intended and unintended developments, and between gradual and sudden change. It could also be used as a test case to explore these developments while trying not to use the concept of decivilizing.

# References

Blumer, H. ([1969] 1998). *Symbolic interactionism: Perspective and method.* Berkeley, CA: University of California Press.

Elias, N. ([1939] 2012). *On the process of civilisation: Sociogenetic and psychogenetic investigations (The collected works of Norbert Elias, Vol. 3).* Dublin: University College Dublin Press [Previous editions published as *The civilizing process*].

Goode, E., & Ben-Yehuda, N. ([1994] 2009). *Moral panics: The social construction of deviance* (2nd ed.). Chichester: Wiley-Blackwell.

# Index